Unfair Advantage

Workers' Freedom of Association
in the United States
under International Human
Rights Standards

LANCE COMPA

A Human Rights Watch Book

ILR Press
An imprint of
Cornell University Press
ITHACA AND LONDON

Human Rights Watch is dedicated to protecting the human rights of people around the world.

We stand with victims and activists to prevent discrimination, to uphold political freedom, to protect people from inhumane conduct in wartime, and to bring offenders to justice.

We investigate and expose human rights violations and hold abusers accountable.

We challenge governments and those who hold power to end abusive practices and respect international human rights law.

We enlist the public and the international community to support the cause of human rights for all.

CONTENTS

ACKNOWLEDGMENTS

Human Rights Watch is grateful to the Ford Foundation for the support that made this report possible. They are also grateful to Lance Compa, the author of this report, and Cynthia Brown, the principal editor. Research and writing assistance was provided by Human Rights Watch consultant Jennifer Bailey and fellow Carol Pier. Research assistance was provided by Human Rights Watch associate Sam David and intern Manuel Rybach. Senior Researcher Allyson Collins provided program coordination; advice on international law was provided by Wilder Taylor, Legal and Policy Director of Human Rights Watch; and Program Director Malcolm Smart provided additional editorial input.

Technical consultations on labor law and labor markets were provided by labor law Prof. Charles J. Morris of Southern Methodist University (retired) and lawyer/economist Howard Wial of the Keystone Research Center. Photographic research assistance was provided by Keith Ernst of Southern Exposure Magazine. Human Rights Watch extends its thanks as well to John J. Walsh of Carter, Ledyard and Milburn of New York, who provided pro bono legal advice on the text. Frances Benson of Cornell University Press and Widney Brown of Human Rights Watch arranged for Cornell's publication of this edition of *Unfair Advantage*.

INTRODUCTION, 2004

The decision by Cornell University Press to bring out this edition of *Unfair Advantage: Workers' Freedom of Association in the United States under International Human Rights Standards* confirms the continuing timeliness and relevance of this report and reflects a fruitful partnership between two preeminent institutions. Human Rights Watch is the largest U.S.-based independent human rights organization, universally respected for its rigorous investigations and thoroughly documented reports on human rights around the world for more than a quarter century. Cornell University Press, through the ILR Press imprint, is known for its publication of significant books on labor law, industrial and labor relations, and national and international labor policy.

Historically, the labor movement has seen the human rights community as a separate venture, mostly concerned with victims of abuse in other countries. For their part, many human rights advocates and activists have thought little about human rights for workers in the United States. Like many Americans unfamiliar with violations suffered by workers in organizing and bargaining, they saw trade unionists not as victims of abusive treatment but as favored labor elites.

By focusing on case studies of workers' rights violations in the United States in light of international human rights standards, *Unfair Advantage* helped to change that perception. The report analyzes workers' organizing and collective bargaining as fundamental human rights, not simply as labor-management disputes between institutional interests. It aims to promote new consciousness, attitudes, and policy on workers' organizing and bargaining rights. As one Cornell labor and human rights scholar puts it:

> The Human Rights Watch report is historically significant. It reverses the usual approach of judging other nations' labor laws and practices by using United States labor law (or an idealized version of that law) as the standard. As evidenced by its title, the report looks inward at United States labor law and policies using internationally accepted human rights principles as standards for judgment. It is a valuable new perspective because human rights standards have not been an important influence in the making or the integrating and applying of United States labor law.[1]

---

[1]See James A. Gross, review of *Unfair Advantage: Workers' Freedom of Association in the United States under International Human Rights Standards*, 4 *University of Pennsylvania Journal of Labor and Employment Law* 699 (spring 2002).

The Impact of Unfair Advantage

Unfair Advantage garnered significant attention when it was released by Human Rights Watch in August 2000. International, national, and local commentary featured the report's hard-hitting findings, based on exhaustive case studies, which showed that the self-image of the United States as a beacon for human rights flickers badly when it comes to workers' rights.[2]

Since then, *Unfair Advantage* has become an authoritative reference point in U.S. labor law and human rights discourse. Even sooner than might have been expected in a climate inhospitable to workers' exercise of freedom of association, *Unfair Advantage* is helping to inspire new energy in the labor movement and allied social justice communities. It is also prompting the introduction of legislation in Congress based on the report's recommendations.

The report has created new linkages between the human rights and labor communities. The AFL-CIO has made the report a centerpiece of its Voice@Work campaign.[3] Inspired by the report and the prospect of greater links between the labor and human rights communities, a new civil society organization, American Rights at Work (ARAW), has set an ambitious research and education program to drive home the principle that workers' rights are human rights.[4]

Unfair Advantage has become the standard source for labor advocates reaching out to new constituencies using a language of human rights, not just

---

[2]See, for example, Julian Borger, "Workers' Rights 'Abused in US'," *Guardian* (London), August 30, 2000, p. 12; Ned Glascock, "Rights Group Targets Firms," *Raleigh News & Observer*, August 31, 2000, p. A3; Editorial, "Study: Labor Law Fails Millions," *New York Daily News*, August 31, 2000, p. 84; Editorial, "Labor Day Finds Some with Old Troubles," *Greensboro News & Record*, September 4, 2000, p. A8, Robert McNatt, "The List: Union Busters," *Business Week*, September 11, 2000, p. 14; Steven Greenhouse, "Report Faults Laws for Slowing Growth of Unions," *New York Times*, October 24, 2000, p. A20; Lance Compa, "U.S. Workers' Rights Are Being Abused," *Washington Post*, October 30, 2000, p. A27; "O governo dos EUA tem sido ineficiente na defesa dos trabalhadores," *O Estado de Sao Paulo*, November 1, 2000; Roy Adams, "U.S. Immigrants Being Exploited," *Hamilton Spectator* (Ontario), November 21, 2000, p. D10; Arvind Panagariya, "Shoes on the Other Foot: Stunning Indictment of Laws Governing Workers' Rights in the United States," *Economic Times* (India), December 20, 2000, p. 1; Scripps Howard News Service, "Worker Rights," February 21, 2001.

[3]See Web site at www.aflcio.org/aboutunions/voiceatwork; see also AFL-CIO *Issue Brief*, "The Silent War: The Assault on Workers' Freedom to Choose a Union and Bargain Collectively in the United States" (June 2002).

[4]See Web site at www.araw.org.

that of labor-management relations.[5] One example of such a new constituency was the million-plus readership of *Scientific American,* which published a public policy feature on *Unfair Advantage* one year after the report came out.[6] At its national convention in June 2002, Americans for Democratic Action (ADA) presented the first Reuther-Chavez Award to Human Rights Watch for its U.S. labor report.[7]

ADA called *Unfair Advantage* "an exhaustive analysis of the status of workers' freedom to organize, bargain collectively, and strike in the United States, written from the perspective of international human rights standards. It is the first comprehensive assessment of workers' rights to freedom of association in the U.S. by a prominent international human rights organization." In presenting the award, ADA noted that "Human Rights Watch, in preparing and releasing *Unfair Advantage,* has given us what we hope will be enduring evidence in the struggle to regain fair advantage for workers in the U.S."[8]

Unfair Advantage has also become a point of reference in the scholarly community. Many U.S. labor law teachers have added the book as a supplemental law school text. So have professors in human rights, political science, sociology, government, industrial relations, and other academic fields. The American Political Science Association gave a "best paper" award at its 2001 annual meeting to "From the Wagner Act to the Human Rights Watch Report: Labor and Freedom of Expression and Association, 1935–2000."[9]

British Symposium

The British Journal of Industrial Relations devoted two issues in 2001 to a symposium discussing the report. Symposium editors Sheldon Friedman and Stephen Wood attracted contributions from leading labor law, labor history, and

---

[5]See, for example, Judith A. Scott, SEIU general counsel, "Workers' Rights to Organize as Human Rights: The California Experience," Los Angeles County Bar Association Labor and Employment Law Symposium (February 26, 2004).

[6]See Rodger Doyle, "U.S. Workers and the Law," *Scientific American* (August 2001), p. 24.

[7]The Reuther-Chavez Award, named for ADA cofounder and United Auto Workers president Walter Reuther and United Farm Workers leader Cesar Chavez, was created by ADA "to recognize important activist, scholarly and journalistic contributions on behalf of workers' rights, especially the right to unionize and bargain collectively."

[8]See more at ADA Web site, www.adaction.org/reutherchavez.htm.

[9]See Carl Swidorski, "From the Wagner Act to the Human Rights Watch Report: Labor and Freedom of Expression and Association, 1935–2000," *New Political Science* 25 (March 2003): 55.

industrial relations scholars in the United States, Canada, and Britain. In the symposium, University of South Carolina business school professor Hoyt N. Wheeler writes, "It is by explicitly taking a human rights approach that the Human Rights Watch report makes its most important contribution to the understanding and evaluation of American labor policy." University of Texas law school professor Julius Getman calls *Unfair Advantage* "a powerful indictment of the way in which U.S. labor law deals with basic rights of workers." University of California at Davis labor historian David Brody writes, "The Human Rights Watch report on labor rights in America is truly a gift to all those working people struggling for, and being denied, full freedom of association."

In the symposium, McMaster University business school professor Roy J. Adams calls the publication of *Unfair Advantage* "an important event because of the new perspective that it brings to bear on American labor policy." University of Essex human rights professor Sheldon Leader terms the report "an important document . . . that should help us see what difference it makes to connect up the corpus of principles in labor law with the wider considerations of human rights law." K. D. Ewing, a law professor at King's College, London, states:

> In what is perhaps a novel approach for an American study, the report is set in the context of international human rights law . . . [quoting from the report] "where workers are autonomous actors, not objects of unions' or employers' institutional interests.". . . The approach of the HRW report and the methodology that it employs have a universal application; they are particularly relevant for the United Kingdom.[10]

These are the words of serious scholars, and they followed their generous praise for *Unfair Advantage* with constructively critical engagement. Wheeler

---

[10]See Sheldon Friedman and Stephen Wood, eds., "Employers' Unfair Advantage in the United States of America: Symposium on the Human Rights Watch Report on the State of Workers' Freedom of Association in the United States," 39 *British Journal of Industrial Relations* 591 (December 2001) and 40 *British Journal of Industrial Relations* 114 (March 2002), with Hoyt N. Wheeler, "The Human Rights Watch Report from a Human Rights Perspective"; Julius Getman, "A Useful Step"; David Brody, "Labour Rights as Human Rights: A Reality Check"; Lance Compa, "Reply to Wheeler-Getman-Brody papers"; Roy J. Adams, "The Wagner Act Model: A Toxic System beyond Repair"; Sheldon Leader, "Choosing an Interpretation of the Right to Freedom of Association"; K. D. Ewing, "Human Rights and Industrial Relations: Possibilities and Pitfalls."

looks at the foundation of the human rights approach to freedom of association for workers. He probes for deeper roots than the international human rights instruments cited by Human Rights Watch in the report and draws attention to religious, moral, and philosophical first principles as an important complement to the case for workers' rights in *Unfair Advantage*.

Getman criticizes the report for not sufficiently addressing the "deeper causes" of the "toxic system" that U.S. labor law has become. He suggests that one such deeper cause is what he calls a "Capitalist Exception" applied by judges and government officials favoring property rights over workers' associational rights. Getman calls for "a new burst of rank and file-led activism" to bring about changes in law and practice recommended in *Unfair Advantage*.

Brody believes that *Unfair Advantage* should have more historical perspective and that the report too willingly accepts the view that collective bargaining is gained through a bureaucratic process of government certification rather than through workers' direct action. "That a formally democratic process might be at odds with workers' freedom of association," he writes, "seems to fall below the screen of 'human rights analysis.'" Adams also believes that *Unfair Advantage* does not sufficiently break with the "dysfunctional" Wagner Act model and that the report's "prescription for reform, even if followed to the letter, would not cure the sick patient."

Leader addresses two key features of the U.S. labor law model that went unchallenged in *Unfair Advantage*: (1) majority rule (workers achieve bargaining in workplaces where a majority chooses it); and (2) exclusive representation (once a union is established, no other organization may speak for subgroups in the "bargaining unit"). He suggests that a broader, more dynamic application of freedom of association principles should do more for workers who seek to bargain without a majority (sometimes called "members-only" bargaining) and for subdivisions of a bargaining unit such as women workers in a mostly male workplace.[11]

Ewing warns that the human rights approach "does not answer all the questions that are posed by an industrial relations system." He cautions that "in our readiness to embrace the rhetoric of human rights, we cannot overlook the fact that others may claim human rights that may directly contradict our own. These 'others' may be employers and workers who are opposed to trade unions."

---

[11]For a thorough treatment of law and practice on nonmajority unionism in the United States, see Charles A. Morris, *Blue Eagle at Work* (Ithaca: Cornell University Press, 2004).

Readers of *Unfair Advantage* can judge for themselves the merits of the report and these experts' analyses. But by engaging the report so deeply, these scholars, as well as many others who have written about *Unfair Advantage*, stretch the report's boundaries back toward assumptions and forward toward implications in ways that validate the significance of its findings and recommendations.[12] As James Gross notes:

> The report is about moral choices we have made in this country. These moral choices are about, among other things, the rights of workers to associate so they can participate in the workplace decisions that affect their lives, their right not to be discriminated against, and their right to physical security and safe and healthful working conditions. The choices we have made and will make in regard to those matters will determine what kind of a society we want to have and what kind of people we want to be. Human rights talk without action is hypocrisy. This report could be an important first step toward action.[13]

Little Change . . . and a Broken Strike

Cornell's republication of *Unfair Advantage* is especially timely and useful in light of the continuing struggle for workers' freedom of association in the United States. The reality of labor law and practice in the United States described in *Unfair Advantage* has not changed much since the report's initial publication in 2000. Many workers who try to exercise the right to organize still suffer widespread harassment, threats, spying, and dismissals for their efforts. In the fiscal year ending September 30, 2002, the last period for which official records are available, the NLRB issued reinstatement or back pay

---

[12]See, for example, Harry Arthurs, "Reinventing Labor Law for the Global Economy: The Benjamin Aaron Lecture," 22 *Berkeley Journal of Employment and Labor Law* 271 (2001); Steve Early, "How Stands the Union" (book review), *The Nation*, January 22, 2001, p. 22; Andrew S. Levin, "What Thirty Million Workers Want<M>But Can't Have," 3 *University of Pennsylvania Journal of Labor and Employment Law* 551 (spring 2001); James A. Gross, "Worker Rights as Human Rights: Wagner Act Values and Moral Choices," 4 *University of Pennsylvania Journal of Labor and Employment Law* 479 (spring 2002); Ann-Marie Cusac, "Brazen Bosses," *Progressive*, February 1, 2003, p. 23; Kate E. Andrias, "A Robust Public Debate: Realizing Free Speech in Workplace Representation Elections," 112 *Yale Law Journal* 2415 (June 2003).

[13]See James A. Gross, supra note 1.

orders for 17,700 workers who had suffered discrimination for union activity.[14] This is down from the more than twenty thousand victims reported in *Unfair Advantage* for 1998. But it reflects a slowed economy and fewer organizing efforts by workers, not more respect for their rights.[15] When they succeed in forming unions, workers still face obstacles in bargaining. Workers lodged nearly ten thousand allegations of bad-faith bargaining against employers in fiscal 2002.[16]

The remarkable thing is that each year hundreds of thousands of workers overcome these obstacles to form new local unions in U.S. workplaces. The organizing impulse springs from a bedrock human need for association in a common purpose to make things better, as corny as that sounds amid predominantly individualistic social pressures. Polls indicate that more than forty million workers would join unions immediately in their workplaces if they did not risk reprisals from employers.[17]

Striker Replacement: Continuing Violation, Continuing Abuse

Many workers who exercise the right to strike suffer the consequences of the permanent striker replacement doctrine discussed in the *Unfair Advantage* case study of Oregon Steel in Pueblo, Colorado. A recent, dramatic example of the use of permanent replacements to break a strike came at a Tyson Foods plant in Jefferson, Wisconsin. Tyson, the world's largest meat and poultry producer, purchased a locally owned sausage processing plant in that small Midwest town, where workers had decent wages and benefits and a longstanding good relationship with previous company ownership. In 2003 bargaining, Tyson demanded drastic wage and benefit cuts from plant employees. They went on strike in February 2003 against the company's cutbacks.

Workers' exercise of the right to strike is recognized in international law

---

[14]See "Remedial Actions Taken in Unfair Labor Practice Cases Closed, Fiscal Year 2002," *Annual Report of the National Labor Relations Board 2002* (2003), table 4, p. 90.

[15]See Steven Greenhouse, "Worried about Labor's Waning Strength, Union Presidents Form Advisory Committee," *New York Times*, March 9, 2003, p. 22.

[16]See "Types of Unfair Labor Practices Alleged, Fiscal Year 2002," *Annual Report of the National Labor Relations Board 2002* (2003), table 2, p. 82. The "merit rate" (cases in which evidence indicates that violations occurred) of these allegations is not further broken down by type of unfair labor practice, but the average merit rate of 35 to 40 percent yields 3,500 to 4,000 instances of bad faith bargaining. See ibid., "Unfair Labor Practice Merit Factor," chart 5, p. 9.

[17]See David Moberg, "Labor Fights for Rights," *The Nation*, September 15, 2003, p. 23; Richard B. Freeman and Joel Rogers, *What Workers Want* (New York: Russell Sage Foundation, 1999).

as integral to their freedom of association. However, U.S. labor law permits permanent replacement of striking workers.[18] The International Labor Organization's (ILO) Committee on Freedom of Association has condemned this legal doctrine as a violation of freedom of association.[19]

Tyson's Jefferson plant produces pepperoni and other sausage products, many sold to national pizza and other fast food chain companies. "It was a good job," said Sharon Guttenberg, a striking worker. "We weren't getting rich, but we were making a living."[20] A labor economist explained, "They [Tyson] want to make their wages and benefits in Wisconsin more or less equal to what they have in the non-union chicken processing plants in Mississippi."[21]

On April 4, 2003, Tyson announced it would hire permanent replacement workers to take the jobs of workers exercising their right to strike.[22] The replacement move sparked anger and resentment in the community, especially against prison inmates paroled to halfway houses who were recruited by Tyson to take strikers' jobs.[23] "The community is being torn apart, both emotionally and economically," said a retired employee.[24] Local food retailers and the University of Wisconsin responded by withdrawing Tyson products from stores and from campus food services, but sales to national pizza chains sustained the company's reduced operation in Jefferson.[25]

In January 2004, Tyson crushed the strike. Faced with the prospect of a decertification vote by replacement workers, union members voted to accept

---

[18]See *NLRB v. Mackay Radio & Telegraph Co.*, 304 U.S. 333 (1938).

[19]See International Labor Organization, Committee on Freedom of Association, *Complaint against the Government of the United States Presented by the American Federation of Labor and Congress of Industrial Organizations (AFL-CIO)*, Report no. 278, Case no. 1543 (1991).

[20]See Lisa Schuetz, "Tyson Standoff Grinds On," *Wisconsin State Journal*, August 3, 2003, p. A1.

[21]Economist Frank Emspak of the University of Wisconsin, in "Strike Continues at Pepperoni and Sausage Plant in Southern Wisconsin," *Morning Edition*, National Public Radio, July 15, 2003.

[22]See "Tyson to Hire Permanent Replacements for Striking Workers at Plant in Wisconsin," *Daily Labor Report*, Bureau of National Affairs, April 14, 2003, p. A4.

[23]See Bill Novak, "Union: Probe Parolees at Tyson," *Madison Capital Times*, July 10, 2003, p. 2A.

[24]See Lisa Schuetz, supra note 20.

[25]See Joe Potente, "UW Bans Tyson Products Till Strike Over," *Madison Capital Times*, August 23, 2003, p. 3A.

the company's offer.[26] However, union members could not return to work. In violation of international labor standards, they had been permanently replaced. They must wait until replacement workers vacate positions before any who exercised the right to strike may return to their jobs.[27]

U.S. Supreme Court: Two Blows against Workers' Rights

Since publication of *Unfair Advantage*, the U.S. Supreme Court has delivered two damaging decisions further impairing workers' rights. One decision dealt with the National Labor Relations Act's (NLRA's) exclusions clause, which defines categories of workers excluded from coverage of the act. The other dealt with remedies for undocumented immigrant workers illegally fired for union activity.

Exclusions and Kentucky River

One of the key findings of *Unfair Advantage* was the extraordinary reach of the NLRA's "exclusions" clause. Section 2 excludes the following categories of private sector workers from the provisions of the act: agricultural employees, household domestic employees, independent contractors, and supervisors. Their exclusion denies them two rights:

- They have no protection of the right to organize a union; employers can discharge them for union activity with impunity.

- They have no right to bargain collectively when a majority—even 100 percent—desires it; employers can ignore their bargaining requests or proposals with impunity.

Public employees are also excluded from the NLRA's coverage, but they have First Amendment rights of association in the public sector workplace, which prevent reprisals against them for union activity. However, twenty-seven states make collective bargaining illegal for many, most, or all public employees, even those in traditional hourly employment or for low-ranking clerical and technical staff.

A 2002 report by the U.S. General Accounting Office on workers without

---

[26]See Bill Novak, "Concessions End Tyson Plant Strike," *Madison Capital Times*, January 30, 2004, p. 3A.

[27]See Joel Dresang and Tom Daykin, "Tyson Workers Battled against All Odds, and Lost," *Milwaukee Journal Sentinel*, February 8, 2004, p. 1D.

collective bargaining rights put these numbers to excluded categories of workers:[28]

Independent contractors	8.5 million
Low-level supervisors	8.6 million
Public employees	6.9 million
Household domestic workers	532,000
Agricultural workers	357,000

These twenty-five million workers represent almost 20 percent of the total labor force, and almost 30 percent of the non-managerial workforce. A 2001 decision by the U.S. Supreme Court expanded the scope of the exclusions clause, stripping away rights of organizing and bargaining from even more workers. In its *National Labor Relations Board v. Kentucky River Community Care, Inc.* decision, the Court nullified the results of a 1997 NLRB election in which a majority of the hospital's 110 employees voted in favor of union representation.[29] The employer refused to bargain with the union, arguing that six "charge nurses" in the voting group were supervisors. The Supreme Court agreed, saying that charge nurses who oversee the work of lower-ranking nurses and nurses' aides, even though they have no disciplinary power over them, are supervisors unprotected by the NLRA.

Health care employers crowed that the decision gave them new ammunition to break workers' organizing efforts, calling it "welcome news" that could give them "an edge in union organizing campaigns." The decision "may make it easier for employers to prove that certain employees are supervisors—and therefore ineligible to vote in union elections." It "has significant and far-reaching implications for all professional and technical employees who direct the work of less-skilled employees. . . . Other labor organizations targeting professional and technical employees who direct the work of other employees can expect to be similarly affected."[30]

Immigrant Workers and Hoffman Plastic

Many of the abuses described in the *Unfair Advantage* case studies of Washington apple workers, North Carolina slaughterhouse workers, New York

---

[28]See U.S. General Accounting Office, *Collective Bargaining Rights: Information on the Number of Workers with and without Bargaining Rights*, GAO-02-835 (September 2002).
[29]See *NLRB v. Kentucky River Community Care, Inc.*, 532 U.S. 706 (2001).
[30]See John E. Lyncheski and Ronald J. Andrykovitch, "Who's a Supervisor? U.S. Supreme Court Redefines Supervisors in National Labor Relations Board Case," *Human Resources Magazine* (September 2001).

City sweatshop workers, and others are directly linked to the vulnerable immigration status of workers in many American industries. Immigrant workers' defenselessness creates a vicious cycle of abuse. Fearful of being found out and deported, undocumented workers shrink from exercising rights of association or from seeking legal redress when their workplace rights are violated. Fully aware of workers' fear and sure that they will not complain to labor law authorities or testify to back up a claim, employers heap up abuses and violations of their rights. A recent dramatic example involved Wal-Mart, after federal immigration agents raided stores in twenty-one states in October 2003 and arrested more than two hundred undocumented people working in overnight cleaning jobs.[31] Workers lodged a class-action lawsuit against Wal-Mart alleging failure to comply with minimum wage, overtime, health and safety and social security laws.[32] In an amended complaint, workers also alleged violations of civil rights laws by the company's practice of locking doors to prevent workers from leaving the stores.[33]

Unfair Advantage does not challenge the capacity of the United States or any country to set conditions for admission of noncitizens into the country and to enforce those conditions. However, immigration rules must be formulated and enforced in compliance with basic human rights standards.

In this light, the 2002 decision of the U.S. Supreme Court in the case of *Hoffman Plastic Compounds v. National Labor Relations Board* highlights the human rights dimensions of a crisis in immigration policy. The Court decided that an undocumented worker, because of his immigration status, was not entitled to back pay for lost wages after he was illegally dismissed for exercising rights protected by the NLRA. The Supreme Court's 5–4 ruling overturned an NLRB decision, upheld by a federal appeals court, that granted back pay to the worker. The decision strips away from millions of workers in the United States their only protection of the right to freedom of association, the right to organize, and the right to bargain collectively.[34]

From a human rights and labor rights perspective, workers' immigration

---

[31]See Steven Greenhouse, "Wal-Mart Raids by U.S. Aimed at Illegal Aliens," *New York Times*, October 24, 2003, p. A1.
[32]See Steven Greenhouse, "Illegally in U.S., and Never a Day Off at Wal-Mart," *New York Times*, November 5, 2003, p. A1.
[33]See Steve Strunsky, "More janitors sue Wal-Mart for violations of civil rights; Say they were locked inside during their cleaning shifts," *Bergen Record*, February 3, 2004, p. L11.
[34]*Hoffman Plastic Compounds, Inc. v. NLRB*, 535 U.S. 137 (2002).

status does not diminish or condition their status as workers holding fundamental rights of association. Most undocumented workers are employed in workplaces with documented migrant workers and with U.S. citizens. Before the *Hoffman* decision, union representatives assisting workers in an organizing campaign could say to all of them, "We will defend your rights before the National Labor Relations Board and pursue back pay for lost wages if you are illegally dismissed." Now they must add: "except for undocumented workers—you have no protection." The resulting fear and division when a group of workers is deprived of their protection of the right to organize has adverse impact on all workers' right to freedom of association and right to organize and bargain collectively.[35]

International Human Rights Bodies' Rulings on *Hoffman Plastic*

Two authoritative international human rights bodies have examined the *Hoffman Plastic* doctrine and found that it violates workers' rights. In September 2003, the Inter-American Court of Human Rights (IACHR) issued an advisory opinion in a case filed by Mexico in the wake of the *Hoffman Plastic* decision. In November 2003, the International Labor Organization's Committee on Freedom of Association issued its decision in a case filed by the AFL-CIO and the Mexican Workers' Confederation.

IACHR Ruling

The IACHR held that undocumented workers are entitled to the same labor rights, including wages owed, protection from discrimination, protection for health and safety on the job, and back pay as citizens and those working lawfully in a country. The court said:

> The migrant quality of a person cannot constitute justification to deprive him of the enjoyment and exercise of his human rights, among them labor rights. . . . The State has the obligation to respect and guarantee human labor rights of all workers, independent of their condition as nationals or foreigners, and to not tolerate situations of discrimination that prejudice them. . . . The State must not permit

---

[35]See Alfredo Corchado and Lys Mendez, "Undocumented Workers Feel Boxed In," *Dallas Morning News*, July 14, 2002, p. 1J; Nancy Cleeland, "Employers Test Ruling on Immigrants," *Los Angeles Times*, April 22, 2002, p. 1; David G. Savage and Nancy Cleeland, "High Court Ruling Hurts Union Goals of Immigrants," *Los Angeles Times*, March 28, 2002, p. 20.

that private employers violate the rights of workers, or that a contrac-
tual relationship weakens minimum international standards. . . .
Workers, by being entitled to labor rights, must be able to count on
all adequate means to exercise them. Undocumented migrant workers have the same labor rights that correspond to the rest of workers
in the State of employment, and the State must take all necessary
measures for this to be recognized and complied with in practice.[36]

The court held that, as part of its principal obligation to interpret the
Charter of the Organization of American States (OAS), it must apply the
American Declaration of the Rights and Duties of Man and other international
conventions on human rights in the hemisphere. It declared its decision bind-
ing on all members of the OAS, whether or not they have ratified certain of the
conventions that formed the basis of the opinion. The IACHR based its deci-
sion on the nondiscrimination and equal protection provisions of the OAS
Charter, the American Declaration, the International Covenant on Civil and
Political Rights, the American Convention on Human Rights, and the Universal
Declaration of Human Rights.[37]

ILO Ruling

In November 2003, the ILO's Committee on Freedom of Association
issued a decision that the U.S. Supreme Court's *Hoffman Plastic* ruling violates
international legal obligations to protect workers' organizing rights. The committee stated:

The Committee recalls that the remedies now available to undocumented workers dismissed for attempting to exercise their trade
union rights include: (1) a cease and desist order in respect of violations of the NLRA; and (2) the conspicuous posting of a notice to
employees setting forth their rights under the NLRA and detailing
the prior unfair practices. . . . The Committee considers that such

---

[36]See Inter-American Court of Human Rights, *Legal Condition and Rights of
Undocumented Migrant Workers*, Consultative Opinión OC-18/03 (September 17, 2003).
[37]Ibid. For thorough discussion, see Sarah Cleveland, Beth Lyon and Rebecca Smith,
"Inter-American Court of Human Rights Amicus Curiae Brief: The United States Violates
International Law When Labor Law Remedies Are Restricted Based on Workers' Migrant
Status," 1 *Seattle Journal of Social Justice* 795 (spring/summer, 2003).

remedies in no way sanction the act of anti-union discrimination already committed, but only act as possible deterrents for future acts. Such an approach is likely to afford little protection to undocumented workers who can be indiscriminately dismissed for exercising freedom of association rights without any direct penalty aimed at dissuading such action.[38]

The ILO committee concluded that "the remedial measures left to the NLRB in cases of illegal dismissals of undocumented workers are inadequate to ensure effective protection against acts of anti-union discrimination." The committee recommended congressional action to bring U.S. law "into conformity with freedom of association principles, in full consultation with the social partners concerned, with the aim of ensuring effective protection for all workers against acts of anti-union discrimination in the wake of the *Hoffman* decision."[39]

Unfair Advantage Case Study Updates
Many of the case studies supporting the findings and recommendations of *Unfair Advantage* continued to develop after the report's initial publication in 2000. Some ended in total defeat for workers' rights of association, organizing, and bargaining. Some had positive endings, but at enormous cost. Some are still enmeshed in the labor law system's wearying delays. Here is a summary.

South Florida Nursing Homes: Five Cases, One Contract
Workers' organizing efforts at the Palm Garden nursing home in North Miami collapsed under the weight of the company's rights violations. Years after the organizing drive, the key leader, Marie Sylvain, eventually received modest back pay, but she had moved on to new work outside the nursing home industry. Her coworkers were too frightened to revive the effort.[40]

The NLRB affirmed an administrative law judge's findings of spying,

---

[38]See ILO Committee on Freedom of Association, Complaints against the Government of the United States Presented by the American Federation of Labor and the Congress of Industrial Organizations (AFL-CIO) and the Confederation of Mexican Workers (CTM), Case no. 2227: Report in which the committee requests to be kept informed of developments (November 20, 2003).

[39]Ibid.

[40]This summary is based on February 2004 interviews with staff of the Service Employees International Union who assisted workers in the organizing campaigns and on NLRB cases recounted in *Unfair Advantage*.

threats, and other violations of workers' rights at the Villa Maria nursing home in Miami.[41] Buying time for employee turnover and discouragement to fatally undermine workers' organizing resolve, management appealed the case to a federal appeals court, then to the U.S. Supreme Court. Both courts refused to hear the appeals, but by then the organizing effort was defunct. It has not been revived.[42]

The employer's dismissals of organizing leaders, threats, and other violations of workers' rights at The Palace nursing home in Miami had their intended effect: workers abandoned their organizing attempt altogether.

Fired for his organizing in 1994, Ernest Duval gained modest back pay from the King David nursing home and returned to work for a short time before leaving, feeling he was still a target for retaliation and wanting to work in a more comfortable environment. Company management bowed to a bargaining order from the NLRB, but no contract was reached after more than a year of negotiations. Management then sold the home to another chain and walked away from the bargaining table. Workers were seeking to bargain with the new owner in early 2004.

At the Avante nursing home in Lake Worth, workers succeeded in holding their organization together and achieving a first contract in May 2003, with what union representatives call a "civilized relationship."

Hotel Workers at San Francisco Marriott: Finally, a Settlement

The long dispute at the San Francisco Marriott hotel discussed in chapter 5 ended with union recognition, a good first contract, and a decent relationship between management and the Hotel Employees and Restaurant Employees union, HERE. The resolution came fifteen years after the hotel opened, when management reneged on an agreement to abide by the results of a "card-check" determination of workers' organizing choice. A card-check agreement is an accepted, legal alternative means for workers to choose collective bargaining. Under it an employer and a union set a period of time for workers to sign cards authorizing the union to represent them.

Workers had to secure a court order to enforce the card-check agreement,

---

[41]See *Villa Maria Nursing and Rehabilitation Center, Inc. and UNITE*, 335 NLRB 1345 (September 26, 2001).
[42]See *Villa Maria Nursing and Rehabilitation Center, Inc. v. NLRB*, 49 Fed. Appx. 289 (11th Cir. 2002); *cert. denied*, *Villa Maria Nursing and Rehabilitation Center, Inc. v. NLRB*, 538 U.S. 922 (2003).

and a solid majority of workers chose union representation in 1996. Management came to the bargaining table but launched a campaign of resistance to a collective bargaining agreement. Workers fought back with noisy demonstrations and calls on associations and groups to cancel stays at the hotel. That was the status of the case in 2000 when *Unfair Advantage* was first published.

Management gradually accepted the fact that a large majority of workers remained fiercely loyal to their union and that peace with its employees was better than conflict. The company began making constructive proposals. When it saw a new management approach to bargaining, HERE's negotiating committee made its own compromise proposals. In August 2002 the parties reached agreement on a first contract, and workers voted 479–75 to approve it. The contract provides a wage of $14.25 an hour for housekeepers and $18.45 an hour for cooks—enough to move them out of the ranks of the working poor into the working class. The contract also provides comprehensive health insurance, a pension plan, and seniority consideration for holiday and vacation scheduling and for promotions.[43]

Shipbuilders at Avondale: Recognition, Agreement, and a Safer Workplace

Shortly before *Unfair Advantage* went to press in 2000, the Avondale shipyard management that had engaged in widespread workers' rights violations sold the shipyard to another firm, a division of Litton Industries. Avondale's former management had unlawfully refused to bargain with the workers' union after a majority voted for representation in 1993.

Litton Avondale, as the company was now called, quickly agreed to a card-check procedure that confirmed the desire of an overwhelming majority of workers for representation and bargaining. Litton Avondale and the workers' chosen representative, the Metal Trades Department of the AFL-CIO, reached a first collective bargaining agreement in December 2000.[44]

In July 2001, an administrative law judge issued a 275-page decision making further findings of massive workers' rights violations by the previous

---

[43]See Carolyn Said, "A Long, Hard Fight, But Respect Endured," *San Francisco Chronicle*, August 30, 2002, p. A21; George Raine, "Hard-Fought Accord for Marriott, Union," *San Francisco Chronicle*, August 30, 2002, p. A1; Wyatt Buchanan, "Workers OK Union Contract at Marriott," *San Francisco Chronicle*, September 13, 2002, p. A24.
[44]See Joe Gyan Jr., "Litton Avondale Signs Labor Deal," *Baton Rouge Advocate*, December 20, 2000.

Avondale management. He also found that management deliberately delayed and obstructed the board's legal proceedings. The judge said, "On learning of the union's organizing campaign, management waged an aggressive counter-campaign that was broad in scope, reckless in implementation, and is likely to have a continuing coercive effect on the free exercise of employee rights for some time to come."[45]

The judge ordered the company to reinstate fired workers, to pay the legal fees of the NLRB and the union, and to reimburse the U.S. Navy $5.4 million for the legal costs of resisting the workers' organizing and bargaining efforts. An Avondale attorney had denied during the trial that it billed the navy for such costs, a representation that turned out to be false.

Litton had assumed Avondale's legal liabilities as part of the earlier acquisition deal and was faced with the costs of applying the judge's order. However, with a collective bargaining agreement in place and in the context of what the company called "an evolving partnership" and the union "a mutually beneficial relationship," Litton settled the NLRB case. The company agreed to reinstate more than fifty fired workers and pay them more than $2 million in back pay. As part of the overall settlement, the NLRB agreed to drop the portion of its order requiring the $5.4 million payment to the navy.[46]

Several Avondale workers died in shipyard accidents while the company was devoting its energies to violating workers' organizing and bargaining rights. Once the new contract came into force the company and the union instituted a far-reaching labor-management safety committee and rapid response system that cut the rate of workplace injury by half. There have been no fatalities since the union was recognized.[47]

Colorado Steelworkers: A Return to Work—After Six Years

After six years of bitter conflict provoked by Oregon Steel Mill's use of permanent replacements against one thousand steelworkers exercising their right to strike at its Rocky Mountain Steel plant in Pueblo, Colorado, the company and the workers reached a settlement that ended the dispute in early 2004.

The 1997 strike lasted one month. Replacements remained in the plant for

---

[45]See Keith Darce, "Avondale Ordered to Rehire 22: Firm Also Must Pay Navy $5.4 Million for Legal Defense," *New Orleans Times-Picayune*, July 11, 2001, p. 1.

[46]See John M. Biers, "Avondale, Union Settle Labor Dispute," *New Orleans Times-Picayune*, December 21, 2001, p. 1.

[47]See Barbara Powell, "Shipyard Injuries Down Dramatically<M>Sea Change Occurs in Emphasis on Employee Safety," *Memphis Commercial-Appeal*, May 25, 2003, p. D10.

six years. The NLRB ruled that the strike was instigated by company unfair labor practices. Management vowed to continue appealing this ruling, but it faced mounting back pay liabilities to replaced workers if it lost the appeals. Under the permanent striker replacement doctrine in U.S. labor law, workers who strike in response to employer unfair labor practices cannot be permanently replaced. As *Unfair Advantage* noted, however, it takes years to obtain a final judicial ruling about a strike's motivation in such cases, years in which workers are jobless and families and communities are torn apart.

During the six-year period of legal appeals while replacement workers stayed on the job, the Steelworkers union conducted a vigorous nationwide "corporate campaign" publicizing increased injuries and fatalities in the plant, challenging company bids for public transit purchases of steel rails, filing a public interest lawsuit for Clean Air Act violations, and pressing investors for a change in management due to mounting losses.[48]

In July 2003, Oregon Steel's board of directors jettisoned the CEO who made the decision to use permanent replacements in Pueblo and who spent the next six years battling the workers and their union.[49] The new management entered intensive talks with the workers' union to put an end to the conflict. In January 2004 they reached an agreement. Despite the cost of the settlement, news that the long dispute was ending caused the price of company stock to nearly double in value.[50]

Oregon Steel agreed to offer a generous early retirement package to two hundred eligible workers and to rehire all other strikers who had not returned to work. The agreement established a $21-million "labor dispute settlement trust" funded by company stock to provide back pay to workers. Oregon Steel agreed to add a Steelworkers union representative to its board of directors and

---

[48]See Stephen Franklin, "Union Fights at Another Level," *Chicago Tribune*, July 2, 1999, p. B1; John Norton, "OSHA Inspects Pueblo, Colo., Steel Mill after Second Fatal Accident," *Pueblo Chieftain*, March 3, 2000, p. 1; John Norton, "Steel Company Sues California Transit Board over Boycott," *Pueblo Chieftain*, February 16, 2000, p. 3; Gail Pitts, "Court Ruling against Oregon Steel Mills Delights Workers," *Pueblo Chieftain*, March 5, 2003, p. 1; John Norton, "Oregon-Based Steel Company Sees Stock Drop after Poor Fourth Quarter," *Pueblo Chieftain*, January 31, 2000, p. B1.

[49]See Tom McGhee, "CEO of Pueblo Steel Mill Parent Quits," *Denver Post*, July 30, 2003, p. C3.

[50]See John Norton, "Union, Steel Mill End Six-Year Fight with Settlement," *Pueblo Chieftain*, January 15, 2004, p. 1.

to reserve one-fourth of its operating income for a ten-year period, capped at $45 million, for worker profit-sharing.[51]

"It's a huge relief," said the Pueblo plant manager. "We've been struggling with a split workforce."[52] Workers' reaction was "cautiously optimistic," according to reports. "I'm ready to go back, but I want to make sure that conditions are going to be right," said Elmer Espinoza. "I am hopeful with the new leaders at Oregon Steel that they will provide dignity for the stewards and that we won't be subjected to hazardous conditions any longer." Another worker, George Chapo, said, "Before Oregon Steel took over, this was a happy place to be. I hope this settlement brings that back."[53] On March 12, 2004, workers approved the new contract.[54]

North Carolina Slaughterhouse Workers: Abuses Confirmed, No End in Sight

When it was published in August 2000, *Unfair Advantage* noted that an NLRB judge had earlier presided over a trial of evidence on unfair labor practices and an unfair election at the giant Smithfield Foods pork slaughtering factory in Tar Heel, North Carolina, where five thousand workers kill and process twenty-five thousand hogs a day. The judge reviewed documents and heard testimony from all parties and evaluated the credibility of company and union witnesses. All witnesses faced challenging cross-examinations by lawyers from the other side. *Unfair Advantage* appeared before his decision came out.

In a 442-page single-spaced decision in December 2000, the judge made detailed findings of massive abuse against workers trying to exercise their freedom of association. Based on the evidence, the judge found that Smithfield illegally:

- threatened to discharge union supporters and to close the plant if workers chose union representation;

[51]See John Norton, "Strike Settlement at Pueblo Mill Will Cost Oregon Steel $32 Million," *Pueblo Chieftain*, January 16, 2004, p. 1.

[52]See Kelly Pate Dwyer, "Oregon Steel Strike Settled," *Denver Post*, January 16, 2004, p. C8.

[53]See Gayle Perez, "Steelworkers Cautiously Optimistic after Settlement at Pueblo, Colo. Mill," *Pueblo Chieftain*, January 16, 2004, p. 1.

[54]See John Norton, "Steelworkers Approve New Labor Contract, Ending Long Dispute," *Pueblo Chieftain*, March 15, 2004, p. 1; Gayle Perez, "Union Members Happy, Relieved as Pact Signed with Steel Mill," *Pueblo Chieftain*, March 13, 2004, p. 1.

- threatened to call the INS to report immigrant workers if workers chose union representation;

- threatened the use of violence against workers engaged in organizing activities;

- threatened to blacklist workers who supported the union;

- harassed, intimidated, and coerced workers who supported the union;

- disciplined, suspended, and fired many workers because of their support for the union;

- spied on workers engaged in lawful union activities.[55]

But the judge had more to say in the matter. In the episode of Margo McMillan's firing by supervisor Sherrie Buffkin, recounted by Buffkin in the *Unfair Advantage* case study, the judge found that a company attorney "intentionally lied under oath at the trial" about an affidavit that Buffkin signed under pressure from management. The judge found that the company attorney fabricated the affidavit to justify the firing of Margo McMillan. The judge said that a second Smithfield attorney "left himself some 'wiggle' room" in connection with the affidavit, but "I do not credit [the second attorney's] testimony." He recommended that the NLRB refer the attorneys' conduct to the general counsel on the grounds that "there is a question of whether [the attorneys] suborned perjury or otherwise violated federal statutes involving criminal penalties."[56]

One of the most chilling conclusions by the NLRB judge confirmed Human Rights Watch's findings that Smithfield orchestrated a campaign to deploy local police forces and company security officials to intimidate employees and, beyond that, to assault and arrest union supporters on the day of the election.

The judge found specifically that "the Respondent's [Smithfield's] use of the Sheriff's Deputies . . . was an intimidation tactic meant to instill fear in the Respondent's employees."[57] The judge found that the top company manager "not only knew that they were there, [the manager] was responsible for them being there. [He] wanted to make a point that the Tar Heel plant was his plant,

---

[55] See *Decision* of ALJ John H. West, JD-158-00, *Smithfield Foods, Inc. and UFCW*, Case Nos. 11-CA-15522 et al., December 15, 2000 (hereafter ALJ Decision).
[56] ALJ Decision, 419–20, 423.
[57] Ibid., 358–359, 382.

the Union was going to pay a price for its attempt to organize the employees who worked there, and employees who supported the union would have an old-fashioned example of what can occur when they try to bring in a Union."[58]

In devising a remedy for the company's violations, the judge made the extraordinary decision that "where, as here, an employer initiates physical violence at or near the polling place just after the election results are announced, and it engages in egregious and pervasive unfair labor practices and objectionable conduct, the reasons for favoring conducting a new election on the Respondent's premises have been substantially undermined. A new election should be conducted off premises at a neutral site."[59]

No new election has taken place. Smithfield has announced its intention to exhaust all appeals, saying that "it would appeal the judge's findings to the full National Labor Relations Board and that, if it failed there, it would appeal to the federal courts."[60] In early 2004, Smithfield's appeal was still pending at the NLRB in Washington—six years after the unfair election was held and three years after the appeal was filed. The board's decision can be appealed to a federal appeals court, meaning that several more years might pass before a final decision in the case.

Apple Workers in Washington State: Some Progress but No Union

More than forty thousand Mexican workers, including some U.S. citizens and green card holders, but mostly undocumented immigrants, labor in the orchards and processing plants of the largest apple-growing region in the United States. *Unfair Advantage* tells how employers crushed their efforts throughout the 1990s to form trade unions, to bargain collectively, to have job health and safety protection, to end discrimination, and to make other workplace gains.

Thanks to creative worker and community organizing and strategic use of the North American Agreement on Labor Cooperation (NAALC), the labor side agreement to the North American Free Trade Agreement (NAFTA), apple workers in Washington made some progress on wages, safety, and housing issues, helped by a state government sympathetic to workers' needs. The Mexican and U.S. labor departments developed a program of public outreach

---

[58]Ibid., 266.
[59]Ibid., 429–430.
[60]See Kevin Sack, "Judge Finds Labor Law Broken at Meat-Packing Plant," *New York Times*, January 4, 2001, p. A18.

and public hearings chaired by officials from the two federal governments and from the state government. The forums took place in 2001 in the apple-growing region of Washington, where large numbers of workers testified about conditions. Worried about possible effects on export sales in Mexico, apple industry employers made modest improvements in wages, health and safety, and housing conditions, and the state labor department added new labor standards enforcement capacity and bilingual inspectors.[61]

Nevertheless, Washington apple workers have not been able to advance their freedom of association, organizing, and bargaining goals. The NLRA still excludes them from protection of the right to organize and bargain collectively. Growers in Washington refuse to recognize apple workers' unions, and Washington has not adopted a state-level agricultural labor relations act, as have California and some other states.[62]

H-2A Workers in North Carolina: NAFTA and Congress

Unfair Advantage reports on widespread abuses against farmworkers in North Carolina, who come to work in the fields there holding H-2A temporary visas for seasonal agricultural labor. Supported by allied advocacy groups in North Carolina and across the nation, the Farm Labor Organizing Committee (FLOC) maintains a campaign targeting the Mt. Olive pickle company for voluntary recognition and bargaining with the union.[63]

Continuing problems impelled a coalition of workers, unions, and allied organizations in the United States and Mexico to file a broad-scale complaint in 2003 under the NAALC for violations of H-2A workers' freedom of association and for wage, job safety, and nondiscrimination guarantees.[64] *Unfair Advantage* served as a basic source for the complaint. The NAFTA labor agreement is not an enforcement system, but it can lead to international scrutiny of labor rights violations.

---

[61]See Marni Leff, "Fair-Trade Apples Sought," *Seattle Post-Intelligencer*, August 3, 2001, p. E6; Carole Pearson, "A Case of Apples: Mexican Farm Workers in Washington," *Our Times* magazine, January 2002.

[62]For a comprehensive analysis of the California legislation, see Philip L. Martin, *Promise Unfulfilled: Unions, Immigration, and the Farm Workers* (Ithaca: Cornell University Press, 2003).

[63]See campaign information at FLOC's Web site, www.floc.com; for Mt. Olive's position, see its Web site at www.mtolivepickles.com.

[64]See Mexico National Administrative Office (NAO) Submission No. 2003-1 (February 11, 2003).

In Congress, farmworker advocates used *Unfair Advantage* to develop a significant legislative proposal titled the Agricultural Jobs, Opportunity, Benefits and Security Act of 2003 (AgJOBS). The bill enjoys broad bipartisan support in Congress.

The AgJOBS bill contains two major parts: (1) a legalization program that allows undocumented farmworkers who have been working in American agriculture to apply for temporary immigration status and gain permanent immigration status upon completing a multi-year agricultural work requirement; and (2) revisions to the H-2A program that reduce employers' paperwork and time frames for H-2A applications, modify the wage-setting process, and, for the first time, give H-2A guest workers the right to enforce the terms of their employment contracts in federal courts. Farmworker unions believe this last point will allow them to effectively represent workers and perhaps persuade employers to bargain with them voluntarily rather than spend time and resources on litigation.

In its advocacy for passage, the AgJOBS coalition points to *Unfair Advantage*:

> A few labor contractors and agricultural employers argue that the proposed reform of the H-2A temporary foreign agricultural worker program is not good enough. We note that the most vociferous opponent thus far has been . . . the "North Carolina Growers Association." The abuses committed by this H-2A recruitment and consulting agency have been the subject of several exposés, including by Human Rights Watch in its report *Unfair Advantage* and in the award-winning series in the *Charlotte Observer* called "Desperate Harvest."[65]

New Hope for Freedom of Association: The Employee Free Choice Act of 2003

Inspired by *Unfair Advantage* and drawing directly from its recommendations, Senator Edward Kennedy of Massachusetts and Representative George Miller of California introduced the Employee Free Choice Act (EFCA)

---

[65]See Bruce Goldstein, Co-Executive Director, Farmworker Justice Fund, Letter to Judiciary Committee, November 3, 2003, at www.fwjustice.org/fjfagjlett.htm.

in November 2003.[66] They quickly gathered more than two hundred cosponsors in the Senate and House.

In a statement accompanying his submission of the bill in the House, Rep. Miller said:

> In August 2000, Human Rights Watch, which usually reviews condi-tions in developing nations, documented "a systemic failure to ensure the most basic right of workers in the United States: their freedom to choose to come together to negotiate the terms of their employment with their employers." No impartial observer of our law could reach any other conclusion.[67]

The EFCA would allow workers to opt for card-check certification of their desire for union representation as an alternative to the NLRB election sys-tem, whose delays, frustrations, and resulting bitterness are described in excru-ciating detail in *Unfair Advantage*. As the Avondale organizing effort and its aftermath show, the card-check method can be a rapid, fair, peace-promoting system of mutual benefit for workers and employers.

The legislation would also create a system of first-contract arbitration when workers and employers cannot reach an agreement. Whether to overcome deliberate bad-faith bargaining, as in the Acme Die Casting case study in *Unfair Advantage*, or in situations in which simple fear of the unknown keeps parties from reaching an agreement, first-contract arbitration, using average settlement guidelines, can get newly formed unions and newly organized com-panies over the threshold of their first experience in bargaining. Second con-tracts are normally settled more easily and peacefully than first contracts, once the parties have gotten used to working together in administering an agreement.

Finally, the EFCA would strengthen penalties for violations of workers' organizing rights. For workers fired for organizing efforts, the bill calls for more vigorous use of the NLRB's injunction-seeking capability to gain their rapid reinstatement. The EFCA would require triple back pay for fired work-ers, and a system of civil fines, as for other labor law violations.

All these measures are contained in the recommendations in *Unfair*

---

[66]See "The Right to Organize," testimony of Kenneth Roth, executive director, Human Rights Watch, before the Senate Committee on Health, Education, Labor and Pensions, June 20, 2002.

[67]See "Statement by the Honorable George Miller (D-CA): On Introducing the Employee Free Choice Act," November 13, 2003.

Advantage. On December 10, 2003, International Human Rights Day (the anniversary of the signing of the Universal Declaration of Human Rights), the AFL-CIO and allied civil society groups in seventy cities across the country mounted large-scale rallies, marches, and demonstrations in support of the EFCA and of workers' human rights. *Unfair Advantage* was the source universally cited in this mobilization.[68]

Cornell University Press offers this edition of *Unfair Advantage* to a broad readership of national and international activists, advocates, scholars, journalists, policy makers, agency officials, candidates for office, and others at the intersection of labor and human rights affairs. But more: this edition is meant to reach people who may fit none of those categories but who care about working people, human rights, social justice, and the kind of society we and our children will live in.

LANCE COMPA

Ithaca, New York

---

[68]See, for example, editorial, "Rights at Work," *Boston Globe*, December 9, 2003, p. A22; John Sweeney (AFL-CIO president), "Workers' Rights Inseparable from Basic Human Rights," *Chicago Tribune*, December 10, 2003, p. 55; Nancy Cleeland, "Workers, Labor Leaders Rally in Los Angeles for Union Rights," *Los Angeles Times*, December 11, 2003, p. C2; Steven Greenhouse, "Labor Rallies in Support of Bill to Back the Right to Join Unions," *New York Times*, December 11, 2003, p. A41.

NOTE ON METHODOLOGY

Human Rights Watch selected case studies for this report on workers' freedom of association in the United States with several objectives in mind. One was to include a range of sectors—services, industry, transport, agriculture, high tech—to assess the scope of the problem across the economy, rather than to focus on a single sector. Another objective was geographic diversity, to analyze the issues in different parts of the country. The cases studied here arose in cities, suburbs and rural areas around the United States.

Another important goal was to look at the range of workers seeking to exercise their right to freedom of association—high skill and low skill, blue collar and white collar, resident and migrant, women and men, of different racial, ethnic and national origins. Many of the cases involved the most vulnerable parts of the labor force. These include migrant farmworkers, sweatshop workers, household domestic workers, undocumented immigrants, and welfare-to-work employees. But the report also examines the rights of U.S. workers with many years of employment at stable, profitable employers. These include packaging factory workers, steel workers, shipyard workers, food processing workers, nursing home workers, and computer programmers.

The cases studied here offer a cross-section of workers' attempts to form and join trade unions, to bargain collectively, and to strike. The cases reflect violations and obstacles workers met in the exercise of these rights. In many cases, workers' voices recount their experiences. Human Rights Watch also made written requests for responses and comments from employers identified in the report. Most of them declined. Of those who did respond, most did not want to be identified by name. In several cases, the names of individual managers are known to Human Rights Watch, but they are omitted so as not to profile them unduly in a human rights report with wide distribution to the public. This report is intended to illuminate systemic problems in U.S. labor law and practice, not conduct of individuals.

In addition to interviews, the report relies on documented evidence in proceedings under U.S. labor law. Researching and writing a report like this is different from other international human rights investigations and reports carried out in zones of armed conflict, in refugee camps, or in countries without functioning legal systems. The United States has an elaborate system of constitutional, statutory and administrative labor law. In many of the cases studied here there are legal records and decisions by neutral adjudicators.

In many cases, the report relies both on interviews with workers and on records available from the National Labor Relations Board (NLRB) or federal court decisions. Workers in the private sector who are covered by the National Labor Relations Act (NLRA) can file charges with the NLRB for violations of their

1

statutory rights to organize, to bargain collectively, and to strike. Decisions of the NLRB are subject to review by the federal courts This gives rise to investigations and resulting legal procedures that produce an often extensive written record. Where such a record is available, Human Rights Watch relies on it to shed light on the nature and extent of workers' rights violations.

To supplement its on-the-ground research and official records, Human Rights Watch used credible news accounts of instances where workers' rights appear to have been impaired. Books published by university presses and based on extensive field research are also used, as are law review and social science journal articles.

No Human Rights Watch assertion in this report is based on unfair labor practice *charges* against employers. Workers can file such charges with the NLRB claiming a violation of their rights, but the charge by itself is an allegation. Human Rights Watch begins relying on NLRB records with the issuance of *complaints* by the general counsel of the agency. Complaints are issued when an investigation finds merit in the charge.

The NLRB is scrupulous in evaluating charges and issuing complaints. Fewer than 15 percent of unfair labor practice charges result in complaints. However, the NLRB makes intensive efforts to settle meritorious cases before issuing complaints, as well as after issuing complaints but before a hearing. Human Rights Watch refers to such settlements in this report. Their use is not intended to characterize conduct cited in the settlements as unlawful under the NLRA, but to provide an account of the conduct in light of international standards.

Findings of merit in unfair labor practice charges are based on detailed investigations of charges by regional agents of the NLRB and evaluations by experienced labor law attorneys in the regional offices. These investigations include interviewing and taking affidavits from workers who filed charges and from potential witnesses. They also involve consulting extensively with employers and offering them an opportunity to rebut any charges through written position statements and dialogue with the NLRB regional officials. Based on these investigations and evaluations of the evidence, labor law enforcement officials decide whether charges have merit. Only upon finding that charges are meritorious does the NLRB seek pre-complaint settlements or, failing settlement, issue complaints and set cases for trial before administrative law judges, normally several months in the future.[1]

---

[1]While the proceeding before an administrative law judge is a trial in the normal sense of the word—the presentation of evidence and examination and cross-examination of witnesses—it is called a "hearing" in U.S. labor law parlance. Further references to this stage of U.S. labor law procedures will use the term "hearing," but it should be understood that it involves a formal legal proceeding under rules of evidence, not an informal proceeding more often

NLRB records show that in the past decade a very consistent 35-40 percent of unfair labor practice charge cases are deemed meritorious following an investigation.[2] Two-thirds of these are settled before complaints are issued, with settlements containing some form of relief. Relief often involves back pay for workers who suffered discrimination, along with posting by employers of notices in the workplace stating that they will not engage in the conduct cited in the settled charges.[3]

The NLRB general counsel's method of interviewing witnesses, obtaining corroborating evidence, and giving employers an opportunity to respond before issuing a complaint or settling a meritorious charge is analogous to the standard research methods of Human Rights Watch and other organizations that seek to document human rights abuses, most often in areas of conflict where a legal system is inoperative, if it even exists. In the United States, however, succeeding stages of NLRB and federal court proceedings provide further foundation for Human Rights Watch's analyses in this report.

Decisions of administrative law judges are based on testimony and documents subject to the rules of evidence and related examination and cross-examination of witnesses. Decisions normally are issued several months after a hearing is concluded. In cases that were not yet decided as this report goes to press but that have available transcripts of hearing testimony, Human Rights Watch uses testimony from the transcripts in its analysis. Where written decisions of administrative law judges are available, Human Rights Watch uses them and not prior testimony from transcripts or complaints.

Administrative law judges' decisions are appealable to the NLRB's five-member board in Washington. The NLRB can take one, two, or three years to issue its decisions. In several of the cases studied here, the findings of administrative law judges have been appealed and are still pending. Most such findings are upheld by the NLRB on appeal.

Where the NLRB has ruled on appeals from administrative law judges' decisions, Human Rights Watch uses the board's rulings, not the prior decisions, as the basis of its analysis. However, board rulings are themselves subject to appeals

---

associated with the term "hearing."

[2]See National Labor Relations Board, 1998 *Annual Report* (hereafter NLRB Annual Report), Chart 5, p. 9.

[3]Settlements normally contain a non-admission clause by which employers do not concede that they broke the law. In using such settlements as a documentary basis for analyzing workers' exercise of freedom of association, Human Rights Watch is not asserting that employers violated the NLRA. However, the information is relied on in some cases in discussions of violations of international norms regarding workers' freedom of association.

to a federal circuit court. In some cases in the report, such appeals are pending. Indeed, circuit court rulings can be appealed to the U.S. Supreme Court, although such appeals are rare and none of the cases studied are in this position. Where decisions of federal appeals courts are available, Human Rights Watch uses them. Federal courts of appeals uphold NLRB rulings in approximately 80 percent of appealed cases.[4]

In sum, where using NLRB and federal court records as the basis for analyzing cases in terms of workers' freedom of association under international human rights standards, Human Rights Watch uses the "last best" documented evidence and determinations. However, where noted, some determinations were still pending on appeal as this report goes to press and could be reversed. It must again be stressed that Human Rights Watch uses information from documented legal proceedings to inform the analysis of workers' rights under international standards, not to assert conclusively that U.S. law was violated except where, in fact, there has been a final, conclusive determination to that effect under U.S. law.

This report could not address all the issues in U.S. labor law and practice with implications for workers' freedom of association. For example, minority unionism—the right of workers to organize and bargain collectively when they are a minority of the employees in a workplace, a right recognized in many other countries' labor law systems—is not discussed here.[5] Neither is denying workers the right to have a coworker present at a disciplinary interview with management when there is no union in the workplace, a recurring issue in U.S. labor law that concerns freedom of association.[6] Nor is the issue of workers' right not to associate or to disassociate from a union considered here.

An important distinction in U.S. law between "mandatory" and "permissive" subjects of bargaining is also not treated here, although many analysts suggest that it unfairly restricts the scope of workers' bargaining rights, especially over workplace closures.[7] The application of antitrust laws to block organizing efforts

---

[4]See NLRB 1998 Annual Report, Table 19A, p. 182. NLRB decisions are upheld in full in almost 70 percent of the cases; other decisions are affirmed in part or modified by the courts.
[5]The case has been made that minority unionism and minority bargaining are possible under U.S. labor law, but workers have not pressed the issue. See Clyde Summers, "Unions Without Majority – A Black Hole?", 66 *Chicago-Kent Law Review* 531 (1990).
[6]See *NLRB v. J. Weingarten, Inc.*, 420 U.S. 251 (1975; *Materials Research Corp.*, 262 NLRB 1010 (1982); *Sears, Roebuck & Co.*, 274 NLRB No. 55 (1985); Epilepsy Found. of N.E. Ohio, 331 NLRB No. 92 (2000).
[7]See, e.g., Abner J. Mikva, "The Changing Role of the Wagner Act in the American Labor Movement," 38 *Stanford Law Review* 1123 (1986); *First National Maintenance Corp. v. NLRB*, 452 U.S. 666 (1981).

by workers deemed independent contractors is another obstacle to freedom of association for affected workers, but it is not taken up here in detail.[8] The issue of secondary picketing for organizational purposes ("organizational picketing") is set aside, while secondary action as a means of strike support ("secondary boycott") is addressed. Both actions implicate workers' freedom of association, but the latter is more severely restricted in U.S. law, and more options are available to workers seeking to form a union.[9]

The denial to state and local public employees in many states of the right to bargain collectively and the right to strike is referred to in discussions of workers excluded from the protection of U.S. labor laws, but without a full analysis or case studies. Brief mention is also made of the denial to federal employees of the right to bargain over economic terms and conditions of employment or to strike, without further treatment. Problems of agricultural workers, domestic household workers and other excluded categories are treated at greater length in this report.

Case studies fall into two broad categories. One involves cases where U.S. law comports with international standards regarding freedom of association, but government enforcement action is not sufficient to protect workers' exercise of their rights in the face of violations by employers. In some cases studied here, governmental power itself interfered with workers' freedom of association.

The second category involves cases where U.S. law conflicts with international labor rights standards and thus places legal obstacles in the way of workers seeking to exercise rights to free association. In practice, distinctions among violations by employers, lack of effective enforcement by government, and legal obstacles cannot always be neatly made, but the general structure of the report approaches the issues with these distinctions in mind. Human Rights Watch's recommendations follow similar lines, suggesting ways to make enforcement of workers' rights more effective under existing U.S. law and proposing changes to U.S. law where it fails to protect workers' freedom of association.

---

[8]See Michael C. Harper, "Defining the Economic Relationship Appropriate for Collective Bargaining," 39 *Boston College Law Review* 329 (March 1998).

[9]Organizational picketing is action taken by workers to compel a non-union employer to recognize and bargain with a union without an NLRB election. A secondary boycott is action taken by workers to have a "secondary" supplier or customer firm cease doing business with (thus cease economically supporting) a "primary" employer involved in a labor dispute with workers at the primary firm. See sections 8(b)(7) and 8(b)(4) of the NLRA.

I. SUMMARY

Everyone shall have the right to freedom of association with others, including the right to form and join trade unions.
—International Covenant on Civil and Political Rights (ratified by the United States in 1992)

Employees shall have the right to self-organization, to form, join, or assist labor organizations, to bargain collectively through representatives of their own choosing, and to engage in other mutual aid or protection.
—National Labor Relations Act (passed by Congress in 1935)

I know the law gives us rights on paper, but where's the reality?
—Ernest Duval, a worker fired in 1994 for forming and joining a union (speaking in 1999)

Every day about 135 million people in the United States get up and go to their jobs in service, industry, agriculture, non-profit, government and other sectors of the enormous and complex American economy. The rate of new job creation in the United States—almost twenty million in the 1990s—is the envy of many other countries.

Under a wide-angle lens the American economy appears strong. Unemployment is low, and wages are inching up after years of stagnation. In focus, though, there are alarming signals for Americans concerned about social justice and human rights. A two-tier economy and society are taking shape. Income inequality is at historically high proportions.[10] Worker self-organization and collective bargaining, engines of middle-class growth and social solidarity in the century just ended, have reached historically low proportions. Although trade unions halted a

---

[10]See Center on Budget and Policy Priorities; Economic Policy Institute, "Pulling Apart: A State-by-State Analysis of Income Trends" (January 2000), showing that the average income of families in the top 20 percent of the income distribution was $137,500, or more than ten times as large as the poorest 20 percent of families, which had an average income of $13,000, and that throughout the 1990s the average real income of high-income families grew by 15 percent, while average income remained the same for the lowest-income families and grew by less than two percent for middle-income families – not enough to make up for the decline in income in the 1980s. See also Richard W. Stevenson, "In a Time of Plenty, The Poor Are Still Poor," *New York Times*, January 23, 2000, Week in Review, p.3; James Lardner, "The Rich Get Richer" What happens to American society when the gap in wealth and income grows larger?", *U.S. News & World Report*, February 21, 2000, p.38.

declining membership trend in 1999, slightly increasing the absolute number of workers who bargain collectively, the percentage of the workforce represented by unions did not increase.[11]

Many Americans think of workers' organizing, collective bargaining, and strikes solely as union-versus-management disputes that do not raise human rights concerns. This report approaches workers' use of these tools as an exercise of basic rights where workers are autonomous actors, not objects of unions' or employers' institutional interests. Both historical experience and a review of current conditions around the world indicate that strong, independent, democratic trade unions are vital for societies where human rights are respected. Human rights cannot flourish where workers' rights are not enforced. Researching workers' exercise of these rights in different industries, occupations, and regions of the United States to prepare this report, Human Rights Watch found that freedom of association is a right under severe, often buckling pressure when workers in the United States try to exercise it.

Labor rights violations in the United States are especially troubling when the U.S. administration is pressing other countries to ensure respect for internationally recognized workers' rights as part of the global trade and investment system. For example, many developing countries charge that U.S. proposals for a working group on labor rights at the World Trade Organization (WTO) are motivated by protectionism, not by a concern for workers' rights. U.S. insistence on a rights-based linkage to trade is undercut when core labor rights are systematically violated in the United States.

This report occasionally touches on rights of association outside the context of trade unionism. One example is the right of workers to seek legal assistance for work-related problems. Most of Human Rights Watch's investigation, however, deals with workers' attempts to form unions and bargain with their employers. Forming and joining a union is a natural response of workers seeking to improve their working conditions. It is also a natural expression of the human right, indeed

---

[11]In 1999 more than sixteen million workers in the United States belonged to trade unions. For the workforce as a whole, 13.9 percent of all workers and 9.4 percent of private sector workers were union members. While more workers gained union representation by forming new unions than lost it through workplace layoffs and closures in 1999 for the first time in many years, the proportion of the total workforce represented by unions remained unchanged because of employment growth in firms and sectors with less union presence. In the 1950s such union "density" reached more than 30 percent of the total workforce and nearly 40 percent in the private sector. See Frank Swoboda, "Labor Unions See Membership Gains," *Washington Post*, January 20, 2000, p. E2.

the human need, of association in a common purpose where the only alternative offered by an impersonal market is quitting a job.[12]

Without diminishing the seriousness of the obstacles and violations confronted by workers in the United States, a balanced perspective must be maintained. U.S. workers generally do not confront gross human rights violations where death squads assassinate trade union organizers or collective bargaining and strikes are outlawed.[13] But the absence of systematic government repression does not mean that workers in the United States have effective exercise of the right to freedom of association. On the contrary, workers' freedom of association is under sustained attack in the United States, and the government is often failing its responsibility under international human rights standards to deter such attacks and protect workers' rights.

The cases studied in this report are not isolated exceptions in an otherwise benign environment for workers' freedom of association. They reflect a broader pattern confirmed by other researchers and borne out in nationwide information and statistics. In the 1950s, for example, workers who suffered reprisals for exercising the right to freedom of association numbered in the hundreds each year. In the 1960s, the number climbed into the thousands, reaching slightly over 6,000 in 1969. By the 1990s more than 20,000 workers each year were victims of discrimination leading to a back-pay order by the NLRB—23,580 in 1998.[14] The frequency and

---

[12]Union-represented workers generally have higher wages and benefits than non-represented employees. In 1999, union members had median weekly earnings of $672, compared with a median of $516 for workers who did not belong to a union. They are also protected against arbitrary discharge or other forms of discrimination under a "just cause" standard contained in nearly every union contract. For most non-represented workers in the private sector, an employment-at-will doctrine prevails. An employer can dismiss a worker for "a good reason, a bad reason, or no reason at all," in the classic formulation, except where laws specifically prohibit discrimination. On comparative weekly earnings, see U.S. Department of Labor, Bureau of Labor Statistics, "Union Membership in 1999" (January 19, 2000). For extensive discussion of the at-will doctrine, see Pauline T. Kim, "Bargaining with Imperfect Information: A Study of Worker Perceptions of Legal Protection in an At-Will world," 83 Cornell Law Review 105 (1997); Richard A. Epstein, "In Defense of the Contract at Will," 51 University of Chicago Law Review 947 (1984).

[13]At the same time, Human Rights Watch did find instances in various case studies of interference with workers' rights by government authorities. They included biased intervention by police and local government authorities and government subsidization of workers' rights violators. While these cases do not rise to a level of systemic abuse, they are no less troubling and, if they are not addressed and stopped, such abuses could spread.

[14]See NLRB Annual Reports 1950-1998; 1998 Table 4, p. 137.

growing incidence of workers' rights violations should cause grave concern among Americans who care about human rights and social justice.

Policy and Reality

Workers in the United States secured a measure of legal protection for the right to organize, to bargain collectively, and to strike with passage of the Norris-LaGuardia Act of 1932 and the Wagner Act of 1935, the original National Labor Relations Act (NLRA).[15] These advances came after decades of struggle and sacrifice from the time, a century before, when trade unions were treated as a criminal conspiracy. The NLRA declares a national policy of "full freedom of association" and protects workers' "right to self-organization, to form, join, or assist labor organizations, to bargain collectively through representatives of their own choosing, and to engage in other concerted activities for the purpose of collective bargaining or other mutual aid or protection . . ."[16] The NLRA makes it unlawful for employers to "interfere with, restrain, or coerce" workers in the exercise of these rights. It creates the National Labor Relations Board (NLRB) to enforce the law by investigating and remedying violations. All these measures comport with international human rights norms regarding workers' freedom of association.

The reality of NLRA enforcement falls far short of its goals. Many workers who try to form and join trade unions to bargain with their employers are spied on, harassed, pressured, threatened, suspended, fired, deported or otherwise victimized in reprisal for their exercise of the right to freedom of association.

Private employers are the main agents of abuse. But international human rights law makes governments responsible for protecting vulnerable persons and groups from patterns of abuse by private actors. In the United States, labor law enforcement efforts often fail to deter unlawful conduct. When the law is applied, enervating delays and weak remedies invite continued violations.

Any employer intent on resisting workers' self-organization can drag out legal proceedings for years, fearing little more than an order to post a written notice in the workplace promising not to repeat unlawful conduct and grant back pay to a worker fired for organizing. In one case cited here, a worker fired for five years

---

[15]The Norris-LaGuardia Act outlawed "yellow-dog" contracts (requiring a worker to renounce union membership as a condition of employment) and *ex parte* labor injunctions (by which judges enjoined strikes and jailed strike leaders after hearing only the employer's argument in a case). The Wagner Act created Section 7 rights, defined unfair labor practices, and set up the NLRB for enforcement. Senator Norris and Congressman LaGuardia were both Republicans; Senator Wagner was a Democrat, reflecting a tradition of support for workers' rights from both major political parties.
[16]29 U.S.C. §§ 151-169, Section 7.

received $1,305 back pay and $493 interest.[17] Many employers have come to view remedies like back pay for workers fired because of union activity as a routine cost of doing business, well worth it to get rid of organizing leaders and derail workers' organizing efforts. As a result, a culture of near-impunity has taken shape in much of U.S. labor law and practice.

Moreover, some provisions of U.S. law openly conflict with international norms and create formidable legal obstacles to the exercise of freedom of association. Millions of workers are expressly barred from the law's protection of the right to organize. U.S. legal doctrine allowing employers to permanently replace workers who exercise the right to strike effectively nullifies the right. Mutual support among workers and unions recognized in most of the world as legitimate expressions of solidarity is harshly proscribed under U.S. law as illegal secondary boycotts. Labor laws have failed to keep pace with changes in the economy and new forms of employment relationships creating millions of part-time, temporary, subcontracted, and otherwise "atypical" or "contingent" workers whose exercise of the right to freedom of association is frustrated by the law's inadequacy.

Workers' Voices

"I know the law gives us rights on paper, but where's the reality?" asks Ernest Duval, a certified nurse assistant at a Florida nursing home. Duval and several coworkers were unlawfully fired in 1994 for activities like wearing buttons, passing out flyers, signing petitions, and talking with coworkers about banding together in a union at their workplace in West Palm Beach. In 1996 a judge found their employer guilty of unlawful discrimination and ordered Duval and his coworkers reinstated to their jobs. In 1999 they were still out of work despite an NLRB order upholding the judge's ruling.[18] The employer continued to appeal these decisions, now to federal courts where years' more delay is likely. Meanwhile, the fired

---

[17]Under the NLRA, back pay awards are "mitigated" by earnings from other employment. Employers who illegally fire workers for organizing need only pay the difference, if any, between what workers would have earned had they not been fired, and what they earned on other jobs during the period of unlawful discharge. Since workers cannot remain without income during years of litigation, they must seek other jobs and income, leaving the employers who violated their rights with an often negligible back pay liability.

[18]See *PVM I Associates, Inc. D/b/a King David Center and U.S. Management, Inc. and 1115 Nursing Home Hospital and Service Employees Union-Florida*, 328 NLRB No. 159, August 6, 1999. In Duval's case, the judge found that management discharged him on fabricated misconduct charges because it was "determined to rid itself of the most vocal union supporter."

workers remain off the job, and their coworkers are frightened into retreat from the organizing and bargaining effort.

"We know our job, we love our job, we love our patients, but management doesn't respect us," Marie Pierre, another nursing home assistant, told Human Rights Watch.[19] Pierre served as a union observer at two representation elections in 1998 and 1999 at a nursing home in Lake Worth, Florida. The union won both elections, but Pierre was fired in December 1999 for speaking Creole with coworkers. The company has refused to accept election results, appealing them to the NLRB and raising the prospect of years more of appeals before the courts.

"They don't let us talk to Legal Services or the union. They would fire us if we called them or talked to them," said a farmworker in North Carolina to an Human Rights Watch researcher examining freedom of association among H-2A migrant laborers.[20] The H-2A program grants migrant workers a temporary visa for agricultural work in the United States. They labor at the sufferance of growers who can fire them and have them deported if they try to form or join a union.

A continent's breadth away, an apple picker in Washington State told Human Rights Watch of threats from "the consultant that was telling [the company] how to beat the union."[21] Part of a growing industry that specializes in telling employers how to defeat workers' self-organization, the consultant told striking apple workers, "You have thirty minutes to get back to work or you're all fired."[22] A convoy of police cars escorted trucks and vans full of workers sent by other apple growers to break the strike. Farmworkers in the United States are excluded from coverage by laws to protect the right to organize, to bargain, and to strike, and can be fired for exercising these rights.

Nico Valenzuela is another kind of victim. He and his coworkers at a Chicago-area telecommunications castings company voted by a large majority in 1987 to form and join a union. Valenzuela is still working, but collective bargaining proved futile in the face of a management campaign to punish workers for their vote. Despite repeated findings by the NLRB that the company acted unlawfully, legal remedies took years to obtain. The workers abandoned bargaining in 1999, twelve years after they formed a union, never having achieved a contract.

---

[19]Human Rights Watch telephone interview, North Miami, Florida, March 8, 2000.

[20]Human Rights Watch interview, near Mount Olive, North Carolina, July 15, 1999.

[21]Human Rights Watch interview, Sunnyside, Washington, November 6, 1999. See Chapter IV., *Washington State Apple Industry* below.

[22]A videotape of the workers' picketing activity, reviewed by Human Rights Watch, shows the consultant making this statement. For more details, see Chapter IV., *Washington State Apple Industry* below.

The delays "took away our spirit," said Nico Valenzuela of the bargaining process. "I don't know how the law in this country can allow these maneuvers."[23]

Lloyd Montiel, a twenty-seven-year veteran employee at a steel mill in Pueblo, Colorado, exercised the right to strike along with 1,000 coworkers in response to management's threats during bargaining. The company permanently replaced them with newly hired strikebreakers, many coming from other states. "How can the government and Congress allow companies to do this?" he asks. "They [the employer] can plan a strike, cause a strike, and then get rid of people who gave them a lifetime of work and bring in young guys who never saw the inside of a steel mill."[24]

At a world of work far removed from steel mills and nursing homes, Barbara Judd, a high-tech contract worker in Redmond, Washington, found herself and coworkers who formed a union caught between the firm where they worked and their temporary employment agencies when they sought to bargain collectively. As "permatemps"—long-term workers at a single firm, but nominally employed by outside agencies—Judd's group had no one to bargain with. Denying their employment status, the firm refused to bargain with the group. Meanwhile, the temporary agencies refused to bargain with workers placed at the firm.[25]

The stories of these and other workers who have tried to exercise the right to freedom of association promised by international human rights instruments and by the U.S. labor law principles are the focus of this report. The cases reported here are not exceptional, and the findings are not novel for those familiar with domestic U.S. discourse on workers' rights to organize and bargain collectively. Congressional committees and presidential commissions have reached the same conclusions, and Human Rights Watch has consulted these sources among others in preparing this report.[26]

---

[23]Human Rights Watch interview, Chicago, Illinois, July 8, 1999. For more details, see Chapter IV., *Northbrook, Illinois Telecommunications Castings* below.

[24]Human Rights Watch interview, Pueblo, Colorado, May 20, 1999. For details on the legal underpinnings of an assertion of unlawful conduct, see the discussion and footnotes in Chapter V., *Colorado Steelworkers, the Right to Strike and Permanent Replacements in U.S. Labor Law* below.

[25]Human Rights Watch interview, Seattle, Washington, November 4, 1999. For details, see Chapter IV., *Contingent Workers* below.

[26]See, for example, Subcommittee on Labor-Management Relations of the House Committee on Education and Labor, 96th Cong., 2d Sess., "Report on Pressures in Today's Workplace" (1980); Subcommittee on Labor Management Relations of the House Committee on Education and Labor, 98th Congress, "The Failure of Labor Law: A Betrayal of American Workers" (1984); U.S. Department of Labor, Bureau of Labor-Management Relations, Report No. 134, "U.S. Labor Law and the Future of Labor-Management Cooperation"

International Human Rights and Workers

Human Rights Watch brings to the discussion an analysis of workers' freedom of association in the United States in light of international human rights standards. An international human rights perspective provides new ways of understanding U.S. labor law and practice and of advocating changes to bring them in line with international standards.

Freedom of association is the bedrock workers' right under international law on which all other labor rights rest. In the workplace, freedom of association takes shape in the right of workers to organize to defend their interests in employment. Most often, workers organize by forming and joining trade unions. Protection of their right to organize is an affirmative responsibility of governments to ensure workers' freedom of association. As one scholar notes, "States are . . . obligated [under the International Covenant on Civil and Political Rights, ratified by the United States] to protect the formation or activities of association against interference by private parties."[27]

But the right to organize does not exist in a vacuum. Workers organize for a purpose: to give unified voice to their need for just and favorable terms and conditions of employment when they have freely decided that collective representation is preferable to individual bargaining or management's unilateral power.

The right to bargain collectively stems unbroken from the principle of freedom of association and the right to organize. Protecting the right to bargain collectively guarantees that workers can engage their employer in exchange of information, proposals and dialogue to establish terms and conditions of employment. It is the means by which fundamental rights of association move into the real and enduring life of workers and employers. The right to bargain collectively is "real" implementation in the economic and social setting of the "ideal" civil and political rights of association and organizing.

At the same time, the right to bargain collectively is susceptible to a higher level of regulation than the right to organize. Bargaining is more than an exercise of the pure right of association by workers, since it implicates another party—the employer—and can carry social effects outside the workplace. Collective bargaining takes a wide variety of forms in different countries reflecting their

---

(1989); U.S. Department of Labor, U.S. Department of Commerce, Commission on the Future of Worker-Management Relations, *Fact Finding Report* (May 1994).

[27]See Manfred Nowak, *U.N. Covenant on Civil and Political Rights: CCPR Commentary* (Strasbourg, N.P. Engel, 1993), p. 387 (noting that "the US was unsuccessful with its motion in the HRComm to protect freedom of association only against 'governmental interference.'").

national histories and traditions. For example, some countries protect bargaining by workers whose unions represents only a minority of employees in workplaces. Others, like the United States, require majority support. Some countries allow multiple union representation among workers in the same jobs. The United States and others require exclusive representation by a single union for workers in a defined "bargaining unit." But regardless of differences in models of collective bargaining, the underlying basic right must be given effect.

The right to bargain collectively is compromised without the right to strike. This right, too, must be protected because without it there cannot be genuine collective bargaining. There can only be collective entreaty. Here, too, a greater level of regulation is contemplated under international norms since strikes can affect not just the parties to a dispute, but others as well. The International Covenant on Economic, Social and Cultural Rights proclaims "[t]he right to strike, provided that it is exercised in conformity with the laws of the particular country."[28] The International Labor Organization (ILO) has long maintained that the right to strike is an essential element of the right to freedom of association, but recognizes that strikes may be restricted by law where public safety is concerned, as long as adequate alternatives such as mediation, conciliation, and arbitration provide a solution for workers who are affected.

The right to organize, the right to bargain collectively, and the right to strike unfold seamlessly from the basic right to freedom of association. But they should not be equated with outcomes for the exercise of these rights. Workers do not have a right to win an NLRB election. They do not have a right to win their collective bargaining demands. They do not have a right to win a strike on their terms. Nothing in this report should be seen to argue for any specific outcome in an organizing, bargaining, or strike dispute. However, employers must respect and the state must protect workers' fundamental rights.

In recent months, the U.S. government has amplified calls for integrating human rights and labor rights into the global trade and investment system in such venues as the World Trade Organization and the Free Trade Agreement of the Americas. Freedom of association is the first such right cited in calls for labor rights in trade agreements. But to give effective leadership to this cause that is not undercut by hypocrisy, the United States must confront and begin to solve its own failings when it comes to workers' rights. Moving swiftly to strengthen labor rights enforcement and deter labor rights violations in the United States will reinforce the sincerity of U.S. concern for ensuring worldwide respect for core labor standards.

---

[28] ICESCR, Article 8 (d).

International Labor Rights Norms

A widely accepted body of international norms has set forth standards for workers' freedom of association. They can be found in the Universal Declaration of Human Rights and other United Nations instruments, in conventions of the ILO, in workers' rights clauses in regional trade agreements, and in other international compacts. They are also grounded in the near-universality of national laws protecting workers' freedom of association in all countries' labor law systems.

Workers' freedom of association in human rights instruments has been complemented by legal guidelines on international labor norms developed in detail by the ILO. These norms set forth the right to organize, the right to bargain collectively, and the right to strike as fundamental rights. They are inextricably tied to the exercise of the right to freedom of association and must be protected by national governments. Nearly every country is a member of the ILO. Each is bound by ILO Conventions 87 and 98 dealing with freedom of association whether or not they have ratified those conventions, since freedom of association is taken to be a constitutional norm binding on countries by virtue of their membership in the organization.[29]

The United States has not ratified Conventions 87 and 98 but has long acknowledged its obligations under them. In 1998, the United States championed adoption at the ILO of a landmark Declaration on Fundamental Principles and Rights at Work stating that

> all Members, even if they have not ratified the Conventions in question, have an obligation, arising from the very fact of membership in the Organization, to respect, to promote and to realize, in good faith and in accordance with the Constitution [of the ILO], the principles concerning the fundamental rights which are the subject of those Conventions, namely: (a) freedom of association and the effective recognition of the right to collective bargaining; . . .[30]

International human rights law prohibits the use of state power to repress workers' exercise of their right to freedom of association. Forming and joining

---

[29]ILO member countries are "bound to respect a certain number of general rules . . . among these principles, freedom of association has become a customary rule above the conventions." See Fact Finding and Conciliation Commission on Chile, (ILO, 1975), para. 466.

[30]See ILO *Declaration on Fundamental Principles and Rights at Work and Its Follow-Up*, adopted by the International Labour Conference at its Eighty-sixth Session, Geneva, 18 June 1998, p. 7.

unions, bargaining collectively, or exercising the right to strike may not be banned or rendered impotent by force of law. Officially or unofficially, authorities may not harass workers, arrest them, imprison them, or physically abuse or kill them for such activities.

Moreover, governments must take affirmative measures to protect workers' freedom of association. Governments have a responsibility under international law to provide effective recourse and remedies for workers whose rights have been violated by employers. Strong enforcement is required to deter employers from violating workers' rights.

In the United States, millions of workers are excluded from coverage by laws to protect rights of organizing, bargaining, and striking. For workers who are covered by such laws, recourse for labor rights violations is often delayed to a point where it ceases to provide redress. When they are applied, remedies are weak and often ineffective. In a system replete with all the appearance of legality and due process, workers' exercise of rights to organize, to bargain, and to strike in the United States has been frustrated by many employers who realize they have little to fear from labor law enforcement through a ponderous, delay-ridden legal system with meager remedial powers.

II. FINDINGS AND RECOMMENDATIONS

General

This section summarizes Human Rights Watch's findings and offers recommendations for addressing workers' rights violations by employers, inadequate enforcement of workers' rights by government, and legal obstacles that hinder workers' exercise of the right to freedom of association under international labor rights standards. Some of the recommendations could be achieved by administrative action. Some could be accomplished by the judicial branch in future labor law cases. But for the most part, action by Congress in the form of new legislation is called for.

U.S. labor law and practice are deeply entrenched, and its elements that frustrate rather than promote workers' freedom of association are not easily changed. Agencies can work incrementally at the margins of established rules but cannot take dramatic new initiatives absent legislation by Congress. In contrast to some areas of U.S. law, courts have often acted in the labor law arena to curtail workers' rights. Indeed, this report suggests that many of the features of U.S. labor law and practice that counter international norms result from court-fashioned doctrine, not just from statutory deficiencies.

As a political reality, Congress must work cooperatively with the administration and executive agencies with a joint commitment to craft and adopt new legislation halting violations, strengthening enforcement, and removing the obstacles to workers' exercise of freedom of association described in this report. For the most part, the recommendations offered here call for legislative action. Where a defined, practically achievable administrative action or judicial approach is called for, it is noted.

But beyond the technicalities of administrative regulations, jurisprudence or statutory reforms, a larger reality looms over labor law and practice in the United States. So long as worker organizing, collective bargaining, and the right to strike are seen only as economic disputes involving the exercise of power in pursuit of higher wages for employees or higher profits for employers, change is unlikely. Reformulating these issues as human rights concerns can begin a process of change.

What is most needed is a new spirit of commitment by the labor law community and the government to give effect to both international human rights norms and the still-vital affirmation in the United States' own basic labor law for full freedom of association for workers. The specific findings and recommendations that follow should be seen in this broader context.

One way to begin fostering such a change of spirit is for the United States to ratify ILO Conventions 87 and 98. This would send a strong signal to workers, employers, labor law authorities, and to the international community that the United

17

States is serious about holding itself to international human rights and labor rights standards as it presses for the inclusion of such standards in new global and regional trade arrangements.

Authorities and courts can take another step toward creating a climate of respect for workers' rights by looking to international human rights standards to inform their analyses and remedies in cases arising under U.S. domestic law. The NLRB, for example, has no support staff specializing in international labor law. Equipped with such expertise, the board could begin to examine the relevance and applicability of human rights norms or ILO conventions in its work. The private bar has a role here, too. Trade union and employer counsel should brief and argue points of international labor law to advance respect for workers' fundamental rights.

Perhaps most important, the primary actors in the labor field—workers themselves who seek to exercise rights enshrined in international law, and trade union leaders and organizers who assist them—should view and carry out their mission as one that includes human rights concerns, not simply as a business of rendering services in exchange for dues payments or as a path to personal advancement or enrichment. At the same time, their employer counterparts should begin to view workers' self-organization as a fundamental human right, and treat it as such.

Finding: Discrimination against Union Supporters

The basic international norm protecting the right to organize is stated in ILO Convention 98: "Workers shall enjoy adequate protection against acts of anti-union discrimination . . . more particularly acts calculated to cause the dismissal of or otherwise prejudice a worker by reason of union membership or participation in union activities." The NLRA's Section 8(a)(3) appears to meet this goal, making unlawful any discrimination against workers for concerted activity, including union activity.

Firing a worker for organizing is illegal but commonplace in the United States. Many of the cases examined by Human Rights Watch for this report reflect the frequency and the devastating effect of discriminatory discharges on workers' rights. An employer determined to get rid of a union activist knows that all that awaits, after years of litigation if the employer persists in appeals, is a reinstatement order the worker is likely to decline and a modest back-pay award. For many employers, it is a small price to pay to destroy a workers' organizing effort by firing its leaders.

Recommendation: Interim Reinstatement; Tougher Remedies

Two measures are needed to give effect to the international norm cited above. First, where the NLRB's investigation finds merit in a worker's charge of discriminatory discharge, the worker should be reinstated while the case continues to be litigated. Only such an interim reinstatement remedy can overcome the devastating impact on individual workers who are dismissed and on the workers' overall organizing effort. In contrast, this remedy creates no more than an inconvenience to the employer—keeping an experienced worker on the job while the worker's claim, already deemed meritorious under the NLRB's rigorous complaint process, is litigated through hearing and appeal stages. This remedy would also curtail appeals lodged solely for purposes of delay.

Second, abuses should carry a meaningful price so that remedies and sanctions have a deterrent value. Workers should receive full back pay regardless of interim earnings. They should receive punitive damages in cases of willful violations of U.S. law. In addition to paying workers victimized by violations, employers who repeatedly engage in discrimination against union supporters should pay substantial fines to the NLRB.

Finding: Imbalance in Communication Power

Employers have wide latitude under U.S. law to campaign aggressively against workers who seek to form and join unions. In written, oral, and filmed communication, employers confront workers with carefully scripted declarations to dissuade them from choosing union representation and collective bargaining. For their part, trade union organizers campaign aggressively to convince workers to choose in favor of representation.

But the battle is highly unequal. Employers oversee workers all day, every day when they are on the job. Indeed, employers begin "campaigning" the first day a worker is hired, communicating the employer's position about wages, working conditions, and treatment by managers. If workers begin an effort to gain a collective voice in the workplace, employers often hire consultants to develop an intensive campaign against forming and joining a union.

The campaign against workers' organizing efforts is most often marked by mandatory captive-audience meetings and mandatory, pressure-filled, one-on-one meetings between individual workers and their supervisors, with the latter coached by consultants on how to present self-organization as risky to employees' interests. Underlying all this employer opposition to workers' organizing is the raw power of the employment relationship—the power to assign work, to pay a wage, to impose discipline, and ultimately to dismiss the worker. Workers hear employers' views with this power in mind.

Recommendation: More Speech for Workers

Many worker advocates call for the repeal of Section 8 (c) of the NLRA, the 1947 "employer free speech" clause that codified court rulings allowing employers to campaign against worker organizing. According to this argument, workers' organizing is their own business; employers should stay out of it. Allowing *any* campaigning by employers invites unlawful interference because of the employers' inherent advantage in the employment relationship. In this view, the employer's "campaign" consists of the wages and working conditions afforded to employees; if workers decide they need collective bargaining to secure improvements, it should be strictly their own affair.

A human rights analysis approaches these issues differently. As outlined in more detail below, Human Rights Watch advocates more free speech for workers, not less free speech for employers. The goal is to achieve a fair balance for workers to hear all views about choosing to form and join a union, and to reduce the level of fear that so routinely accompanies workers' organizing efforts.

Finding: Workers' Lack of Access to Union Representatives

While forced to listen to the employer's arguments when they seek to organize, workers have only haphazard access to union advocates' views and explanations of the sometimes complicated process of forming a union and bargaining collectively. They may not have any face-to-face communication with organizers in a workplace-related setting. Instead, they have to meet union organizers at their homes or at meetings outside of work time, which is often difficult. For farmworkers in grower-owned housing, even meeting a union representative where they live is often prohibited.

Workers may take union leaflets at the perimeter of employment premises as they enter and leave the job, but even here their access to information is restricted. For example, under the law workers may not receive information from union representatives in publicly accessible parking lots of shopping centers or industrial parks. Workers may distribute union literature in the workplace, but employers can often block this under the law by posting a "nondiscriminatory" rule against solicitation. In the end, the most common form of workers' communication with a union is grabbing a leaflet near the workplace entrance by a public road.

Recommendation: Access to Information from Union Representatives at the Workplace

Congress should adopt legislation authorizing the NLRB to develop rules allowing workers to receive information from union advocates in non-work areas on non-work time within the workplace. Addressing such matters as time, place, duration, number of union representatives allowed access, and other details, access rules should be fashioned to balance the employer's interest in an uninterrupted work process with workers' right to receive information regarding their right to associate.

Finding: Forced Attendance and Discipline at Captive-Audience Meetings

Almost without limits, employers can force workers to attend captive-audience meetings on work time. Most often, these meetings include exhortations by top managers that are carefully scripted to fall within the wide latitude afforded employers under U.S. law—allowing "predictions" but not "threats" of workplace closings, for example—to deter workers from choosing union representation. Employers can fire workers for not attending the meetings. They can impose a "no questions or comments" rule at a captive-audience meeting, and discipline any worker who speaks up. Many of Human Rights Watch's case studies here involved the use of captive audience meetings.

The only limitation on captive-audience meetings is an NLRB rule prohibiting such meetings within twenty-four hours of the election. The board has ruled that the "mass psychology" and "unwholesome and unsettling effect" of captive-audience meetings tend to "interfere with that sober and thoughtful choice which a free election is designed to reflect."[31] It is not clear from NLRB doctrine why twenty-four hours is an appropriate number, or why the same concerns do not apply when management holds repeated captive-audience meetings up to the twenty-four-hour deadline with no opportunity for union advocates to have equal access to communicate with workers.

Recommendation: Proportional Access

A principle of proportional access should apply where employers force workers into captive-audience meetings at the workplace. Workers should have access to union representatives under similar conditions to hear information about their right to form and join trade unions and to bargain collectively.

Equal access for unions should not be automatic. It should be triggered by the employer's use of captive-audience meetings where an employer does not otherwise agree to allow access. NLRB rules should also permit reasonable opportunities for non-disruptive discussion and questioning during such employee meetings, whether with employers or union advocates.

Finding: "Predicting" Reprisals

Under U.S. law, employers and consultants have refined methods of legally "predicting"—as distinct from unlawfully threatening—workplace closures, firings, wage and benefit cuts, and other dire consequences if workers form and join a trade union. For example, a prediction that the workplace will be closed if employees vote for union representation is legal if the prediction is based on objective facts

---

[31] See *Peerless Plywood Co.*, 107 NLRB 427 (1953).

rather than the employer's subjective bias. While this distinction might be discernible to lawyers and judges, it is not clear to workers who hear managers holding superior economic power linking "union" and "closing" in captive audience meetings and in one-on-one discussions with employees.[32]

Recommendation: Closer Scrutiny and Tougher Remedies

Human Rights Watch does not recommend repealing Section 8(c) or unduly restricting employer speech. Instead, the NLRB should more closely scrutinize such statements by employers for potentially coercive effect. Where it finds violations, the board should apply strong, swift remedies. Most potently, the NLRB should more often seek *Gissel* bargaining orders, a special remedy now sparingly applied. Based on the name of a Supreme Court case in which the high court upheld the remedy,[33] *Gissel* orders require employers to recognize and bargain with unions in cases where a majority of workers freely signed union cards authorizing union representation and the employers' coercive threats made a fair election impossible. For their part, the courts should signal approval of wider use of the *Gissel* remedy by upholding NLRB orders for *Gissel* relief.

Finding: Election Acrimony

NLRB elections too often involve intense, acrimony-filled campaigns marked by heated rhetoric and attacks on the motives of both employers and union advocates. The bitterness of a representation campaign can poison chances of a mutually beneficial bargaining relationship. Unfortunately, many of the cases examined here appear to be launched on such a road.

Many analysts have articulated powerful critiques of the NLRB election process and urged replacing elections with the quicker, non-confrontational card-check method of determining workers' choice for representation and collective bargaining.[34] The card-check system, by which recognition of workers' majority

---

[32]Indeed, employers often carry out such reprisals to retaliate against workers' attempts to organize. In a comparative study of anti-union plant closings in the United States, Canada, and Mexico, the NAFTA labor commission reviewed 408 federal appeals court and NLRB decisions on full or partial plant closings between 1986 and 1995, finding that employers were found guilty of unlawful discrimination in 367 cases. See Secretariat of the Commission for Labor Cooperation, *Plant Closings and Labor Rights* (Dallas, Texas, Commission for Labor Cooperation, 1997).

[33]See *NLRB v. Gissel Packing Co.*, 395 U.S. 575 (1969).

[34]See, e.g., Craig Becker, "Democracy in the Workplace: Union Representation in Elections and Federal Labor Law" 77 *Minnesota Law Review* 495 (1993). The card-check method is a standard procedure for choosing representation in several Canadian jurisdictions. Elections

sentiment for or against collective bargaining is based on signed authorization cards, is examined in several cases in this report involving hotel workers, shipyard workers, and apple industry workers. As they demonstrate, the card-check method—with sufficient safeguards to ensure that cards are signed voluntarily—allows a reasoned choice in a less coercive atmosphere.

This argument has merit, and perhaps over time the U.S. system could evolve toward a generalized acceptance of the card-check system. But in American culture now and for the foreseeable future, fairly run secret-ballot elections still have a moral primacy. Workers, employers, and the general public see their outcome as more legitimate.

Recommendation: Expanded Use of Voluntary Card-Check Agreements

Human Rights Watch believes that secret-ballot elections should remain a standard method of determining workers' choice whether to bargain collectively with their employer. At the same time, experience demonstrates that where workers and employers can agree to use card checks that genuinely reflect workers' free choice, with safeguards against coercion by management, by union representatives or by coworkers, they can combine the benefits of freedom of choice and a mutually respectful relationship that carries over into collective bargaining. Public policy should encourage the use of voluntary card-check agreements as an alternative means of establishing workers' majority sentiment and collective bargaining rights.

Finding: Delays in NLRB and Court Procedures

Long delays in the U.S. labor law system confound workers' exercise of the right to freedom of association. In representation cases, NLRB elections take place at least several weeks after workers file a petition seeking an election. In many cases, the election can be held up for months by employer-initiated disputes over which workers should be eligible to vote in the election as part of the "appropriate bargaining unit."

An employer can also file objections to an election after it takes place, arguing that the union used unfair tactics. If the NLRB rules in workers' favor and orders the employer to bargain—usually several months, but often one or two years after the election was held—the employer can then undertake what is called a "technical refusal to bargain" to obtain judicial review of the NLRB's decision. That is, the employer can ignore the board's order. In contrast, workers cannot appeal an NLRB decision upholding an employer's objections to an election.

---

would still be needed if workers seek bargaining without having gained a majority signing cards, or in cases where workers are divided between competing unions seeking representation rights.

A technical refusal to bargain forces workers and the NLRB to launch a new case, this time an unfair labor practice complaint against the employer's refusal to bargain. The new case often requires years more to resolve in the courts. In many of the cases studied for this report, workers voted in favor of union representation years ago, sometimes by an overwhelming majority, but they are still waiting for bargaining to begin while employers' appeals are pending in court.

Debilitating delays also occur in unfair labor practice cases. Most cases involve discrimination against union supporters or refusals to bargain in good faith. After the issuance of a complaint, several months pass before a case is heard by an administrative law judge. Then several more months go by while the judge ponders a decision. The judge's decision can then be appealed to the NLRB, where one, two, or three years go by before a decision is issued. The NLRB's decision can then be appealed to the federal courts, where again up to three years pass before a final decision is rendered. Many of the workers in cases studied here were fired years earlier and have won reinstatement orders from administrative judges and the NLRB, but they still wait for clogged courts to rule on employers' appeals.

Recommendation: Rapid Elections, Faster Resolution of Election Disputes

The NLRB should conduct an election as quickly as possible after the filing of a petition. The election should take place among workers in bargaining units they seek to form based on their own evaluation of the "community of interest" most responsive to their needs. Where there are genuine issues of exclusions, such as those related to supervisors or independent contractors, elections can go forward with challenged ballots set aside and disputes over status of those employees resolved after the election, not before.

Many worker advocates argue that collective bargaining should commence when the NLRB has reviewed an employer's objections to an election, ruled that a majority of workers freely selected representation, and issued a bargaining order. This would reduce the effect of a "technical refusal to bargain" in defiance of a board order, which leaves workers without bargaining rights for years more as appeals proceed through the courts. The argument here is that workers' right to bargain collectively should take precedence over employers' gaining an unfair advantage by deliberate delaying tactics.

Human Rights Watch stops short of this policy here. The right of appeal to the civil courts is a basic element of due process. Given the mutual commitment needed for a sustained, respectful relationship between workers and employers, legal uncertainty over representation rights should not cloud the bargaining process. Requiring an employer to bargain in good faith while the employer at the same time refuses to accept the majority status of the workers' bargaining representative is legally and practically untenable.

The solution recommended here is to bring the corresponding rights of workers and employers as close to parallel as possible. Workers have no right to appeal an NLRB decision upholding an employer's objections to an election and ordering a rerun election. Just as workers have to "live with" NLRB decisions on election objections, employers should also have to accept NLRB orders except in extraordinary circumstances. The NLRB is the specialized agency created by Congress to hold representation elections and guarantee their fairness. Human Rights Watch recommends legislation creating a legal standard for court review of NLRB final bargaining orders similar to the standard for review of arbitrators' decisions, which are rarely disturbed by the courts.[35] Along with a new standard for review, a "fast-track" procedure for courts of appeals to decide whether an employer's refusal to accept the board's decision meets the high threshold for judicial review should be established. This will separate truly extraordinary cases from those where an employer undertakes a technical refusal to bargain only to gain time to undermine the workers' choice of a bargaining representative.

Finding: Outmoded Concepts of Bargaining Units

U.S. labor law is still largely based on the model of fixed employee groups working for a single employer. That model is still relevant for a majority of workers, and protection of the rights of association of workers in that majority model must be maintained. But there are many new employment relationships often described as atypical or contingent where workers' freedom of association is frustrated.

Recommendation: Bargaining Units Shaped by Workers' Needs

Labor law must change to encompass the rights and interests of contingent workers, contract workers, and others involved in new occupations and industries as diverse as office cleaning, child or elder caregiving, and temporary workers in high-tech companies and service industries.

Expanding the concept of the "bargaining unit" would allow workers in novel employment relationships to merge their interests with those of others in similar jobs with other employers. Allowed to associate in a collective bargaining arrangement with corresponding multi-employer associations, workers could address their needs in areas beyond traditional wages and benefits. For example,

---

[35]A policy of judicial deference to arbitrators' decisions was established by the Supreme Court in the "Steelworkers Trilogy" cases: *United Steelworkers of America v. American Mfg. Co.*, 363 U.S. 564 (1960); *United Steelworkers of America v. Warrior & Gulf Navigation Co.*, 363 U.S. 574 (1960); *United Steelworkers of America v. Enterprise Wheel & Car Corp.*, 363 U.S. 593 (1960).

they could bargain for improved training and career ladders providing upward mobility in their employment sector. An isolated employer views these as costs creating a competitive disadvantage, but employers collectively could approach them as opportunities to upgrade skills and productivity in the sector as a whole.[36]

Finding: Staff, Budget Cuts at NLRB

Congress has hobbled the NLRB over many years by failing to keep staffing and funding levels in line with the growing volume of cases, especially unfair labor practice cases. The number of cases filed each year has tripled since the 1950s, but the NLRB's staffing level has fallen from nearly 3,000 full-time employees in 1980 to fewer than 2,000 in 1998, only slightly more than staffing levels in 1950.

The NLRB's staff and budget constraints have retarded efforts to recruit investigators, agents, and attorneys with foreign-language skills to protect the rights of foreign-born workers, a rapidly growing part of the labor force. Many of the workers' rights violations recounted in this report were suffered by immigrants who do not speak English.

In its earlier decades the bulk of the NLRB's caseload involved representation cases, i.e. running elections. Now more than 80 percent of its workload involves unfair labor practice cases. Requiring careful investigation, often extensive settlement negotiations, and complicated litigation in cases that go to hearing, unfair labor practice cases are much more staff-intensive than representation cases. Yet the size of the NLRB staff and its inflation-adjusted budget have not been adapted to the fact that time-consuming investigation and litigation have replaced administration of elections as the main task of the agency.

Recommendation: More Staff and Resources for NLRB; Renewed Recruiting Campaign

As the premier federal agency charged with protecting workers' freedom of association in the United States, the NLRB is a critically important human rights enforcement agency. It should have the staff and resources to carry out its mandate effectively. For fiscal year 2000, Congress did approve an increase in the NLRB's budget from $184.5 million to $205.7 million, the first substantial increase in many years.[37] This will allow the NLRB to hire additional staff.

---

[36]For an extensive development of this argument for expanding bargaining "units" beyond the 1930s factory model, see Stephen A. Herzenberg, John A. Alic, and Howard Wial, *New Rules for a New Economy* (Ithaca, New York, Cornell University Press, 1998), pp.161-166.
[37]See Bureau of National Affairs, "NLRB," BNA *Daily Labor Report* No. 6, January 10, 2000, p. S-5.

But the FY 2000 increase should not be a one-time adjustment. A multi-year plan for increasing staffing levels should be joined with a determined campaign by the NLRB to retain experienced, committed staff and to recruit outstanding college and law school graduates, as well as young and mid-career individuals interested in moving into human rights work. In appealing to potential NLRB staffers committed to human rights enforcement, particular attention should be paid to applicants' foreign-language skills so that they can help the sizeable number of migrant and other foreign-born workers who suffer violations of their right to freedom of association.

Finding: Government Involvement in Frustrating Workers' Rights

In some cases studied for this report, government officials and police intervened one-sidedly to deter workers from choosing representation and collective bargaining. In one, a town's mayor passed out leaflets citing plant closings to workers on their way to vote in an NLRB election. The U.S. Navy paid more than $5 million for a company to defend actions deemed "egregious misconduct, demonstrating a general disregard for employees' fundamental rights" by a judge who heard evidence in the case. There are no provisions in U.S. law for withholding lucrative government contracts from companies that repeatedly violate workers' rights.

Welfare recipients required to find jobs under the 1996 welfare reform are especially vulnerable to violations. State agencies administering federal monies for welfare-to-work are required to provide a grievance procedure to protect these workers from unjust firings, but regulations are silent about workers' rights to organize, to bargain, or to strike. In many states, a welfare-to-work employee who exercises the right to strike automatically loses cash assistance or other welfare benefits. The same fate can befall a welfare-to-work employee who refuses to accept a job at a workplace where workers are on strike. Many welfare-to-work laborers are also treated as "trainees" who do not meet the definition of "employee" under labor laws protecting employees' right to organize.

Recommendation: No Interference, No Favoritism; Debarment

National associations of state, county and municipal governments and police organizations should undertake special training and educational programs to make local officials aware of workers' right to freedom of association and related rights to organize, to bargain collectively, and to strike. Such programs should emphasize the importance of non-interference with these rights and ways to ensure that keeping the peace does not become, in effect, a euphemism for intimidation of peaceful workers. Federal law should be interpreted or amended to provide for federal investigation and prosecution of local officials who violate workers' freedom of association, in the same way that federal civil rights enforcement measures are available.

Government subsidies for hiring workers in empowerment zones should be conditioned on compliance with the NLRA and other relevant labor rights laws. This requirement should be enforced by having companies that violate workers' rights repay the government for subsidies paid. Congress should consider a "debarment" law prohibiting the awarding of government contracts to companies that repeatedly violate workers' rights to organize, to bargain collectively, and to strike. Finally, federal regulations should make clear that the right to freedom of association for welfare-to-work employees must be respected by government and private employers in administering assistance programs.

Finding: Surface Bargaining, Superficial Remedies

Employers can continue to thwart workers' choice to form a union and bargain collectively by bargaining in bad faith—going through the motions of meeting with workers and making proposals and counterproposals without any intention of reaching an agreement. This tactic is called "surface bargaining." The problem is especially acute in newly organized workplaces where the employer has fiercely resisted workers' self-organization and resents their success.

Proving surface bargaining is extremely difficult, since a well-coached employer can follow a legal roadmap created by earlier NLRB and court decisions to give an appearance of good faith. Even when the violation is so clear that the NLRB and courts uphold a surface bargaining charge, the only remedy currently available is an order to return to the bargaining table, where the same cycle can repeat itself. In one case studied here, a company was repeatedly found guilty of bad-faith bargaining after workers voted in favor of union representation, yet no contract was reached for twelve years after the vote, and workers ultimately surrendered bargaining rights.

Recommendation: Stronger Remedies, First-Contract Arbitration

Stronger NLRB-ordered and court-ordered remedies, including punitive damages, should be fashioned for willful refusal to bargain in good faith. Where workers have formed and joined a new union in a previously unorganized workplace and the employer is found to bargain in bad faith, workers should have recourse to first-contract arbitration as a remedy. Average contract settlements in comparable industries or facilities can be used as a guidepost for an arbitrator applying the first-contract arbitration remedy.

While this remedy should be extraordinary in a system that advances free collective bargaining as a paramount principle, it may be the only effective step where workers have been deprived of the right to bargain freely by the employer's violation of the rule of good faith. As indicated, this remedy would be available only for first-contract negotiations in a newly organized workplace where the employer is found guilty of bad-faith bargaining. This gives workers an opportunity to establish a bargaining relationship that would most likely have taken shape had the employer bargained in good faith. It also provides a chance to demonstrate to the employer that both parties can act responsibly and respectfully under a collective agreement, making good-faith negotiations more probable in subsequent bargaining.

Finding: Exclusion of Millions of Workers from Protection of Organizing and Bargaining Rights

International norms refer to the right of "every person" to form and join trade unions and to bargain collectively. Several of the cases examined by Human Rights Watch for this report involved workers excluded from coverage by the NLRA, such as agricultural workers, domestic employees, and "independent" contractors who actually work in a dependent relationship with a single employer for years. Moreover, supervisory and managerial exclusions are used to deny organizing rights to many workers inappropriately placed in these categories. In the public sector, many states deny state and local employees the right to bargain collectively. As noted above, many welfare recipients employed in workfare programs are categorized as "trainees" and excluded from organizing and bargaining protection.

In all, millions of workers in the United States are excluded from coverage of laws that are supposed to protect the right to organize and bargain collectively. Workers who fall under these exclusions can be summarily fired with impunity for seeking to form and join a union. Even where the employer does not fire them, workers' requests to bargain collectively can be ignored.

Recommendation: Eliminate Statutory Exclusions, Narrow Supervisory and Managerial Definitions

Congress should bring agricultural workers and domestic workers under NLRA coverage with the same rights and protections as all other covered workers. Legal reform should also subject employers' claims of workers' independent contractor status to strict scrutiny by the NLRB and the courts under standards that make workers' real-life dependence on employers the test for NLRA coverage. Congress should also act to bring low-level supervisors and managers under the mantle of laws protecting rights of association, with adequate safeguards against conflicts of interest among groups of employees. Federal and state legislation should be enacted to protect public employees' exercise of the right to bargain collectively and the right to strike, under conditions established in international norms.   Welfare-to-work and workfare employees should be covered by laws protecting rights of organizing and collective bargaining.

In general, workers who *want* to organize and bargain collectively should have the *right* to organize and bargain collectively, except where there are manifestly no employers to bargain with or where the essence of such workers' jobs is so truly managerial or supervisory that they effectively would be bargaining with themselves.

Finding: Subcontracted and "Leased" Workers are denied Freedom of Association and Effective Remedies

As seen in several cases in this report involving farmworkers, express-delivery employees, and high-technology temporary agency employees, many employers can use subcontracting arrangements, supplier chains and temporary employment agencies to avoid any obligation to recognize workers' rights of organization and collective bargaining.   In effect, workers labor "for" the prime employer while nominally employed "by" a supplier, subcontractor or agency.

The same problems afflict workers in the apparel manufacturing industry, in janitorial services, and other sectors characterized by layers of subcontracting arrangements, where prime contractors often simply cancel the contracts of subcontractors whose employees form and join unions. The result is widespread denial of workers' freedom of association under international norms, often affecting the most vulnerable workers in the labor force.

Recommendation: Make Prime Contractors and Employers of "Permatemps" Responsible for Workers' Rights of Association, Organizing, and Collective Bargaining

Congress should enact legislation cutting through the fiction of subcontracted employment relationships like those cited that are structured to avoid responsibility for recognizing workers' rights. Fixing responsibility should be based on a test of effective economic power to set workers' terms and conditions of employment, not the formality of an employment relationship.   The dominant entity in the employment relationship holding real power over workers' terms and conditions of employment should have legal responsibility to recognize and bargain with workers when a majority choose representation. This principle should apply to large apparel retailers for sweatshop workers, to building owners' associations for janitorial cleaning workers, to agricultural growers who use labor-supplying middlemen, and to other forms of labor contracting.

Finding: Nullification of the Right to Strike By the Permanent-Replacement Doctrine

Employers' power to permanently replace workers in the United States who exercise the right to strike runs counter to international standards recognizing the right to strike as an essential element of freedom of association. International norms limit the right to strike, excepting members of the military and police and authorizing alternatives such as mandatory arbitration when strikes affect public safety. But international norms do not authorize permanent replacements. The ILO has determined that the right to strike "is not really guaranteed when a worker who exercises it legally runs the risk of seeing his or her job taken up permanently by another worker, just as legally."

Permanent replacement crosses the line balancing the rights of workers and employers and undercuts a fundamental right of workers. The prospective pain of a strike or lockout is the most powerful incentive to reach a collective agreement without a strike. The balance of pain after a strike or lockout has begun is an equally powerful incentive to resolve the dispute expeditiously. But with the one-sided pain of a strike marked by permanent replacements, the employer maintains operations, workers who exercised the right to strike are left to languish, and after just one year permanent replacement workers can vote to extinguish the strikers' right to representation and collective bargaining.

U.S. law forbids permanent replacement of workers who strike over employers' unfair labor practices, as distinct from "economic strikers" seeking better contract terms. The latter can be permanently replaced; unfair labor practice strikers are entitled to reinstatement when they end their strike. But it often takes years of NLRB and federal court proceedings before a final decision is made as to whether replaced workers have a right to reinstatement. In a case studied by Human Rights Watch for this report, workers at a Colorado steel mill who ended a strike in 1997 still do not know their fate, despite NLRB decisions firmly in their favor ordering reinstatement. In 2000 their employer vowed "years and years of hearings before there's any conclusion on this."

Recommendation: Reverse the Permanent-Replacement Doctrine

Congress should enact legislation prohibiting the permanent replacement of workers who exercise the right to strike. Some trade union advocates argue that a reform should go even further, prohibiting temporary replacements as in some Canadian jurisdictions, or even requiring an employer to cease operations in a legal strike, as in Mexico.

Human Rights Watch does not recommend such a drastic change. Instead, the balance should be restored to a genuine equilibrium permitting employers to engage temporary replacements, as they now can, alongside non-striking employees or supervisors and managers who maintain operations. However, temporary replacements should give way to employee strikers when the strike ends. In effect, prohibiting permanent striker replacements effectuates a "balance of pain" in a strike that promotes more rapid resolution of a dispute while respecting both workers' right to strike and management's ability to operate.

Finding: Stifling of Solidarity Action by Workers

U.S. labor law creates a total prohibition on workers involved in a labor dispute seeking solidarity help from other workers at companies doing business with their employer. The NLRA backs up the ban by requiring the NLRB to seek an immediate injunction to halt any solidarity action or "secondary boycotts." Meanwhile, the board's authority to seek injunctions to halt employers' unfair labor practices, however egregious and destructive of workers' rights such practices might be, is only discretionary and is rarely used by the NLRB.

In contrast to the United States' total ban, other countries have fashioned rules for balancing the interests of workers and employers, protecting workers' right to join in solidarity and employers' right to avoid unwarranted economic harm if they are truly neutral to a dispute. These legal rules comport with the general principle formulated by the ILO that workers' solidarity action is lawful so long as the primary action is lawful and so long as both are carried out in accordance with legal rules.

Recommendation: Reformulate Rules to Allow Workers' Solidarity Action in Keeping with Principles of Freedom of Association

Human Rights Watch recognizes that the issue of workers' solidarity action in support of workers involved in a primary dispute is complex. A purist view sees any limit to secondary action as a violation of freedom of association. But banning any limits to secondary action would be as absolute, at the other extreme, as the current ban on secondary action itself. Rather than removing any and all restrictions, Human Rights Watch recommends a serious effort by Congress to craft new rules allowing workers to seek and to afford solidarity support, looking to comparative experience in other developed countries and to ILO analysis and principles for guidance. For example, some countries of the European Union apply a rule of "reasonableness" or "proportionality" to workers' invoking of solidarity action rights, allowing workers to affect a secondary firm's dealings with the primary company involved in the dispute, but not to influence dealings with other companies not involved in a labor dispute. Some countries have a "last resort" requirement to exhaust mediation and conciliation mechanisms before solidarity action can be taken.

Immigrant Workers

International human rights principles apply to all persons regardless of immigration and citizenship status. In the United States, Human Rights Watch found workers' rights violations with particular characteristics affecting immigrant workers in nearly every economic sector and geographic area examined in this report, prompting a separate set of recommendations.

Immigrant workers are a fast-growing part of the labor force. Many work in industries with low wages, few benefits, unsafe and unhealthy working conditions, and harsh treatment by managers. These workers are urgently in need of the protection that can be gained through freedom of association, yet they are victimized when they exercise the right. Moreover, violations of their rights to organize and bargain collectively affect their coworkers in many places of employment, diminishing everyone's ability to exercise the right to freedom of association.

Their status often makes immigrant workers less likely to complain about unfair wages and working conditions and afraid to form and join trade unions to defend their rights. For many, the vulnerability of their undocumented status and related fear of deportation are the most powerful forces inhibiting their use of the right to organize and bargain collectively. Still, many undertake efforts to form and join trade unions, only to suffer reprisals.

To address this problem, U.S. labor rights policy must give greater attention to the right to freedom of association in the application of immigration policy than is currently the case. The following findings and recommendations address first the situation of non-agricultural immigrant workers, then conditions of two types of migrant farm labor, one undocumented and one with valid visas for temporary agricultural work in the United States.

With regard to immigrant workers covered by the NLRA (that is, non-agricultural workers), these are Human Rights Watch's findings and recommendations:

Finding: Threats to call the INS; Racial and Ethnic Divisiveness

Human Rights Watch found repeated use of threats by employers during NLRB election campaigns to call the Immigration and Naturalization Service (INS) to have workers deported if they formed and joined a union. In some cases, such threats may take a racially divisive turn, with employers telling immigrants that their U.S.-born coworkers—African-Americans, in cases studied for this report—are forming a union to get rid of immigrants.

Recommendation: INS Forbearance When Workers Exercise Freedom of Association; Stronger Remedies

The current discretionary policy of the INS not to conduct "raids" or other internal enforcement measures while an NLRB election is pending should be made mandatory by legislation or by regulation. A policy foregoing raids or other internal enforcement measures should be applied for reasonable periods from a time when workers have begun organizing efforts to a phase following NLRB elections, whatever the results. Finally, where the NLRB finds evidence of deliberate race- or ethnic-based interference with workers' organizing efforts linked to the vulnerable status of immigrant workers, strong remedial action like injunctive relief and bargaining orders should be taken.

Finding: Fear of Filing Charges or Testifying; Workers Subject to Deportation

Human Rights Watch found that immigrant workers are often afraid to come forward to file unfair labor practice charges or to appear as witnesses in unfair labor practice proceedings because they fear their immigration status will be challenged. Many workers seeking to organize and bargain are in fact undocumented. Vulnerability because of their immigration status chills the exercise of these rights. Workers who persist in exercising the right to freedom of association are often victimized by the employer moving from threat to action: calling the INS to have them deported, even though such an act is an unfair labor practice under the NLRA.[38]

The precarious situation of undocumented immigrants inhibits workers' freedom of association on a national scale.[39] In one widely publicized incident involving hotel workers in Minneapolis, Minnesota, management reported the names of nine leaders, all Mexican women working as maids, to the INS after they

---

[38]The NLRA covers workers' defined as "employees" regardless of immigration status. Courts have ruled that undocumented workers covered by the NLRA can file unfair labor practice charges if they are discriminated against for union activity. They can obtain a reinstatement order if they are fired for union activity. They can vote in NLRB elections. See *Sure-Tan, Inc. v. NLRB*, 467 U.S. 833 (1984); *NLRB v. A.P.R.A. Fuel Oil Buyers Group*, 134 F.3d 50 (2d Cir. 1997).

[39]For an overall description of the problem, see Nancy Cleeland, "Unionizing is Catch-22 for Illegal Immigrants: Undocumented status makes them vulnerable to workplace retaliation . . .," *Los Angeles Times*, January 16, 2000, p. A1.

and coworkers voted in favor of union representation. The workers were fired, arrested and faced deportation.[40]

Recent reports suggest that the demand for immigrant labor in a period of low unemployment has eased pressure for strict enforcement of immigration laws.[41] However, the INS acknowledges that an exception arises in cases where workers seek to exercise rights to organize, to bargain, or to strike. A senior INS official stated that an undocumented worker is at little risk "unless the employer turns a worker in, and employers usually do that only to break a union or prevent a strike or that kind of stuff."[42]

Recommendation: "Don't Ask" in NLRB Proceedings; Protected Status for Workers Exercising Rights of Association

NLRB rules should prohibit any assertion of or inquiry into a worker's immigration status by NLRB agents conducting investigations, or by union or employer attorneys in NLRB proceedings, or by administrative law judges or other NLRB officials at any time. This is the thrust of an NLRB General Counsel memorandum on the subject,[43] but it should be codified in NLRB rules and given wide, prominent publicity. This rule must be publicized to give workers confidence that their right to freedom of association will be respected and that they cannot be questioned about their immigration status in connection with NLRB proceedings.

Congress should establish a new visa category analogous to "S" visas for undocumented persons who are witnesses in criminal proceedings, or proposed "T" visas for victims of trafficking, for undocumented workers who suffer violations of their right to freedom of association through organizing and bargaining collectively. Both victims of violations of these rights, and potential witnesses in NLRB and court proceedings, should be granted such temporary visa status for the duration of

---

[40]See AP Wire Report, "Illegal Immigrants Help Unionize a Hotel but Face Deportation," *New York Times*, January 13, 2000, p. A19. The NLRB issued a complaint finding meritorious the workers' charge that they were fired for union activity. The case was settled with the workers' accepting modest payments without right to reinstatement, but still facing deportation. In April 2000, the INS granted the workers two years' "deferred action" status allowing them to stay. See Kimberly Hayes, "Illegal workers get to stay in U.S.; The INS gives seven undocumented immigrants who tried to form a union at a downtown Minneapolis hotel "deferred-action" status for two years," *Minneapolis Star-Tribune*, April 26, 2000, p. 1B.

[41]See, e.g., Louis Uchitelle, "I.N.S. Is Looking the Other Way As Illegal Immigrants Fill Jobs," *New York Times*, March 9, 2000, P. A1.

[42]Ibid., quoting Robert L. Bach, INS associate commissioner for policy and planning.

[43]See NLRB General Counsel Memorandum GC 98-15 (December 4, 1998).

legal proceedings under the NLRA and appeals through the courts, and for a reasonable period following the conclusion of such proceedings while the INS may consider exercising discretionary authority to allow them to remain in the United States.

Finding: Impossibility of Reinstatement

While under NLRB rules undocumented workers can obtain a reinstatement order, they cannot be reinstated if they cannot regularize their immigration status in short order. This is practically impossible. In one notable case, the attorney for a New York City garment factory—himself a former INS official—called the INS to raid the factory and arrest worker leaders where employees had voted in favor of union representation. The NLRB found this to be an unfair labor practice. However, despite the fact that evidence of the worker's status was obtained by unlawful means, a federal appeals court upheld a deportation order.[44]

Recommendation: Interim Reinstatement for Immigrant Workers Who Suffer Discrimination

Congress should fashion greater balance between immigration laws and laws protecting workers' freedom of association such that immigration rules cannot be used to destroy fundamental rights of association. Workers who obtain a reinstatement order because their right to freedom of association was violated should be immediately reinstated and granted a work authorization card for sufficient time to allow them to seek renewed, extended, or permanent authorization under discretionary authority which may be exercised by the INS in such cases.

Agricultural Workers

With regard to agricultural workers, Human Rights Watch finds and recommends as follows:

Finding: Agricultural Workers' Exclusion

Under current law, all agricultural workers, residents and immigrants alike, are excluded from coverage under the National Labor Relations Act affording protection of the right to freedom of association and rights to organize, to bargain collectively, and to strike. Except in a few states, agricultural workers can be fired with impunity for exercising the right to organize and have no means of obtaining recognition and collective bargaining through elections or other means of demonstrating majority support. No law makes such reprisal an unfair labor

---

[44]See *Montero v. Immigration and Naturalization Service*, Case No. 96-4130 (2d Cir. 1996).

practice, or provides a hearing and enforcement mechanism for redress. Furthermore, because of the intermittent and often itinerant nature of agricultural labor, workers are not able to pursue a claim even if a forum were available.

Recommendation: End the Exclusion with Added Provisions for Farmworkers' Specific Problems

Human Rights Watch recommends including *all* workers under stronger laws effectively protecting freedom of association, including agricultural workers. In a reformed NLRA structure recommended by Human Rights Watch, agricultural workers, like all workers, would have available interim reinstatement power allowing reinstatement while their case is processed, based on the NLRB's initial investigation and finding of *prima facie* merit in a claim of discrimination. However, even the several weeks normally taken by the NLRB to conduct an investigation might be too long a time to protect a farmworker. Instead, agricultural worker protection laws should include new, stronger and swifter non-retaliation provisions guarding against dismissal for associational activity. Finally, under strengthened NLRA coverage, agricultural workers could avail themselves of rapid secret-ballot elections for union representation.

Finding: Violations Due to Labor Contracting System

As in other sectors of the economy, the agricultural labor market is becoming layered with contracting and subcontracting systems. For example, large food processors and growers claim not to be employers of farmworkers even where they openly or effectively determine wages and working conditions. These large employers claim that smaller farmers or individual growers are the employer. In turn, smaller farmers or growers argue that they are not employers because they use labor contractors or crew leaders who supply a labor force. These labor contractors are the real employers, growers claim. Crew leaders—called "coyotes" for their ruthless tactics—are often shadowy figures trafficking in migrant farm labor who extract large fees from workers and then cannot be found when any legal proceeding is brought against them.

Recommendation: Accountability by the Prime Employer

As recommended elsewhere in this report in sections dealing with contingent, atypical, and subcontracted labor, U.S. labor law covering agricultural workers should cut through the layers of claimed non-responsibility to hold employers "up the line" accountable for respecting workers' right to freedom of association. Such employers should also be held liable for violations of the right, as long as such employers decisively influence farmworkers' wages and working conditions.

Where workers have formed and joined trade unions, an agricultural collective bargaining framework should allow for multiple-party negotiations bringing all interests to the table to settle wages and working conditions for farmworkers. Thus, for example, if a majority of workers harvesting agricultural products for a large retail food processor choose to form and join a union, a good-faith bargaining obligation should attach to the processor, to growers who supply the processor, and the farmworkers' union.

Finding: Denial of Legal Services

Legal services organizations are barred from representing undocumented workers and from filing class action lawsuits to vindicate farmworkers' rights. Private attorneys cannot receive attorneys' fees in successful suits for individual farmworkers or groups of farmworkers.

Recommendation: Access to Legal Services

Access to legal counsel and to the justice system is an essential aspect of freedom of association denied to agricultural workers. Congress should remove the ban on representing undocumented workers and on class action lawsuits for farmworkers by legal services organizations, and provide for attorneys' fees for representing farmworkers on the same basis they are provided under the Fair Labor Standards Act and civil rights laws. Where undocumented workers are involved in such cases, they should be protected against any inquiry into their immigration status.

H-2A Workers

With regard to a sub-group of agricultural workers— the temporary, legal migrants who come to the United States with H-2A visas—Human Rights Watch found specific problems and makes separate recommendations:

Finding: a Restricted Labor Force

About 30,000 temporary agricultural workers enter the United States each year under the H-2A program giving them legal authorization to work in areas where employers claim a shortage of domestic workers. Human Rights Watch examined conditions in North Carolina, the state where growers are the largest users of H-2A workers. Some 10,000 H-2A workers are employed in North Carolina.

H-2A workers are tied to the growers who contract for their labor. They have no opportunity to organize for improved conditions, no opportunity to change employers to obtain better conditions, and no access to federal courts to vindicate their rights. Many workers are brought to the United States by associations specializing in H-2A migrants. Representatives of such associations tell workers that farmworker unions and Legal Services attorneys are their enemies. H-2A workers are often denied the right to receive visitors through restrictive clauses in their housing arrangements.

Recommendation: Mobility, Organizing Rights, and Access to Legal Recourse

The H-2A program should allow workers to seek work with a different employer in the same area, under supervision by H-2A enforcement authorities, if the employer they are assigned to violates their rights. Workers should also have access to federal courts when their rights are violated. Where workers are dismissed or discriminated against for exercising rights of association, a strengthened regime is needed to ensure swift reinstatement or placement in another position where they reside. Workers should have unfettered access in their living quarters to advocates who can advise them about their rights, if workers seek such advice.

Labor department regulations governing the H-2A program should define as an unfair labor practice recruiters' characterizations of unions and legal services as "enemies" of H-2A workers. Recruiters who use such tactics should be subject to cease-and-desist orders and contempt enforcement for continued violation. The H-2A program should instead require that workers be fully informed of their rights to organize and bargain collectively, and have access to legal services and to the justice system, as they desire.

It should be noted that many of the problems cited here also apply to workers who enter the United States temporarily under the H-2B program covering non-agricultural workers. Thousands, for example, labor in agricultural-related processing operations and in plants processing chickens, crabs, and other food products.[45] The development of initiatives to address problems of H-2A workers should also apply to other workers facing similar difficulties.

---

[45]For a comprehensive account of conditions of H-2B crab pickers in North Carolina, see the three-part series by Anne Hull, "Una Vida Mejor, A Better Life," *St. Petersburg Times:* "Leaving Paloma," May 9, 1999, p. 1A; "The Smell of Money," May 10, 1999, p. 1A; "Freedom Found," May 11, 1999, p. 1A.

III. WORKERS' FREEDOM OF ASSOCIATION UNDER INTERNATIONAL HUMAN RIGHTS LAW

The International Background

International human rights analysts and advocates have been slow coming to grips with issues of workers' rights. Attention has focused on pressing problems of arbitrary detention and torture, massacres of indigenous peoples and ethnic minorities, atrocities of war and civil war, and other gross human rights violations, not on workers' rights to form and join trade unions and bargain collectively. For their part, worker representatives have been slow to see human rights aspects in their work. The day-to-day challenge of organizing and bargaining in complex frameworks of national labor laws leaves little time to learn from international human rights discourse. In the United States and in many other countries, union and management officials and attorneys, as well as administrators and judges, seldom turn to international law to inform their work.

All that is changing under the pressures of a globalizing economy and new sensitivity to the human rights implications of workers' rights advocacy. For example, employers' organizations, trade unions and governments joined together at the International Labor Organization in 1998 to issue a landmark Declaration on Fundamental Principles and Rights at Work. Their common declaration set out freedom of association and the right to organize and bargain collectively as the first such principles.

At the same time, the 1998 action at the ILO was not a novelty. Freedom of association for workers has long been universally acknowledged as a fundamental right. A widely accepted body of international norms has established standards for workers' freedom of association covering the right to organize, the right to bargain collectively, and the right to strike.[46]

Sources of international labor law on workers' freedom of association include human rights instruments developed by the United Nations and by regional human rights bodies, principles elaborated through worker, employer and government representatives at the ILO, and labor rights clauses in international trade agreements. The United States has acknowledged its international responsibility to honor workers' freedom of association by ratifying human rights instruments, in

---

[46]For additional treatment of human rights principles regarding freedom of association for workers, see James A. Gross, "A Human Rights Perspective on United States Labor Relations Law: A Violation of the Right of Freedom of Association," 3 *Employee Rights and Employment Policy Journal* 65 (Chicago-Kent College of Law 1999); see also papers and other information available at the web site of the Society for the Promotion of Human Rights in Employment (SPHRE) at http://www.mericleinc.com/Sphre/.

particular the International Covenant on Civil and Political Rights. It has also accepted obligations under ILO conventions on freedom of association and under the 1998 declaration.

The United States has committed itself, through international agreement, to effectively enforce U.S. laws protecting workers' rights to organize, to bargain collectively and to strike. It has affirmed obligations to honor workers' freedom of association in its own trade laws and in laws governing U.S. involvement in the World Bank, the International Monetary Fund, and other multilateral bodies. In all these laws, freedom of association is held out as the foremost internationally recognized workers' right.

International Human Rights Instruments

- The Universal Declaration of Human Rights (1948) states that "[E]veryone has the right to freedom of peaceful assembly and association," and "[E]veryone has the right to form and to join trade unions for the protection of his interests."[47]

- The International Covenant on Civil and Political Rights (ICCPR, 1966) declares: "[E]veryone shall have the right to freedom of association with others, including the right to form and join trade unions for the protection of his interests."[48]

- The International Covenant on Economic, Social and Cultural Rights (ICESCR, 1966) obliges governments to "ensure the right of everyone to form trade unions and join the trade union of his choice . . .; the right of trade unions to function freely . . .; the right to strike . . ."[49]

The United States ratified the International Covenant on Civil and Political Rights in 1992. The ICCPR requires ratifying states "to respect and to ensure to all individuals within its territory and subject to its jurisdiction the rights recognized in the present Covenant" and "to adopt such legislative or other measures as may be necessary to give effect to the rights recognized in the present Covenant." The

---

[47]Universal Declaration of Human Rights, G.A. Res.217A(III), U.N. GAOR, 3d Sess., pt. 1, at 71, U.N. Doc. A/810 (1948) (art. 20(1); art. 23(4)).

[48]International Covenant on Civil and Political Rights, Dec. 16, 1966, 999 U.N.T.S. 171 (art.22).

[49]International Covenant on Economic, Social and Cultural Rights, Dec. 16, 1966, 993 U.N.T.S. 3 (art. 8).

ICCPR also constrains ratifying states "to ensure that any person whose rights or freedoms as herein recognized are violated shall have an effective remedy."[50]

When the U.S. Senate ratified the International Covenant on Civil and Political Rights in 1992, it entered several reservations, understandings, and declarations sidestepping certain obligations in the covenant, perhaps most notably reserving the right to impose capital punishment on minors.[51] But it took no reservations, understandings or declarations with respect to Article 22 on the right to form and join trade unions, or to Article 2 requiring an "effective remedy" for rights violations.[52]

Acknowledging the obligation, the U.S. State Department's first report on compliance with the ICCPR stated that "provisions of the First, Fifth and Fourteenth Amendments guarantee freedom of assembly in all contexts, including the right of workers to establish and join organizations of their own choosing.
. . . The rights of association and organization are supplemented by legislation."[53]

Distressingly, however, the United States devalued the importance of protecting the right to freedom of association by claiming that the widespread exclusion of workers from coverage under U.S. labor laws—primarily agricultural workers, domestic workers, and supervisory employees—"means only that they do not have access to the specific provisions of the NLRA . . . for enforcing their rights

---

[50]International Covenant on Civil and Political Rights, Article 2.

[51]See U.S. Senate, Ratification of ICCPR, April 2, 1992. Reservations, understandings, and declarations are accepted under international law as a means of ratifying complex international instruments while taking exception to certain details, so that wider ratification of the instruments can be achieved.

[52]In a written exchange between the Senate and the White House on questions posed by Senator Daniel Moynihan, first as to whether ICCPR Article 22 alters or amends U.S. labor law, the administration responded, "No," asserting that Article 22's "general right of freedom of association, including the right to form and join trade unions . . . are fully contemplated by the First Amendment to the U.S. Constitution." On the question whether ratification of Article 22 commits the U.S. to ratify ILO Convention 87, the administration again responded in the negative, saying "the two agreements are different in the scope of the rights and obligations they provide." This exchange, not reflected in the instrument of ratification, does not lessen the United States' obligation to fully comply with Article 22 of the ICCPR.

[53]See Office of the Legal Advisor, U.S. Department of State, "Civil and Political Rights in the United States: Initial Report of the United States of America to the U.N. Human Rights Committee under the International Covenant on Civil and Political Rights," Department of State publication 10200 (July 1994; released September 1994).

to organize and bargain collectively."[54] "Only" lacking access to enforcement mechanisms means these workers' rights can be violated with impunity. There is no labor board or other authority to remedy violations.

Regional Instruments

Regional human rights instruments reaffirm the consensus on workers' freedom of association as a basic right:

- The American Declaration of the Rights and Duties of Man (1948) states: "Every person has the right to assemble peaceably with others in a formal public meeting or an informal gathering, in connection with matters of common interest of any nature. Every person has the right to associate with others to promote, exercise and protect his legitimate interests of a political, economic, religious, social, cultural, professional, labor union or other nature."[55]

- The later American Convention on Human Rights (1969) declares: "[E]veryone has the right to associate freely for ideological, religious, political, economic, labor, social, cultural, sports, or other purposes."[56]

- Reflecting the international consensus on workers' freedom of association, though it does not involve the United States, the European Convention for the Protection of Human Rights and Fundamental Freedoms (1950) says: "Everyone has the right to freedom of peaceful assembly and to freedom of association with others, including the right to form and to join trade unions for the protection of his interests."[57]

---

[54]See U.S. Department of State, "Civil and Political Rights in the United States: Initial Report of the United States of America to the U.N. Human Rights Committee under the International Covenant on Civil and Political Rights" (July 1994), p. 166.

[55]American Declaration of the Rights and Duties of Man, 1948, in Final Act, Ninth International Conference of American States, Bogota, Colombia, Articles 21,22. "American" here refers to the Americas, including North, Central and South America and the Caribbean region.

[56]American Convention on Human Rights, OAS Official Records, OEA/Ser.A/16 (English), T.S. No. 36 (Nov. 7-22, 1969), Article 16.

[57]European Convention for the Protection of Human Rights and Fundamental Freedoms, Nov. 4, 1950, E.T.S. No. 5 (entered into force, Sept. 3, 1953), Article 11.

- The European Union's Community Charter of Fundamental Social Rights of Workers (1989) holds: "[E]mployers and workers of the European Community shall have the right of association in order to constitute professional organisations or trade unions of their choice for the defence of their economic and social interests . . . the right to negotiate and conclude collective agreements under the conditions laid down by national legislation and practice . . . the right to strike, subject to the obligations arising under national regulations and collective agreements.[58]

ILO Conventions and OECD Guidelines

Building on this international consensus, the ILO, a U.N.-related body with nearly universal membership and tripartite representation by governments, workers, and employers, recognizes freedom of association and protection of the right to organize as core workers' rights. Over decades of painstaking treatment of allegations of violations of workers' rights, the ILO's Committee on Freedom of Association has elaborated authoritative guidelines for implementation of the right to organize, the right to bargain collectively, and the right to strike.

- ILO Convention No. 87 on freedom of association and protection of the right to organize says that "Workers and employers, without distinction whatsoever, shall have the right to establish and, subject only to the rules of the organization concerned, to join organizations of their own choosing without previous authorization."[59]

- ILO Convention No. 98 declares that "Workers shall enjoy adequate protection against acts of anti-union discrimination in respect of their employment . . . Such protection shall apply more particularly in respect of acts calculated to—a) make the employment of a worker subject to the condition that he shall not join a union or shall relinquish union membership; b) cause the dismissal of or otherwise prejudice a worker by reason of union membership or because of participation in union activities."

  In greater detail, Convention 98 goes on to say: "Workers' and employers' organizations shall enjoy adequate protection against any acts of interference by each other. . . Machinery appropriate to national conditions shall be

---

[58]European Union, Community Charter of Fundamental Social Rights of Workers, in Roger Blanpain and Chris Engels, eds., *European Labour Law* (The Hague, Kluwer Law International, 1998), Articles 11-13.
[59]ILO Convention No. 87, Articles 2, 11.

established, where necessary, for the purpose of ensuring respect for the right to organize . . . Measures appropriate to national conditions shall be taken, where necessary, to encourage and promote the full development and utilization of machinery for voluntary negotiation between employers' and workers' organizations, with a view to the regulation of terms and conditions of employment by means of collective agreements."[60]

- The ILO's <u>Declaration of Fundamental Principles and Rights at Work</u> says expressly: "All members, even if they have not ratified the Conventions in question, have an obligation arising from the very fact of membership in the Organization, to respect, to promote, and to realize, in good faith and in accordance with the [ILO] Constitution, the principles concerning the fundamental rights which are the subject of those Conventions, namely: (a) freedom of association and the effective recognition of the right to collective bargaining; . . ."

ILO core conventions were officially recognized at the 1995 World Social Summit conference in Copenhagen. In addition to those covering freedom of association and the right to organize and bargain collectively, ILO norms on forced labor, child labor, and employment discrimination were defined as essential to ensuring human rights in the workplace. Signed by the United States, the Copenhagen summit's final declaration called on governments to ratify these ILO conventions, to respect them even if they have not ratified them, and to use international labor standards as a benchmark for their national legislation.[61] The U.N. High Commissioner for Human Rights includes these ILO conventions in an authoritative list of "international human rights instruments."[62]

At the Organization for Economic Cooperation and Development (OECD), the United States subscribes to a statement that "[e]nterprises should, within the framework of law, regulations and prevailing labor relations and employment practices, in each of the countries in which they operate: respect the right of their employees to be represented by trade unions . . . and engage in constructive

---

[60]ILO Convention No. 98, Articles 1, 3, 4.

[61] Cited in OECD, *Trade, Employment and Labour Standards: A Study of Core Workers' Rights and International Trade* (1996) (hereafter *Trade, Employment and Labour Standards*); see also Hilary Barnes and Andrew Jack, "Nations agree on fighting poverty," *Financial Times*, March 13, 1995, p .6.

[62]See *ILO Focus* (Winter/Spring 1997); the Conventions cited are nos. 87 and 98 on freedom of association and the right to organize and bargain collectively, 29 and 105 on forced labor, 100 and 111 on non-discrimination, and 138 on child labor.

negotiations . . . with such employee organizations with a view to reaching agreements on employment conditions."[63] The OECD has characterized freedom of association and the right to organize and bargain collectively as labor standards that "reflect basic human rights which should be observed in all countries, independently of their levels of economic development and socio-cultural traditions."[64]

U.S. Commitments in the Multilateral Setting

The United States championed the 1998 adoption of the ILO's Declaration on Fundamental Principles and Rights at Work that set out freedom of association as the first such principle and right. Upon adoption, U.S. Labor Secretary Alexis Herman declared, "The ILO has underlined and clarified the importance of the fundamental rights of workers in an era of economic globalization . . . ILO members have accepted the need to be accountable, and with this action there will now be a process within the ILO to demonstrate that accountability."[65]

Whether or not a country has ratified Conventions 87 and 98, the ILO has determined that ILO member countries are "bound to respect a certain number of general rules which have been established for the common good . . . among these principles, freedom of association has become a customary rule above the Conventions."[66] Though it has so far not ratified Conventions 87 and 98, the United States has accepted jurisdiction and review by the ILO Committee on Freedom of Association (CFA) of complaints filed against it under these conventions.

Several ILO cases involving the United States in the past fifteen years have raised issues cited in this Human Rights Watch report. The United States has defended itself in these cases by describing its elaborate system of labor laws and procedures and asserting that the system generally conforms to ILO standards.[67] In many cases, the CFA "noted with concern" and "drew the attention of the U.S. government" to problems the Committee perceived. In some cases, the committee recommended changes in policy and practice. However, the ILO has no enforcement powers, and the United States took no action to implement the recommendations.

---

[63] Organization for Economic Cooperation and Development, "Guidelines for Multinational Enterprises" (1976).
[64] See OECD, *Trade, Employment and Labour Standards* (1996).
[65] See U.S. Labor Department News Release, June 18, 1998, available at www.dol.gov.
[66] See Fact Finding and Conciliation Commission on Chile, International Labor Organization, Geneva, Switzerland (1975), para. 466.
[67] See ILO, CFA Cases nos. 1130 (1987), 1401 (1987), 1416 (1988), 1420 (1988), 1437 (1988), 1467 (1988), 1543 (1991), 1523 (1992), 1557 (1993), available at www.ilolex.ilo.ch.

Reporting on compliance and defending against complaints, the United States likewise has taken the position that its labor law and practice are generally in conformance with the conventions but that some elements of U.S. federal and state labor laws conflict with the conventions' detailed requirements. Ratification of ILO conventions, it is contended, would amount to "back door" amendment of U.S. labor laws without following the normal legislative process because the ratification of an international treaty would supersede pre-existing domestic law under the United States' constitutional system.[68] The leading U.S. employer representative to the ILO cautioned against making U.S. law subject to ILO supervision because "this machinery is not in our control" and the United States could be embarrassed by holding its "domestic laws and practices up to greater international scrutiny and criticism than is presently the case."[69]

Before 1999, U.S. reports to the ILO on compliance with freedom of association standards offered boilerplate descriptions of American labor law and asserted that U.S. law and practice "appears to be in general conformance" with Conventions 87 and 98.[70] Significantly, however, the United States in a 1999 report acknowledged for the first time that "there are aspects of this [U.S. labor law] system that fail to fully protect the rights to organize and bargain collectively of all employees in all circumstances."

The 1999 U.S. report stated that "the United States is concerned about these limitations and acknowledges that to ensure respect, promotion and realization of the right to organize and bargain collectively, it is important to reexamine any system of labor laws from time to time to assure that the system continues to protect

---

[68]To take one example, the exclusion of agricultural workers from protection of the right to organize clashes with ILO norms. The argument against ratification is developed in detail in Edward E. Potter, *Freedom of Association, the Right to Organize and Collective Bargaining: The Impact on U.S. Law and Practice of Ratification of ILO Conventions No. 87 and No. 98*, Labor Policy Association (1984). Ratification of ILO conventions is further complicated by the fact that, in the U.S. system, later-in-time statutes passed by Congress and signed by the president supersede earlier-ratified international treaties.

[69]See statement of Abraham Katz, president, U.S. Council for International Business, "Examination of the Relationship Between the United States and the International Labor Organization," U.S.. Senate, Hearing before the Senate Committee on Labor and Human Resources, 99th Cong., 1st Sess. 1 (1985), pp. 74-101.

[70]See, e.g., U.S. *Report* for the period ending 31 December 1997 under Article 19 of the ILO Constitution on the position of national law and practice in regard to matters dealt with in Conventions 87 and 98, available from the U.S. Department of Labor and on file with Human Rights Watch.

these fundamental rights."[71] An ILO Committee of Expert-Advisors that reviewed country reports called the U.S. statements "striking for their open recognition of difficulties still to be overcome or situations they deemed relevant to achieving full respect for the principles and rights in the Declaration."[72]

U.S. Trade Laws

The United States has also affirmed the importance of international norms and obligations regarding workers' freedom of association in its own trade statutes. Although these laws create obligations for trading partners, they underscore the U.S. commitment to freedom of association under international standards. In these statutes governing trade relationships with other countries, Congress defined freedom of association and the right to organize and bargain collectively as "internationally recognized workers' rights."

Labor rights amendments have been added to statutes governing the Generalized System of Preferences (GSP) in 1984,[73] the Overseas Private Investment Corporation in 1985,[74] the Caribbean Basin Initiative in 1986,[75] Section 301 of the Trade Act of 1988,[76] Agency for International Development (AID) funding for economic development grants overseas,[77] and U.S. participation in the World Bank, International Monetary Fund and other international lending

---

[71]See *Annual Report for 1999* to the ILO regarding aspects of Conventions 87 and 98, available from the U.S. Department of Labor and on file with Human Rights Watch.

[72]See "Review of annual reports under the follow-up to the ILO Declaration on Fundamental Principles and Rights at Work," ILO Governing Body, March 2000, para. 44.

[73]19 U.S.C.A. § 2461 *et.seq.* The GSP program permits a developing country to export goods to the United States on a preferential, duty-free basis as long as they meet the conditions for eligibility in the program.

[74]22 U.S.C.A. § 2191 *et.seq.* OPIC insures the overseas investments of U.S. corporations against losses due to war, revolution, expropriation or other factors related to political turmoil, as long as the country receiving the investment meets conditions for eligibility under OPIC insurance.

[75]19 U.S.C.A. § 2702 *et seq.* A 1990 labor rights amendment to what is now called the Caribbean Basin Economic Recovery Act (CBERA) expanded the worker rights clause to comport with GSP and OPIC formulations. CBERA grants duty-free status to exports into the United States from Caribbean basin countries on a more extensive basis than under GSP provisions.

[76]19 U.S.C.A. § 2411 *et.seq.* Section 301 defines various unfair trade practices, now including worker rights violations, making a country that trades with the United States liable to retaliatory action.

[77]Amendment to the Foreign Assistance Act, 22 U.S.C.A. §§ 2151 et seq.

agencies.[78] All these measures hold out the possibility of economic sanctions against trading partners that violate workers' rights. In every case, freedom of association and the right to organize and bargain collectively are the first rights listed.

In formulating the labor rights clauses in U.S. trade laws, Congress has relied on ILO guidance. In its report on legislation governing U.S. participation in international financial institutions, Congress pointed to "the relevant conventions of the International Labor Organization, which have set forth, among other things, the rights of association [and] the right to organize and bargain collectively."[79] Analyzing the application of workers' rights provisions in U.S. trade laws, the General Accounting Office underscored the fact that "the international standards have been set by the International Labor Organization, which is part of the U.N. structure."[80]

Since passage of the 1984 GSP labor rights amendment, the U.S. State Department's annual *Country Reports on Human Rights Practices* refer to ILO Convention 87 as the basis of U.S. policy on workers' freedom of association. The reports say, "The 'right of association' has been defined by the International Labor Organization to include the right of workers to establish and to join organizations of their own choosing" and "the right to organize and bargain collectively includes the right of workers to be represented in negotiating the prevention and settlement of disputes with employers; the right to protection against interference; and the right to protection against acts of antiunion discrimination."[81]

Regarding strikes, the State Department's human rights policy is that "the right of association includes the right of workers to strike. While strikes may be restricted in essential services (i.e., those services the interruption of which would endanger the life, personal safety or health of a significant portion of the population) and in the public sector, these restrictions must be offset by adequate guarantees to safeguard the interests of the workers concerned."[82] The State Department's formulation of the right to strike reflects the determination by the ILO that the right to strike is an essential element of the right to freedom of association.

---

[78]22 U.S.C. § 1621 (1994).

[79]See H.R. Conf. Rep. No. 4426, 103rd Cong., 2d Sess., §1621 (a) (1994), codified at 22 U.S.C. §1621 (a).

[80]See General Accounting Office, "Assessment of the Generalized System of Preferences Program," GAO/GGD-95-9 (November 1994), pp. 99-100.

[81]See U.S. Department of State, *Country Reports on Human Rights Practices for 1999* (February 2000), Appendix B, "Reporting on Worker Rights."

[82]Ibid.; see also Hodges-Aeberhard and Odero de Diós, "Principles of the Committee of Association concerning Strikes," 126 *International Labour Review* 544 (1987).

The North American Free Trade Agreement

The North American Free Trade Agreement (NAFTA) among the United States, Canada and Mexico brought with it a labor side agreement, the North American Agreement on Labor Cooperation (NAALC). Freedom of association and protection of the right to organize, the right to bargain collectively, and the right to strike are the first three "labor principles" of the NAALC. This international agreement was negotiated at the insistence of the United States government following a commitment made during President Clinton's 1992 electoral campaign.[83]

The NAALC characterizes the first labor principle as "the right of workers exercised freely and without impediment to establish and join organizations of their own choosing to further and defend their interests." The agreement formulates the right to bargain collectively as "the protection of the right of organized workers to freely engage in collective bargaining on matters concerning the terms and conditions of employment." It describes the right to strike as "the protection of the right of workers to strike in order to defend their collective interests."[84] With its North American trading partners, the United States committed itself to promote the NAALC labor principles and to "effectively enforce its labor law" to achieve their realization.[85]

* * * * *

To sum up, an argument that international human rights and labor rights law is not relevant to U.S. labor law and practice cannot be sustained. Basic U.N., ILO and regional human rights instruments have forged an international human rights consensus on workers' freedom of association that includes the United States. The consensus is strengthened by the accelerating international engagement of the United States at the ILO and in regional and multilateral trade fora, where it actively supports the cause of internationally recognized workers' rights. To fulfill both the obligations it has assumed and the objectives that it promotes in the international community, the United States must live up in its own labor law and practice to international labor rights norms on workers' freedom of association and rights to organize, to bargain, and to strike.

---

[83]See Gov. Bill Clinton, "Expanding Trade and Creating American Jobs," Address at North Carolina State University, Raleigh, North Carolina (1992).
[84]North American Agreement on Labor Cooperation, Annex 1, Labor Principles 1-3.
[85]Ibid., Article 2.

IV. FREEDOM OF ASSOCIATION UNDER U.S. LABOR LAW

The U.S. Legal Framework for Workers' Freedom of Association

Constitutional Underpinnings of U.S. Labor Law

The U.S. Constitution makes no specific mention of the right to organize, to bargain collectively, or to strike. However, the First Amendment of the U.S. Constitution (1789) protects freedom of assembly, free speech, and the right to petition the government for redress of grievances. Laws or regulations that violate these rights may be struck down as unconstitutional by the Supreme Court of the United States. The 14th Amendment (1866) and its mandate for "equal protection of the law" applies the Bill of Rights to the individual states. Moreover, each state has its own constitution and bill of rights providing equivalent guarantees. The U.S. Supreme Court has specifically applied the First Amendment to protect workers' organizing, political and legislative action, peaceful picketing and other lawful activity.[86]

The "commerce clause" in Article I, Section 8 of the United States Constitution empowers Congress to "regulate commerce among the several states." Citing "burdens and obstructions" on interstate commerce when employers refuse to deal with workers' organization, the Supreme Court upheld the constitutionality of the National Labor Relations Act based on the commerce clause.[87] The same constitutional clause is the basis of federal jurisdiction over most U.S. labor law regarding workers' freedom of association, since most commerce is interstate.

Statutory Sources

Landmark federal legislation in the twentieth century set the framework for protection of workers' rights to organize, to bargain and to strike (note that U.S. laws often carry the name of their congressional sponsors and are often referred to by those names):

The Railway Labor Act of 1926 (RLA) established the right of workers in the railroad industry to organize and bargain collectively through representatives of their own choosing. That law was limited to railway labor because of the central importance of rail transportation in the national economy. In 1964 the RLA was

---

[86]See *Hague v. C.I.O.*, 307 U.S. 496 (1939); *Thornhill v. Alabama*, 310 U.S. 88 (1940).
[87]See *NLRB v. Jones & Laughlin Steel Corp.*, 301 U.S. 1 (1937).

extended to workers and employers in the air transportation sector. Today, nearly one million U.S. rail and air transport workers are covered by the RLA.

The Norris-LaGuardia Act of 1932 outlawed contracts between workers and employers in which the worker promised never to join a union. Such "yellow-dog" contracts, as they were called, were a common demand made upon workers by employers to prevent exercise of rights to organize and bargain collectively. The Norris-LaGuardia Act also sharply constricted the ability of employers to obtain labor injunctions as a strike-breaking measure. Finally, it relieved workers' leaders of personal criminal and civil liability for the acts of individual workers unless the leaders participated in or ratified the acts.

The National Labor Relations Act (NLRA or Wagner Act) of 1935 extended to most private sector employees "the right to self-organization, to form, join or assist labor organizations, to bargain collectively through representatives of their own choosing, and to engage in other concerted activities for the purpose of collective bargaining or other mutual aid or protection." The NLRA created a new concept in American law: the unfair labor practice. The law defined five unfair labor practices, including discrimination against workers for engaging in mutual aid or protection and refusal to bargain with workers' freely chosen representatives. It made such practices unlawful.

The Labor Management Relations Act (LMRA or Taft-Hartley Act) of 1947 amended the NLRA, in a number of respects sought by U.S. employers who argued that the Wagner Act was too pro-labor. The LMRA created a new set of unfair labor practices under which unions could be held liable. It established an "employer free speech" clause permitting managers to openly and aggressively campaign against worker self-organization. The Taft-Hartley amendments allowed individual states to enact "right to work" laws barring voluntary agreements between workers and employers to require payment of union dues by all represented employees. The law prohibited "secondary boycotts," where workers involved in a "primary" labor dispute seek solidarity action by workers at a supplier or customer of their own employer, and instructed the NLRB to seek immediate injunctions against such action.

The Labor Management Reporting and Disclosure Act (LMRDA or Landrum-Griffin Act) of 1959 established a "bill of rights" for individual trade union members in internal union affairs, including a right to democratic elections of leaders. The LMRDA set forth detailed financial reporting and disclosure requirements for unions. It also extended prohibitions on secondary action by workers.

Today, the Wagner Act, the Taft-Hartley Act and the Landrum-Griffin Act are the most important federal labor laws governing private sector labor-management relations. While they are separate statutes, these laws often overlap and refer to one another in a complex legislative structure. For convenience, this bundle of statutes is often called "the NLRA," a practice followed in this report. Other laws such as the Fair Labor Standards Act, the Occupational Safety and Health Act, the Equal Pay Act, the Agricultural Workers Protection Act and so on cover minimum wage, hours of work, child labor, workplace safety, nondiscrimination in employment, migrant labor conditions and other matters separate from labor-management relations.

Labor Law Jurisdiction

United States labor laws on the right to organize, to bargain collectively and to strike fall almost entirely within federal jurisdiction. Under the commerce clause of the U.S. constitution, federal law prevails over state laws on matters of interstate commerce—an extremely broad jurisdiction in the complex modern economy.

U.S. labor laws covering freedom of association mainly are enforced by federal government authorities and federal courts. Occasional state efforts to pass legislation on labor relations matters are usually struck down by the courts as pre-empted by federal law. The states are allowed a limited legislative or law enforcement role where predominantly local interests are at stake.

Basic Labor Law Policy

Section 1 and Section 7 of the 1935 Wagner Act set forth the central precepts of U.S. labor law.

Section 1 states: "It is hereby declared to be the policy of the United States to eliminate the causes of certain substantial obstructions to the free flow of commerce and to mitigate and eliminate these obstructions when they occur by encouraging the practice and procedure of collective bargaining and by protecting the exercise by workers of full freedom of association, self-organization, and designation of representatives of their own choosing, for the purpose of negotiating the terms and conditions of their employment or other mutual aid or protection."

Under Section 7 of the NLRA, "Employees shall have the right to self-organization, to form, join, or assist labor organizations, to bargain collectively through representatives of their own choosing, and to engage in other mutual aid or protection." The Taft-Hartley Act of 1947 added to Section 7 the terms "and shall also have the right to refrain from any or all of such activities except to the extent that such right may be affected by an agreement requiring membership in a labor organization as a condition of employment as authorized in Section 8(a)(3)."

An important feature of U.S. labor law is that it protects "concerted activity" and "mutual aid or protection." That is, employees do not have to be involved in trade union activity to be protected by the law. Indeed, they may have no intention at all to unionize, but as long as they act in concert their activity is protected under the law.[88]

Exclusions from coverage of the NLRA

Legal protection for concerted activity, including the right to organize, to bargain collectively and to strike, are afforded to "employees" as defined in the law. The definition specifically excludes agricultural workers, domestic workers, managers, supervisors, confidential employees and independent contractors from coverage. The exclusion means that employers can discharge these workers with impunity for attempting to form and join a union. Victimized workers have no legal recourse (see the discussion in Chapter V., *Defenseless Workers: Exclusions in U.S. Labor Law.* below).

Unfair labor practices

The central instrument in U.S. law for protecting workers'rights to organize, to bargain collectively, and to strike is the definition of five unfair labor practices in Section 8(a) of the National Labor Relations Act. An unfair labor practice violates the NLRA and is subject to the remedies provided by the law.

*Section 8(a)(1) of the NLRA makes it an unfair labor practice to "interfere with or coerce" employees engaged in concerted activity.

*Section 8(a)(2) of the NLRA makes employer "domination" of a labor organization an unfair labor practice.

*Section 8(a)(3) protects the right to organize by defining an unfair labor practice of discrimination against workers for protected concerted activities, including union activity.

*Section 8(a)(4) makes it unlawful to retaliate against a worker for filing unfair labor practice charges or giving testimony in NLRB proceedings.

*Section 8(a)(5) defines as an unfair labor practice an employer's "refusal to bargain" with a certified collective bargaining representative of employees.

U.S. labor law is remedial, not punitive. It does not provide for civil or criminal sanctions or penalties in unfair labor practice cases. An employer that commits an unfair labor practice must "cease and desist" from unlawful conduct and post a notice in the workplace promising not to repeat the conduct. Steps must also be taken to restore the *status quo ante*, such as reinstatement and back pay for

---

[88]See *NLRB v. Washington Aluminum Co.*, 370 U.S. 9 (1962), where the Supreme Court ruled that workers who engaged in a spontaneous walkout because their workplace was too cold had engaged in a protected concerted activity, even though they were not unionized or seeking to unionize. The employer had fired the workers for their concerted activity; the court upheld an NLRB reinstatement order.

workers discharged for organizing, or a return to the bargaining table in refusal-to-bargain cases. In back pay awards for workers, the amount of any interim earnings obtained by the worker is deducted from the back pay paid by the employer.

How Workers Form and Join Trade Unions in the United States

Workers usually take the first steps to exercise freedom of association in the workplace with informal meetings among themselves. In small groups at lunch or during breaks, or at a nearby restaurant or coworker's home, they discuss wages, benefits, safety conditions, treatment by management and other problems at their workplace. They might react to a policy move by management—a change in benefit plans, for example, or a new incentive pay system. They often compare their employment conditions to other work experience they have had, or to what they know about unionized workplaces in the same community.

Enter a Union

Sometimes workers' discussions remain gripe sessions, and nothing more happens. But sometimes workers call a local union office for help.[89] A union staff organizer—an employee of a union whose job is to help workers form new unions—normally arranges a series of meetings with workers. Like the workers' own initial meetings, these are usually in small groups starting at a worker's home or at a nearby restaurant.

As the circle of interested workers grows wider, meetings start to be held in larger union halls or rented meeting space. Workers tell organizers about conditions in the workplace. Organizers tell workers how the union operates and what the union has achieved in other locations. If the organizing effort takes root, the most active workers form an organizing committee to advocate openly for the union inside the workplace.

---

[89]Sometimes the selection of which union to call is completely haphazard, depending on nothing more than seeing a union's name in the newspaper, or the location of the nearest union office, knowing the largest union in the community, or having a friend who belongs to a union and calling that union. There is no requirement in the United States, as there is in many other countries, that only a union for a particular industry may organize workers in that industry. So, for example, some nurses have joined the steelworkers union. Some insurance company clerks have joined the autoworkers union. What unions call "jurisdiction" is jumbled, and unions often compete to represent the same group of workers. One of the main activities of the AFL-CIO, the federation of some seventy national unions, is to set rules and regulations for resolving unions' jurisdictional disputes so that they do not squander resources in internecine battles when 85 percent of U.S. workers are not represented by unions.

The union organizer distributes cards for workers to sign indicating their desire to join the union and have the union represent them in collective bargaining with the employer. These authorization cards can be signed at any time, beginning with the first workers involved in the organizing, then by more workers as the organizing effort proceeds. Alternatively, some unions prefer to have employees active in the organizing committee distribute cards and obtain signatures from coworkers in a shorter period after the committee takes shape and the organizing effort is out in the open. Under legal rules, workers usually can hand out cards and other literature in non-work areas on non-work time, typically in a break or lunch room.

Moving to an Election

Once cards are signed by at least 30 percent of the workers in the "bargaining unit"[90] they seek to form, workers can petition the nearest regional office of the NLRB to hold a secret-ballot election. If a majority votes for representation, the NLRB will certify the results, creating a legal obligation for the employer to bargain with the workers' chosen representative. Normally, workers wait until a supermajority—two-thirds is a common rule of thumb—have signed cards before they petition for an election. Union organizers have learned from experience that the percentage of favorable votes in an election usually falls from the percentage that signed cards. They want to enter the election campaign phase with a margin of security, hoping to retain a majority when the election is held.[91]

The Election Campaign

Most NLRB elections take place four to eight weeks after workers file their petition. About 20 percent of elections are held more than eight weeks later, often when the employer contests the makeup of the bargaining unit sought by the

---

[90]The concept of a defined "bargaining unit" is critical for understanding and applying U.S. labor law. Under the law, a group of workers seeking to form a union must have sufficient "community of interest" to bargain as a single group with the employer of their group. Litigation over bargaining unit definition (should a janitor be in the same unit with a skilled computer programmer, for example) and the employer-employee relationship (can "leased" employees from a temporary agency bargain with the employer at the place where they work) is often complex and causes serious delays in the exercise of freedom of association for workers in the United States.

[91]Trade unionists attribute the dropoff in union support to employers' campaigns of fear and intimidation. Employers call workers' change in sentiment a sincere reversal after hearing management's side in the campaign.

union—for example, arguing that workers included in the union's petition are supervisors who should be excluded.

The NLRB calls the weeks between a petition and an election the "critical period" because an employer cannot claim no knowledge of a union organizing effort during this time. Such lack of knowledge is often used as a defense against an unfair labor practice charge when management dismisses a union supporter before a petition is filed.[92]

The pre-election period is usually marked by vigorous campaigning on all sides. Union supporters hold rallies, wear buttons and T-shirts with a pro-union message, and distribute pro-union flyers to coworkers. Management often engages consultants who specialize in designing and implementing forceful campaigns against workers' efforts to form and join a union. They write scripts for employers' letters to workers' homes, flyers distributed in the workplace, and speeches to workers in "captive-audience meetings" that are a staple of employers' campaigns against workers' attempts to form and join a union.[93] Such meetings are called "captive" because attendance is mandatory for workers, and workers can be prohibited from asking any questions or making any comments under pain of discipline, including discharge. In addition, consultants typically train supervisors to present management's anti-union views in smaller individual and group meetings with the workers under each supervisor.

It is common for some workers within the group being organized to oppose forming and joining a union. They often form a "Vote No" committee and join managers and supervisors in campaigning against the union. It is illegal for employers to instigate or assist such a committee. Intensive discussions and arguments are common in the workplace during the pre-election period. After several weeks, the final days before the election usually reach a high pitch of tension, often with accusations of lies and dirty tricks.

NLRB agents conduct a secret-ballot election, usually in the workplace at times and places allowing all workers to vote during work time. When balloting ends, the NLRB agents count the votes immediately in the presence of company and union observers.

---

[92]Litigating employer "knowledge" of a worker's union activity is often difficult. Some unions take the step of sending the employer a letter early in the organizing effort, before a petition is filed, identifying organizing committee members so that the employer cannot claim lack of knowledge if a worker on the list suffers reprisals.

[93]Captive-audience meetings are meetings held by management at the workplace on work time to inveigh against union formation and collective bargaining. Speeches, videos, movies, overhead projector presentations, role-playing, and even skits using professional actors are some of the features of management's captive-audience meetings.

The NLRB conducts more than 3,000 elections each year at companies where workers seek to form and join a trade union for the first time. A few hundred other elections involve decertifications, where workers seek to get rid of a union; elections between competing unions; and unit "clarification" elections. Nearly two-thirds of elections are held in workplaces with fewer than fifty employees.

For many years now, workers have chosen union representation in approximately half of all NLRB elections. Aggregate vote totals in all elections also divide in roughly equal proportion.[94]

After an Election

Either party may file objections to the election claiming unfair tactics by the other side. The NLRB will investigate these allegations and hold a hearing if necessary. This "objections" case hearing is usually less formal than an "unfair labor practice" case hearing, which is more like a full-scale trial before a judge. Based on the results of an objections case hearing, the NLRB can certify the results of the election or order a new election.

Moving Toward Bargaining

If the NLRB finds that the election was fairly conducted and certifies that a majority of workers chose collective bargaining, the employer is obligated under the law to bargain in good faith with the workers' chosen representative. However, the employer can legally defy the NLRB's order by engaging in what is called a "technical refusal to bargain." Using this tactic, the employer refuses the union's bargaining request and forces it to file a new unfair labor practice charge with the NLRB. The NLRB's General Counsel must then initiate an unfair labor practice case based on the employer's refusal to bargain, and seek support for the NLRB ruling from a federal appeals court. Years of litigation can follow.

Collective Bargaining

The NLRA makes refusal to bargain in good faith an unfair labor practice, and the good-faith bargaining obligation applies to both parties.[95] In 1998, workers charged employers with refusal to bargain in good faith in 7,187 cases, while employers charged unions with such refusals in 172 cases.[96]

The law requires meeting at reasonable intervals and exchanging proposals on "mandatory subjects of bargaining"—issues of wages, hours and working conditions

---

[94]In 1998, a majority of workers chose union representation in 48 percent of "select-or-reject bargaining rights" elections conducted by the NLRB. See NLRB 1998 Annual Report, p.13.
[95]NLRA Section 8(a)(5); 8(b)(3).
[96]See NLRB 1998 Annual Report, Table 2, p. 130.

affecting represented employees. The "good faith" bargaining obligation has been defined as "an obligation . . . to participate actively in the deliberations so as to indicate a present intention to find a basis for agreement
. . . a sincere desire to reach an agreement."[97] To bargain in good faith, "a sincere effort must be made to reach a common ground."[98]

But there are no objective measures of intentions or sincerity. Good-faith bargaining does not require either party to agree to a proposal from the other.[99] Advised by skilled counsel, some employers go through the motions of good-faith bargaining to avoid a finding by the NLRB or the courts of bad-faith bargaining or "surface bargaining," defined as the "desire not to reach an agreement."[100] A typical maneuver is to make a "killer proposal" that the employer knows the union could never agree to, while showing flexibility on other issues. Even if found guilty of bad-faith bargaining, the only remedy the employer faces is an order to return to the bargaining table, where the cycle can simply repeat itself.[101]

"Impasse" in Bargaining and Unilateral Implementation

Collective bargaining can end with an agreement. It can also end with each party making final offers without coming to an agreement. When such an "impasse" is reached, the employer is allowed to "post conditions." That is, the employer can unilaterally implement its final offer unless the parties agreed earlier to extend prior terms and conditions indefinitely (an increasingly rare contract term). Workers must then live with the imposed terms or strike to obtain their own proposal or a compromise that might result from a strike.

The impasse doctrine is not contained in the NLRA. It was elaborated by the courts, first by implication in a case where the Supreme Court ruled that unilateral changes prior to impasse are unlawful.[102] The court said that "even after an impasse is reached he [the employer] has no license to grant wages increases greater than any he has ever offered the union at the bargaining table."[103] This has been taken

---

[97]See *NLRB v. Montgomery Ward & Co.*, 133 F.2d 676 (9th Cir. 1943).
[98]Ibid.
[99]See section 8(d) of the NLRA.
[100]See *NLRB v. Reed & Prince Mfg. Co.*, 205 F.2d 131 (1st Cir. 1953), *cert. denied*, 346 U.S. 887 (1953).
[101]The U.S. Supreme Court has ruled that the NLRB has no power to remedy an employer's refusal, made in bad faith for the sole purpose of avoiding an agreement, to accept or even to bargain over a proposal from workers other than to order the employer to resume bargaining. See *H.K. Porter Co. v. NLRB*, 397 U.S. 90 (1970).
[102]See NLRB v. Katz, 369 U.S. 736 (1962).
[103]Ibid., at 745.

to mean that the employer may implement his last offer to the union upon impasse, and this is now the rule in U.S. labor law.[104]

Strikes and Lockouts

Whether or not impasse has been reached in bargaining, workers can strike or employers can "lock out" workers in a test of economic strength to achieve their bargaining goals, unless a no-strike/no-lockout clause in a prior contract is still in effect. Workers can withhold their labor and set up picket lines at the workplace, but they cannot prevent the employer from continuing operations.

Employers have many options for continuing operations during a strike. In many workplaces managers and supervisors can maintain activity. As long as employers do not use threats to coerce them or promises to entice them, they are legally permitted to try to persuade workers not to join strikes or to "cross over" picket lines and return to work, which trade unionists call "scabbing."

Employers may subcontract operations to other employers during a strike. They can recover lost income from a mutual aid fund among employers, just as workers depend on a union strike fund for assistance. Even during a strike, employers and unions can agree, as many do, to have striking workers maintain certain equipment or functions to prevent safety hazards or to assure a rapid resumption of operations when the strike ends. Absent such an agreement, an employer may use contractors to this end.

Striker Replacements

Most important, employers may hire replacements for striking workers. These can be temporary replacements who leave the worksite when the strike ends. But management may also hire permanent replacements, leaving workers who exercise the right to strike jobless, able to be recalled to work only when a job is vacated by a replacement worker. Replacement workers, too, are called "scabs" by workers loyal to the strike. After one year, an NLRB election to decertify the union can be held, with strikers not eligible to participate in the vote.[105]

How the National Labor Relations Board Works

The National Labor Relations Act (NLRA) is the main U.S. law meant to protect workers' rights to organize, to bargain collectively, and to strike under U.S.

---

[104]For a thorough discussion, see Ellen J. Dannin, "Legislative Intent and Impasse Resolution under the National Labor Relations Act: Does Law Matter?", 15 Hofstra Labor and Employment Law Journal 11 (Fall 1997).
[105]Se below, Chapter V., *Coloradao Steelworker, the Right to Strike, and Permanent Replacements in U.S. Labor Law*, for treatment of the permanent replacement doctrine.

law.[106] The National Labor Relations Board (NLRB) is the main government agency that enforces those rights. But these are not the only laws and agencies that cover workers' freedom of association. The Railway Labor Act and the National Mediation Board (NMB) play parallel roles for workers in the railroad and airline industries. A Federal Labor Relations Act and Federal Labor Relations Board cover federal government employees' organizing and bargaining rights.

In states that allow public employees to form unions and bargain collectively, various labor relations laws and boards regulate organizing and collective bargaining by state, county and municipal employees. States also have "little NLRBs" for private sector workers in extremely small enterprises that fall short of the NLRB's jurisdictional requirements. The NLRB requires that the employer have annual gross revenues of $250,000 including $50,000 in interstate commerce to come under its jurisdiction.

While millions of private sector workers (agricultural workers, supervisors, managers and others) are excluded from coverage by the NLRB, a substantial majority of private sector workers in the United States do come under the board's jurisdiction.[107] Its operations come up repeatedly in this study, making a "primer" on NLRB procedures an important reference. Knowing how the NLRB works is especially needed for understanding how, despite an enforcement staff committed to the purposes of the law and a successful record conducting elections and prosecuting unfair labor practice cases, legal entanglements in the board and the courts often frustrate workers' freedom of association rights.[108]

The NLRB has three independent branches: the five-member board in Washington, D.C.; a general counsel also based at NLRB headquarters, and a

---

[106]Unless otherwise noted, reference to "U.S. labor law" or "U.S. labor law and practice" in this report involves the NLRA and related NLRB and federal court decisions and doctrine dealing with freedom of association, the right to organize, the right to bargain collectively, and the right to strike. Where laws or legal matters related to other worker issues like wages, hours or working conditions are discussed, those laws or matters will be separately identified.

[107]Using the Bureau of Labor Statistics' Current Population Surveys, Human Rights Watch estimates that half of all workers in the United States come under NLRB jurisdiction. The rest are public employees, railway and airline employees, self-employed individuals, microenterprise workers (presumably under state "little NLRA " laws) and workers excluded from NLRB coverage including independent contractors, domestic workers, managers, and supervisors.

[108]A comprehensive history of the NLRB is found in James A. Gross, *Broken Promise: The Subversion of U.S. Labor Relations Policy, 1947-1994* (Philadelphia, Temple University Press 1995).

division of administrative law judges. A network of thirty-three regional offices carries out NLRB tasks around the country.

Structure and Functions of the Board

The five-member NLRB is appointed by the president to individual five-year terms, subject to Senate confirmation. A board member's term is fixed regardless of any change in the presidency, so members remain in office when administrations change. It usually takes some time before a new president puts his or her "stamp" on the NLRB so that it comes to be known, for example, as "the Eisenhower board," (1952-1960) or the "Reagan board" (1980-1988) or the recent "Clinton board" (1992-2000).

By tradition, no more than three board members can belong to the same political party. Appointments often give rise to controversy, since nominees of necessity must be experienced labor law scholars or practitioners and thus have a record of writing or advocacy that can be identified as pro-labor or pro-management.[109] Appointments often come in balanced "packages" with relatively moderate candidates identified as having a labor background or a management background. Such balanced appointments usually satisfy Republicans and Democrats in Congress and the administration in the White House.

Labor and management partisans often attack as biased an NLRB closely linked to an administration they are otherwise unhappy with. Trade unions vilified the Reagan board of the 1980s, and management forces have attacked the Clinton board of the 1990s.[110] In general, though, while Democratic or Republican majority boards might lean one way or another, the NLRB carries out its mandate within a centrist range established by the law. Charges of bias are unwarranted. However, this report demonstrates that the range is established between legal margins that often frustrate workers' rights under international human rights standards.

---

[109]The famous labor song "Which Side Are You On?" contains the line "There are no neutrals there." In general, labor law professionals cast their scholarship or their working lot with unions or with management early in their careers and remain on one side of the line. As this report demonstrates, labor-management relations are highly contentious, and finding a middle ground on matters of policy or on appointments to the NLRB is more often a process of hard bargaining and painful compromise, not easy consensus.

[110]See, for example, "The NLRB: An Agency In Crisis," Prepared Statement by Daniel V. Yager, Vice President and General Counsel, Labor Policy Association, before the Senate Labor and Human Resources Committee, September 17, 1996, on file with Human Rights Watch (arguing that the NLRB under President Clinton "has abandoned the neutrality and impartiality essential to the administration of a law intended to create a level playing field for management and labor").

The NLRB has two main functions. First, it oversees the representation election process by which workers in a bargaining unit choose whether to bargain collectively with their employer. The board conducts a secret-ballot election and certifies whether a majority has favored union representation. If so, the employer is obligated to bargain in good faith with the workers' chosen representative. Upon filing of "objections to the election" by a losing party, the board also decides whether election campaign behavior has tainted election results. If so, the board orders a re-run election.

Second, the board serves as an appeal panel that reviews written decisions by administrative law judges in cases involving unfair labor practices. The most common unfair labor practices are discriminatory reprisals against workers attempting to form and join trade unions (usually firings), and refusal to bargain in good faith with workers' chosen representatives. Unfair labor practices are legally and procedurally distinct from the election process and from "objections" to election conduct decided by the board in administrative proceedings. Performing its appeal function in unfair labor practice cases, the board is more like a court of appeals than an administrative agency.

The General Counsel

The general counsel of the NLRB is independent of the five-member board. The general counsel has an extremely powerful role in the structure of the agency, because he or she has the sole authority to issue a complaint in an unfair labor practice case. There is no appeal to the NLRB or to the courts if the general counsel does not issue a complaint.

Acting through the directors and staff in regional offices, the general counsel conducts investigations of unfair labor practice "charges" filed by workers, unions or employers. Key steps in the investigation include interviewing and taking statements from workers, employers, and others involved in a case and evaluating the evidence gathered. Employers are informed of any charges and have the opportunity to meet privately with board investigators and to present written arguments contesting a charge. Following the investigation a rigorous evaluation of the evidence is conducted by a team of experienced NLRB attorneys acting on the general counsel's behalf. Complex or novel issues can be referred to the general counsel's office for advice.

The median time lapse to conclude an investigation and evaluation of an unfair labor practice charge is nearly three months.[111] If the general counsel finds "merit" in the charge that an unfair labor practice occurred, a "complaint" is issued

---

[111]See NLRB 1998 Annual Report, Table 23, p. 187.

specifying the violations in detail and setting a date for hearing before an administrative law judge. If the hearing takes place (many cases are settled after the issuance of a complaint and before hearing), the general counsel acts as prosecutor at no cost to the party who filed the charge. The general counsel is representing the public interest and advancing the public policy of the United States, which outlaws actions defined in the NLRA as unfair labor practices.

Regional Offices and Regional Directors

Obviously, the five-person board or the single general counsel does not conduct every election or prosecute every unfair labor practice. The NLRB has thirty-three regional offices to handle cases around the country, each with a staff of attorneys and agents headed by a regional director. Depending on the nature of the case, the regional director and staff handle "R" cases (representation elections) or "C" cases (unfair labor practice charges).

In all proceedings, regional staff and regional directors strive to achieve voluntary settlements of cases without going to hearings. Parties can submit position papers to the regional staff and informally argue their positions with the regional director. The general counsel finds "merit" in 35-40 percent of the unfair labor practice charges filed with the board.[112] As in any litigation system, most of these cases are settled. Of cases where complaints are issued, about 15 percent reach the stage of a completed hearing before an administrative law judge.

In some 90 percent of cases where the general counsel found merit in the charge, relief is obtained—most often back pay for a worker who suffered discriminatory reprisals. In 1998 nearly 24,000 workers received back pay from employers because of discrimination for union activity. Of these, almost 18,000 received back pay under an informal settlement of their unfair labor practice case, while some 6,000 received back pay under an order by an administrative law judge, the NLRB, or a federal court.[113] Total back pay paid to victimized workers in 1998 was nearly $90 million.[114]

While superficially these totals can appear to indicate an enforcement system that is working, other problems discussed in this report such as delays in reinstatement and the fact that very few workers awarded reinstatement actually return to work have a chilling effect on workers' exercise of the right to organize. Failure to swiftly remedy violations by the most determined anti-union employers

---

[112]In 1988-1998, the "merit factor" (cases where the investigation determined that an unfair labor practice occurred) ranged from 35 percent (1994) to 39.6 percent (1996). The merit factor in 1998 was 36.3 percent. See NLRB 1998 Annual Report, Chart 5, p. 9.
[113]See Ibid., Table 4, p. 137.
[114]Ibid., Chart 9, p.13.

signals to other employers that they can get away with similar conduct. The dramatic rise in the frequency of discrimination against workers who try to organize (a four-fold increase since the 1960s) demonstrates that the labor law system has a rapidly diminishing deterrent effect on workers' rights violations.

Administrative Law Judges

Administrative law judges are independent of the board and of the general counsel. A corps of experienced labor law experts, the approximately seventy-five NLRB judges preside over unfair labor practice hearings in much the same way that civil and criminal court judges preside over non-jury trials (there are no juries in NLRB proceedings). The judges manage proceedings to give parties full opportunity to prosecute and defend while avoiding repetition and unnecessary prolonging of a hearing. Applying rules of evidence, they decide on the admissibility of evidence and objections by counsel in the examination and cross-examination of witnesses. They also evaluate the credibility of witnesses.

This last power is significant since most unfair labor practice hearings involve conflicting accounts of what happened. In the most common cases involving the firing of worker activists, workers charge—and the general counsel supports the charge in a complaint—that they were discharged because of organizing activity while the employer claims that the worker was fired for another reason unrelated to such activity. As a general principle, the NLRB or the courts do not overrule an administrative law judge's "credibility" findings because the findings rest on witnesses' demeanor at the hearing, something the reviewer of a written record cannot see.

The median time lapse between the issuance of a complaint and a hearing before an administrative law judge is six months.[115] Depending on the complexity of the case the hearing can last several months. After a hearing ends, the judge reviews the evidence, the transcript of witnesses' testimony, and written briefs by the parties, and issues a written decision with findings of fact and conclusions of law on whether unfair labor practices occurred. As noted above, the findings of fact often depend on the judge's determinations on witnesses' credibility, since much testimony involves disputes about who said what or did what to whom. The median time between the close of the hearing and the judge's decision is four to five months.[116]

---

[115]See NLRB 1998 Annual Report, Table 23, p. 187.
[116]Ibid.

Appeal to the NLRB

A party aggrieved by an administrative law judge's decision can appeal it to the NLRB in Washington. The board reviews the evidence, the transcript, and the judge's written decision and opts to uphold it, reverse it, or modify it. The NLRB's own written decision can adopt the judge's ruling without comment or offer the board's separate reasoning based on its reading of the case record. The median time for the NLRB's decision is ten months. In complex or controversial cases the board often takes two or three years to issue its decision.[117]

Appeal to the Federal Courts

The NLRB's decision can be appealed to a U.S. federal circuit court of appeals in one of twelve geographically distinct parts of the country. Each circuit is composed of several states except the District of Columbia Circuit, which handles many NLRB appeal cases. Most appeals are decided by three-judge panels.

In the same way that the board reviewed the administrative law judge's decision, the court panel reviews the board's decision along with the hearing record and the judge's decision. While there is a general policy of deference to the administrative expertise of the NLRB, appeals courts sometimes make their own judgment on the merits of a case. Some circuit courts are more deferential to the NLRB, while others are more prone to discount the board's reasoning in a case. Subsequently, if the board disagrees with the holding of a circuit court's decision, it will apply that holding only in similar cases arising in the states within that circuit and not in the rest of the country. As a result, there are some conflicting applications of labor law in different parts of the country despite a general policy of uniformity under federal law.

Only a small percentage of unfair labor practice cases reach the stage of a trial and decision before an administrative law judge or go farther, to appeal stages before the NLRB or federal courts. But even these relatively few cases affect many workers. In all, administrative law judges completed 779 initial unfair labor practice hearings in 1998.[118] Also in 1998, 873 cases from earlier years were resolved in appeal stages that follow the administrative law judge's hearing, either by the NLRB or by federal circuit courts of appeals.[119] While unfair labor practice cases are not broken down by size of the employee groups involved, using as a proxy the average size of workplaces where NLRB elections were held (workplaces that most likely give rise to unfair labor practice cases)—sixty-six employees[120]—it

---

[117]Ibid.
[118]Ibid., Table 3A, p. 132.
[119]Ibid.
[120]Ibid., p. 12.

can be estimated that more than 100,000 workers in the United States were affected directly or indirectly by unfair labor practices cases that reached the stage of an administrative law judge hearing or beyond in 1998 alone.

Rulemaking and Adjudication

Unlike many federal agencies, the NLRB does not issue rules in the form of written regulations to supplement the basic content of labor laws governing labor-management relations. Instead, the board acts through adjudication of individual cases to set precedents for similar situations.

Case-by-case NLRB decisions, as upheld or modified by the courts, create a "common law" for organizing, collective bargaining, and the right to strike in the United States. Depending on an infinite variety of facts and circumstances in any situation, the same conduct—for example, a speech by a plant manager to workers in a captive-audience meeting, or the content of a leaflet issued by a union—might be lawful or unlawful. A high level of expertise in "board law" is needed by advocates advising workers and employers about how to behave in union organizing campaigns, by regional directors deciding what makes up an appropriate bargaining unit or whether to issue a complaint in an unfair labor practice case, and by administrative law judges deciding cases.

Remedies

A common expression of U.S. labor law says that the NLRA is remedial, not punitive. The NLRB cannot penalize an employer for breaking the law. It can only order a "make-whole" remedy restoring the *status quo ante* as the remedy for unfair labor practices. The non-punitive character of U.S. labor law was established soon after adoption of the Wagner Act. In the *Consolidated Edison* case, the Supreme Court decided that punitive measures were not authorized by the NLRA.[121] In the *Republic Steel* case, the court overturned a board order to the employer to reimburse the Works Project Administration, a federal jobs program, for the amount of wages subtracted from a back-pay remedy for workers who had been employed by the WPA while they were unlawfully discharged for union activity. The board's decision reasoned that the employer should not reap the benefit of the employees' interim earnings from public works employment. The court held that "[t]he Act is essentially remedial . . . The Act does not prescribe penalties or fines in vindication of public rights."[122] Several commentators have observed that in neither case did

---

[121]*Consolidated Edison v. NLRB*, 305 U.S. 197 (1938).
[122]*Republic Steel Corp. v. NLRB*, 311 U.S. 7 (1940).

the Supreme Court cite any statutory language or legislative history to support the distinction between remedial and punitive measures.[123]

Not only are there no punitive measures for workers' rights violations. Employers can ignore orders by administrative law judges or by the NLRB and force the board to seek enforcement by a federal appeals court, adding years to the enforcement of its rulings. The NLRB has no enforcement authority of its own.

The standard remedy for an unfair labor practice is to have the employer post a notice at the workplace promising not to repeat the unlawful conduct. Discriminatory discharge cases are the most common category of charges filed with the NLRB. Here the standard remedy includes an order to reinstate victimized workers with back pay. However, any interim earnings fired workers received during the period of discharge are subtracted from the employer's back-pay liability.

In practice, many discriminatory discharge cases are settled with a small back-pay payment and workers' agreement not to return to the workplace. At a modest cost and with whatever minor embarrassment comes with posting a notice, the employer is rid of the most active union supporters, and the organizing campaign is stymied.

In the other most common unfair labor practice cases involving charges that employers refused to bargain in good faith with the workers' chosen representative,[124] the remedy is an order to post a notice acknowledging the conduct and to return to the bargaining table and bargain in good faith. There is no further remedy, so the same cycle can repeat itself indefinitely without an agreement being reached.

10(j) Injunctions

In unfair labor practice cases where the severity of an employer's unlawful conduct makes standard remedies inappropriate, the NLRB is empowered under Section 10(j) of the NLRA to seek a federal court injunction to halt the unlawful

---

[123]See, for example, Jeffery A. Smisek, "New Remedies for Discriminatory Discharges of Union Adherents During Organizing Campaigns, 5 *Industrial Relations Law Journal* 564 (1983).

[124]In 1998, 8,734 unfair labor practice charges were filed against employers alleging discrimination against workers exercising the right to freedom of association. Refusal to bargain allegations gave rise to 7,187 charges. Separately, a combination of discrimination and refusal to bargain were alleged in 2,113 charges. Together, these charges accounted for more than 75 percent of the total number of unfair labor practice charges against employers. In comparison, 38 discrimination charges, 172 refusal-to-bargain charges, and 2 combined charges were filed against unions. See NLRB 1998 Annual Report, Table 2, p. 130.

conduct. For example, a 10(j) injunction may be sought to obtain immediate reinstatement of workers fired for union activity. However, this power is rarely invoked. In 1998 the NLRB sought injunctions in only forty-five cases, and some of these included mandatory injunctions against unions to halt secondary boycott actions.[125]

Non-Self-enforcement

Final orders of the NLRB are not self-enforcing. That is, the board must obtain a federal court order to enforce its decisions. In many cases, this adds months or years to the resolution of a case, leaving workers with no effective remedy while the case winds its way through the court system. Even when workers prevail at every stage of the NLRB process, no final remedy takes place until a court orders it. By that time, the remedy is often impotent.

Delays

The problem of delays is endemic in U.S. labor law practice. Using NLRB data on median time lapses for reaching various stages of legal proceedings in unfair labor practice cases that are deemed meritorious (as distinct from the 60-65 percent of cases that are not found to have merit, which are quickly disposed of), it takes nearly three months for an investigation to be wrapped up and a complaint to be issued. It then takes six months to finish a trial before an administrative law judge. Five more months go by before the judge issues his or her decision in the case. If that decision is appealed to the NLRB, it takes ten more months for the board to issue a ruling.[126] By now two years have passed, and appeals can then be made to federal courts, where further delays of up to three years can be expected.

These are median time lapses. That is, half of all meritorious cases take longer than the time frames just noted. In general, these longer cases involve more complex disputes involving multiple unfair labor practices by employers that the NLRB found to be intent on preventing workers' organizing or preventing a contract being reached—exactly those cases with the most serious consequences for workers' freedom of association.

---

[125]See NLRB 1998 Annual Report, p. 19. The report does not break down the nature of injunction proceedings and what type of unfair labor practices they entail.
[126]Ibid., Table 23, p. 187.

Over time, the slow unfolding of the legal mechanisms and the availability of appeal after appeal make workers' organizing efforts suffer from employee turnover and frustration and discouragement among workers who stay. Such sentiments were expressed by many workers interviewed by Human Rights Watch for this report. The result is a frequent denial of workers' fundamental rights.

V. CASE STUDIES OF VIOLATIONS OF WORKERS' FREEDOM OF ASSOCIATION

Context: The Increase in Workers' Rights Violations under U.S. Law

By the 1990s . . . one of every eighteen employees involved in union election campaigns was subjected to discharge or other discrimination to discourage union representation.

—Researcher Charles Morris, based on NLRB records for 1992-1997

The cases described in this section were selected for diversity of sectors, areas of the country, and kinds of workers. The cases were not selected because they are exceptional. According to Prof. Theodore St. Antoine, former dean of the University of Michigan School of Law and president of the National Academy of Arbitrators, the nation's leading organization of labor-management neutrals, "[t]he intensity of opposition to unionization which is exhibited by American employers has no parallel in the western industrial world."[127]

Workers' rights violations in the United States are widespread and growing. The NLRB used to devote most of its work to running elections for workers to choose or reject representation. Now the bulk of the agency's work involves unfair labor practices, most having to do with employers' violations of workers' rights.[128]

The accelerating pace of violations is not a new phenomenon. Myriad studies document the rising volume of workers' rights violations. Congressional hearings and reports in the 1970s revealed extensive employer violations and ineffective enforcement of laws supposed to protect workers' rights. These revelations led to a significant movement for labor law reform in 1977-78. Despite passing the House of Representatives and gaining majority Senate support, the reform legislation failed, halted by a minority filibuster in the Senate.

More hearings, reports, and studies in the 1980s confirmed that violations of workers' freedom of association and rights to organize and bargain collectively were becoming more acute.[129] While the numbers of workers fired for exercising

---

[127]See Theodore St. Antoine, "Federal Regulation of the Workplace in the Next Half Century" (hereafter Federal Regulation), 61 *Chicago Kent Law Review* 631 (1985), 639.

[128]See NLRB 1998 Annual Report, Chart 15, p. 20, showing that less than 40 percent of its caseload in 1948 involved unfair labor practices, compared to more than 80 percent in 1998. The report, at p. 6, states that 80 percent of unfair labor practice cases involve charges against employers.

[129]See Subcommittee on Labor-Management Relations of the House Committee on Education and Labor, 96th Cong., 2d Sess., "Report on Pressures in Today's Workplace" (1980); Subcommittee on Labor Management Relations of the House Committee on

these rights during the 1950s was measured in hundreds each year, by the 1980s thousands suffered such discrimination annually.

Reviewing NLRB records, Prof. Paul Weiler at Harvard Law School found that unfair labor practice charges against employers increased by 750 percent between 1957 and 1980, while the number of NLRB elections (a measure of workers' organizing activity) increased by less than 50 percent.[130]

Research in the 1990s continued examining workers' right violations in light of domestic legal principles and the original intent of the NLRA. In 1994 a report by Prof. Richard Hurd of Cornell University documented one hundred recent cases of flagrant workers' rights violations by employers and the failure of U.S. labor law enforcement authorities to remedy the violations. Hurd concluded that "the right to an independent voice for workers has become a mirage."[131]

The Hurd report was prepared for a presidential commission on worker-management relations chaired by John Dunlop, the dean of American industrial relations scholars and a former secretary of labor. The Dunlop Commission issued its broad study in 1994, reporting these findings:[132]

- The stagnation of real earnings and increased inequality of earnings is bifurcating the U.S. labor marker, with an upper tier of high-wage skilled workers and an increasing "underclass" of low-paid labor.

- The decline in collective bargaining in the private sector has created an arena for employee-management relations in which most employees have no independent organization to discuss issues with management.

- Adjusted for the number of certification elections and union voters, the incidence of unlawful firing of workers exercising the right to organize increased from one in every twenty elections adversely affecting one in 700

Education and Labor, 98th Congress, "The Failure of Labor Law: A Betrayal of American Workers" (1984); U.S. Department of Labor, Bureau of Labor-Management Relations, Report No. 134, "U.S. Labor Law and the Future of Labor-Management Cooperation" (1989).

[130]See Paul Weiler, "Promises to Keep: Securing Workers' Right to Self-Organization Under the NLRA," 96 *Harvard Law Review* 1769 (1983), 1779-80.

[131]See Richard W. Hurd, "Assault on Workers' Rights," a report for the Dunlop Commission (1994), p. iv.

[132]See U.S. Department of Labor, U.S. Department of Commerce, Commission on the Future of Worker-Management Relations (hereafter Dunlop Commission), *Fact Finding Report* (May 1994).

union supporters [in the early 1950s] to one in every four elections victimizing one in fifty union supporters [by the late 1980s].

- Most unlawfully fired workers do not take advantage of their right to reinstatement on the job, and most who are reinstated are gone within a year.

- In a national poll, 59 percent of workers said it was likely they would lose favor with their employer if they supported an organizing drive. And 79 percent agreed that it was "very" or "somewhat" likely that "nonunion workers will get fired if they try to organize a union." Among employed nonunion respondents, 41 percent believed that "it is likely that I will lose my job if I tried to form a union."

A 1997 study by the Secretariat of the North American Commission for Labor Cooperation under NAFTA's labor side accord reported that employers threaten to close the workplace in half of the organizing campaigns undertaken by workers in the United States, but rarely in Canada or Mexico. Such threats are used even more intensively in U.S. industries where workers feel most vulnerable to shutdowns and relocations. Employers threatened closings in nearly two-thirds of organizing efforts in manufacturing facilities and warehouses.[133]

Professor Charles Morris updated the inquiry into the accelerating volume of discrimination against workers who exercise freedom of association. Using NLRB records showing that more than 125,000 workers received back pay because they suffered reprisal for associational activity from 1992 to 1997, Morris concluded that "a substantial number of employers involved in union organizational campaigns deliberately use employment discrimination against employees as a device to remove union activists and thereby inject an element of fear in the process of selecting or rejecting union representation."[134] Morris estimated that by the late

---

[133]See Commission for Labor Cooperation, *Plant Closings and Labor Rights* (1997) (available at the web site of the Commission, www.naalc.org). The findings were based on research directed by Prof. Kate L. Bronfenbrenner of the New York State School of Industrial and Labor Relations at Cornell University.

[134]See Charles J. Morris, "A Tale of Two Statutes: Discrimination for Union Activity Under the NLRA and RLA," 2 *Employment Rights and Policy Journal* 327 (1998), p. 331. Reaching back to 1990 and adding workers found by the NLRB to be victims of discrimination in 1998, the total reaches more than 184,000. See ibid., NLRB 1998 Annual Report, Table 4, p. 137.

1990s, one out of every eighteen workers involved in an organizing campaign was a victim of discrimination for union activity.[135]

A recent study by professors Richard Freeman of Harvard University and Joel Rogers of the University of Wisconsin found that 53 percent of managers said they would oppose any unionization effort in their workplace. One-third said that it would hurt their advancement in the company if the employees they managed formed a union; more than half of these said it would hurt their careers a great deal.[136] Freeman and Rogers noted that under U.S. law, managers who refuse to oppose their employees' organizing efforts can be summarily fired.[137]

In preparing this report Human Rights Watch took into consideration viewpoints of analysts who take opposite views. In general, these analysts view workers' efforts to form and join trade unions and their protection under the NLRA as an unwarranted interference with a free market in labor. They point to favorable treatment for workers and unions in U.S. law, such as exemptions from some antitrust rules.[138] They cite the ability to obtain recognition through "card checks" (more on this below) rather than elections.[139]

------

[135]Ibid., p. 330.

[136]See Richard B. Freeman and Joel Rogers, *What Workers Want* (Russell Sage Foundation 1999), pp.62, 88.

[137]Ibid, p. 62. Freeman and Rogers reported that 15 percent of surveyed managers in non-union firms stated they would welcome an effort to form a union among their employees, and that "[w]hen we reported these results to business leaders, they were . . . interested in the 15 percent of managers who were pro-union 'so we can get them fired immediately.'" Ibid., p. 88. See also *Parker-Robb Chevrolet, Inc. v. Automobile Salesmen's Union*, 262 NLRB 402, petition for review denied sub. nom *Automobile Salesmen's Local 1095 v. NLRB*, 711 F.2d. 383 (D.C. Cir. 1983), where a supervisor who protested management's order to fire workers for union activity because he felt they were his best employees was himself fired. The NLRB upheld the firing on the grounds that supervisors are excluded from protection of the NLRA. The appeals court upheld the board's ruling.

[138]See Richard Epstein, "A Common Law for Labor Relations: A Critique of New Deal Labor Legislation," 92 *Yale Law Journal* 1357 (1983); "In Defense of the Contract at Will," 51 *University of Chicago Law Review* 947 (1984). Professor Epstein goes so far as to defend the "yellow dog" contract, outlawed in the 1932 Norris-LaGuardia Act, by which employers made workers promise not to join a union as a condition of hire.

[139]See Daniel V. Yager, Timothy J. Bartl, and Joseph J. LoBue, *Employee Free Choice: It's Not In The Cards; How Organized Labor Uses Authorization Cards to Avoid Secret Ballot Elections on the Question of Unionization*, Labor Policy Association (1998).

Other analysts criticize union-backed proposals for labor law reform and defend Congress's refusal to enact reforms.[140] Some defend employers' ability to permanently replace strikers.[141] Others see the decline of union representation as a result of market forces, not workers' rights violations.[142]

The research and analysis of U.S. labor law and practice outlined above was undertaken entirely in a national context. Neither critics nor defenders of the current system looked to international human rights standards to inform their work. What follows here is a series of case studies carried out by Human Rights Watch in a dozen states, covering a variety of industries and employment sectors, analyzing the U.S. experience in light of both national law and international human rights and labor rights norms.

Service Sector Workers

South Florida Nursing Homes

The law gives you something with one hand then takes it away with the other hand.

—Marie Sylvain, a nursing home worker fired for organizing in 1996

Nursing homes fill the landscape of southern Florida serving the peninsula's enormous senior citizen population. To maintain a residential rather than institutional atmosphere, most nursing homes are relatively small facilities employing fewer than one hundred employees. In all, hundreds of nursing homes employ tens of thousands of workers in southern Florida. The largest single group of employees is certified nursing assistants (CNAs). Most are women, many of them are immigrants, and nearly all work at or near minimum wage levels. Benefits like health insurance are available only with a sharp pay deduction that few can afford.

---

[140]See, e.g., Daniel V. Yager, "Has Labor Law Failed? An Examination of Congressional Oversight and Legislative Proposals 1968-1990," National Foundation for the Study of Employment Policy (1990).

[141]See, e.g., John S. Irving, "Permanent Striker Replacements Should Not Be Banned," *Government Union Review* (Spring 1993).

[142]See, e.g., Leo Troy, "Is the U.S. Unique in the Decline of Private Sector Unionism?", 11 *Journal of Labor Research* 111 (1990); "Convergence in International Unionism, etc.: The Case of Canada and the USA, 30 *British Journal of Industrial Relations* 1 (1992); "Beyond Unions and Collective Bargaining," *Working USA*, January-February 2000, p. 102.

Nursing home aides work in the third most dangerous job in the country, after mining and construction.[143] Many CNAs make ends meet by working overtime, which is often required anyway because of severe understaffing in the homes.[144] But understaffing and long hours make for rampant health and safety hazards. Workers are frequently injured in lifting, pulling and pushing equipment, lifting and moving residents, and even in assaults by confused but still physically strong residents.

Responding to low pay, long hours, and health and safety hazards, nursing home workers often try to come together with a common voice. The most acute violations of these workers' freedom of association arise during workers' efforts to form and join unions and to bargain collectively. Examining several cases, Human Rights Watch found a pattern of threats, intimidation, and firings of nursing home workers trying to form and join unions and of employers' refusal to bargain when workers succeeded. The cases—several of which have led to NLRB complaints against the nursing homes involved—grow out of a "Unite for Dignity" union organizing campaign in the southern Florida nursing home industry cosponsored by the Service Employees International Union (SEIU) and the Union of Needletrades, Industrial and Textile Employees (UNITE).

Palm Garden: a Close Election Loss

At the Palm Garden nursing home in North Miami, the Unite for Dignity campaign narrowly lost an election, 35-32, in April 1996. Palm Garden management resorted to massive unlawful means including repeated threats to cut pay and benefits if workers chose union representation. Managers forged signatures on warning notices against Leonard "Ted" Williams, a key Unite for Dignity activist. They backdated the notices, then fired Williams shortly before the election.[145]

Palm Garden management did not disguise its bias against workers' forming a union. Its personnel manual states:

---

[143]See Lorraine Adams, "The Hazards of Eldercare: Overexertion, Assault Put Aides at High Risk for Injury," *Washington Post*, October 31, 1999, p. A1.

[144]Employers may impose mandatory overtime on workers in the United States and dismiss workers who refuse overtime, except where workers have negotiated limits or refusal rights in collective bargaining agreements.

[145]These and other unfair labor practices described here were confirmed by the NLRB in its Decision, Order, and Direction of Second Election, *Palm Garden of North Miami and UNITE*, 327 NLRB No. 195 (March 31, 1999), pp. 6-8, 13-14.

This is a non-union health center . . . If you are approached to join a union, we sincerely hope you will consider the individual freedoms you could give up, and the countless risks you could be taking. *We intend to protect those freedoms and prevent those risks for you by opposing unionization of this health care center by every lawful means available.*[146]

Company officials unlawfully threatened loss of benefits and wage cuts if workers chose union representation. One powerful threat was to stop helping workers fill out food stamp applications.[147] With such low wages, many employees were eligible for food stamps and needed assistance with English-language forms.[148]

In a captive-audience meeting, two managers staged a "mock negotiation" portraying a stubborn company proposing to cut pay down to the minimum wage and an inept union bargainer. Then they told workers, "That's what will happen in negotiations," unlawfully communicating to workers that it would be futile to choose the union.[149]

Marie Sylvain, another union supporter unlawfully fired by Palm Garden, gave voice to workers' concerns in an interview with Human Rights Watch. Sylvain is a single parent supporting two children in Florida and two older children and an elderly parent in Haiti. She told of low pay—Sylvain received food stamps—and health insurance too expensive to afford at more than $60 per pay period, every two weeks.[150]

Sylvain spoke of severe patient overload, sometimes with a single CNA responsible for twenty residents in a single shift. For each of these, she said, "We have to sit up the patient, brush their teeth, feed them breakfast, take food trays back and forth to the kitchen, change sheets, dress them, take them to lunch, get them into

---

[146]Cited in ibid., p. 4 (emphasis in original).

[147]The food stamp program is a feature of social assistance in the United States that provides food subsidies to low income persons in the form of vouchers, called "food stamps," that can be used only to purchase food or other essential items in stores that accept the stamps. Full-time workers paid at or near the minimum wage are often eligible for food stamps. See, for example, Ted Rohrlich, "Living Wage Movement Targets County Government: Low-Paid Contract Workers Use Costly Public Benefits, Backers Say," *Los Angeles Times*, November 4, 1998, p. B1; U.S. General Accounting Office, "Welfare Reform: State and Local Responses to Restricting Food Stamp Benefits," Report RCED-98-41 (1998).

[148]See NLRB Decision, March 31, 1999, p. 12.

[149]Ibid., pp. 12-13.

[150]Human Rights Watch interview, Miami, Florida, July 22, 1999.

their chairs—most of the patients need total help walking, eating, going to the bathroom, everything."[151]

Sylvain said managers always accepted patient complaints against CNAs or accusations against CNAs from other nursing staff members without hearing the CNA's side of the story. "They don't have respect for us," she concluded. "If you had respect, it would be OK."[152]

Because "I saw so many bad things," said Sylvain, she became active in the organizing effort.[153] "I talked to the other Haitian workers," she told Human Rights Watch. She distributed and collected union cards and spoke up at organizing meetings. She eagerly served as the union's election observer during the NLRB ballot in April 1996. Her dismay at the lost election was made worse, though, when the company fired her at the end of April, telling her that she had given "too much problem at this place" and that she "brought the union to the work place."[154]

In January 1998, an administrative law judge ordered Palm Garden to offer Marie Sylvain and Ted Williams reinstatement to their jobs, with back pay from the date of their unlawful dismissal.[155] The company refused to accept the ruling and appealed to the NLRB in Washington, D.C. In March 1999, the NLRB upheld the judge's order. Palm Garden appealed to the federal court, where the case is still pending with more delays likely before any remedy takes hold.

"Why does it take so long?" Marie Sylvain asked Human Rights Watch. "I've been fired for more than three years" (now four years). "Everything takes too long. Where is the justice? Everything is at the boss's advantage with all these delays. The law gives you something with one hand then takes it away with the other hand." Asked if she would accept reinstatement, Sylvain said, "I would like to come back for one week just to show them the union can win."[156]

A worker still employed at Palm Garden, who asked not to be identified, described conditions at the home while the NLRB case languishes in the courts. She makes $6.31 per hour for seventy-five hours' work every two weeks. She has four children but does not take health insurance because it is too expensive, more

---

[151]Ibid.

[152]Ibid.

[153]Ibid.

[154]The quoted statements are from Sylvain's credited testimony in the unfair labor practice hearing. See NLRB Decision (March 31, 1999), p. 14.

[155]The ALJ's decision dated January 30, 1998 is incorporated in the NLRB Decision, March 31, 1999. Under NLRB rules, back pay is "mitigated" by any earnings the unlawfully fired worker obtains during the period after dismissal.

[156]Human Rights Watch interview, July 22, 1999.

than $60 per pay period. She uses a cash-only emergency clinic for primary health care.

"Everybody is scared now," she explained to Human Rights Watch. She said everyone knows Ted Williams and Marie Sylvain were fired for their union support. "I would get fired if I took up for the union," she added. She said that people still want a union, but "people want it to be automatic, not with a lot of trouble."[157]

The administrative law judge who ordered Williams and Sylvain reinstated to their jobs also ordered a second election at Palm Garden. The company appealed that part of the ruling, too. The NLRB upheld this order in its March 1999 decision, but Palm Garden appealed to the federal court where the case is awaiting a ruling.[158]

Villa Maria: a Spy-filled Election

The Archdiocese of Miami operated the Villa Maria nursing home in Miami, where workers began an effort to form and join a trade union in 1995 and narrowly lost an NLRB election in May 1996. "The workload doubled in the five years before the election," a Villa Maria worker (who asked not to be identified) told Human Rights Watch. "I have twelve or thirteen patients." While workload increased, benefits shrank, she said. "Health insurance used to be free, but now it's $30 a pay period [every two weeks]."[159]

Despite extensive Catholic Church pronouncements supporting workers' freedom of association and the right to organize and bargain collectively,[160] Villa Maria management launched a concerted attack on the workers' attempt to form a union. An administrative law judge found, for example, that a supervisor infiltrated a union meeting by signing a union card with a false name to spy on workers and report attendance back to management.[161] In a series of captive-

---

[157]Human Rights Watch interview, Miami, Florida, July 22, 1999.

[158]See ALJ Decision, January 31, 1998; NLRB Decision, March 31, 1999.

[159]Human Rights Watch interview, Miami, Florida, July 23, 1999.

[160]See, for example, National Conference of Catholic Bishops/United States Catholic Conference, "A Fair and Just Workplace: Principles and Practices for Catholic Health Care" (August 25, 1999), noting that "All church institutions must also fully recognize the rights of employees to organize and bargain collectively with the institution through whatever association or organization they freely choose," and "[I]t is up to workers—not bishops, managers, union business agents, or management consultants—to exercise the right to decide through a fair and free process how they wish to be represented in the workplace . . . . Catholic tradition respects their decision."

[161]This and other unfair labor practices recounted here were confirmed by an administrative law judge who conducted a hearing on the evidence. See Decision of Administrative Law Judge Robert C. Batson, *Villa Maria Nursing and Rehabilitation Center, Inc. and the Service Master Company and UNITE! Union of Needletrades, Industrial and Textile*

audience meetings in January 1996, management told workers that if they signed any union papers "we would lose our pension . . . we would lose our home."[162] The company assigned CNAs to additional weekend work to discourage union activity.[163]

The administrative law judge found that Villa Maria management mobilized new armed security guards during the union organizing campaign to intimidate workers and spy on union activity. In addition to newly hired security agents at the site, archdiocese administrators sent additional security forces from other facilities to Villa Maria during shift change times, when union advocates distributed flyers to coworkers. Security guards held clipboards and appeared to write the names or license numbers of workers who accepted union flyers.

As found by the administrative law judge, management instructed some supervisors to stand on the roof of the nursing home to observe workers entering a nearby restaurant to meet with union representatives. Other supervisors were told to follow workers to the restaurant and report back on those who met with union representatives. Consultants hired by the company to direct its anti-organizing campaign also joined in the illegal surveillance scheme.[164]

Security guards "walked the floor" in the weeks before the election, a Villa Maria worker who requested anonymity told Human Rights Watch.[165] "You didn't know who they were. They had walkie-talkies. We felt like we were being watched all the time." Two consultants also "walked the floor," the worker told Human Rights Watch, "talking against the union." In captive-audience meetings management warned of strikes, lost pensions, lost insurance and other harm.

The results of the NLRB election were 65-59 against union representation, although a majority of workers had earlier signed cards authorizing representation. An administrative law judge found Villa Maria guilty of unfair labor practices and illegal election campaign conduct and ordered a new election.[166] The company refused to accept the judge's ruling and appealed it to the NLRB in Washington, D.C., where the case is pending nearly four years after the first, tainted election.

The Palace: Organizing Nipped in the Bud

Some workers' organizing attempts are terminated at early stages by firing key worker activists. "When I look for a new nursing home job, they tell me not to

Employees, Cases 12-CA-18137, 12-RC-7957, January 9, 1998, p. 6.
[162]Ibid., p. 7.
[163]Ibid., pp. 9-10.
[164]Ibid., pp. 7-8.
[165]Human Rights Watch interview, Miami, Florida, July 23, 1999.
[166]Ibid., p. 15.

come back after they learn about the Palace," Jewel Parham told Human Rights Watch.[167] Parham was a CNA making $5.50 per hour when she sought to form and join a union at this 200-employee Miami nursing home in late 1997. As documented in an NLRB complaint, management retaliated by firing her and four other movement leaders in a single week in January 1998, crushing the organizing effort before it could reach an election.[168]

She was not especially interested in unions at first, Parham told Human Rights Watch. "But I thought it was a good idea" when another worker approached her, she said. "We needed something. We had way too many patients each. Health and safety was a big problem. Our pay was low, but they paid part-time agency employees a lot more for the same work."[169] Citing one health and safety problem, she said the employer refused to furnish protective clothing for CNAs when they bathed residents, even with a scabies outbreak among those they were bathing.[170]

Parham became active in the organizing movement, inviting coworkers to meetings, including one at her home in January 1998. Management learned of the organizing effort.[171] The first victim of what Parham called a "rampage" was Dorothy Grace, another activist who had meetings at her home. She was fired on January 26, 1998. The following day, Jewel Parham and others distributed a letter protesting Grace's dismissal. The Palace fired Jewel Parham on January 28 and three other activists on January 29.

"They told me, 'We no longer need your services,' with no other reason given," Parham told Human Rights Watch. Revealing the fragility of workers' confidence in their rights, Parham sees the main injustice as management's not giving her a chance to *drop* her union activity. "I think it was unfair," she told Human Rights Watch, "because they never let me say, 'I'll stop what I'm doing if you let me keep my job.' I was just trying to see if the other people were interested in the union. We wanted to make it better for the residents."[172]

Parham and her fired coworkers filed unfair labor practice charges with the NLRB. The regional office found merit in their charges and issued a complaint several months later.[173] The complaint noted that management supplemented the firings with threats of more discharges, lost benefits, and closing the home if

---

[167]Human Rights Watch interview, Miami, Florida, July 23, 1999.
[168]See NLRB Region 12, Complaint and Notice of Hearing, *The Palace at Kendall and Home Nurse Corp.*, Case 12-CA-19278, August 28, 1998.
[169]Human Rights Watch interview, July 23, 1999.
[170]Ibid.
[171]Ibid.; according to Jewel Parham, other workers " snitched on us."
[172]Ibid.
[173]See NLRB Complaint and Notice of Hearing, August 28, 1998.

workers selected union representation. But by then management's retaliation had worked. "After the firings everybody clammed up," Parham told Human Rights Watch. "They were afraid . . . Even now I'm shunned by people who used to be my friends there. They're afraid of losing their jobs."[174] Palace workers and the Unite for Dignity campaign abandoned the organizing effort.

The Palace management settled the NLRB case with modest payments to the fired workers and their agreement to forego reinstatement.[175] By then "everybody had other jobs and didn't want to go back," said Parham. But she herself had difficulty. When she first applied for a new job she did not list The Palace as her prior employer, fearing a blacklist effect. But, she told Human Rights Watch, the new home found out she had worked at The Palace and refused her a post for not properly completing the application. However, she adds, after listing The Palace, she still was unable to find work even with a demand for experienced CNAs in the industry. Parham said she is now going back to school and looking for work in a new field.[176]

King David: an Election Won—and a Five-Year Wait
The mostly Haitian CNAs and dietary workers at the King David Center in West Palm Beach voted 48-29 in favor of union representation in an NLRB election in August 1994. "I had a determination to get respect," said Jean Aliza, the first of several workers fired for organizing activity at King David. "I am a citizen, and I deserve respect."[177]

Union adherents prevailed in the face of a massive illegal campaign by management. The campaign began with a common tactic: suddenly applying attendance rules harshly against union supporters after years of granting exceptions to accommodate employees' needs. As the administrative law judge who heard the evidence found, "It is abundantly clear that prior to the onset of union activity the strict provisions of these rules were seldom enforced and . . . that management and employees viewed the handbook more as a loose guideline. . . ." However, said the judge, after workers began organizing, the company "dusted off its handbook and

---

[174]Human Rights Watch interview, July 23, 1999.
[175]The settlement agreement contains a standard non-admission clause to the effect that settling the case and paying the workers do not constitute an admission of unlawful conduct.
[176]Human Rights Watch interview, July 23, 1999.
[177]Human Rights Watch interview, Palm Beach, Florida, July 24, 1999.

began to utilize it to harass and discriminate against its employees who supported the union."[178]

Workers openly began their organizing effort early in 1994. In May 1994, King David management issued a new rule barring workers from speaking Creole to each other with residents in earshot, calling it "verbal abuse" of patients. Management then proceeded to "write up" key union supporters. The administrative law judge found that King David "created the rule as a vehicle by which it could limit the employees' ability to engage in union activity. It is clear that management considered the union organizing activity to be Haitian business."[179]

King David management proceeded systematically to fire active union supporters. Jean Aliza, Lude Duval, Marie Larose, Marie Pierre Louis, Michelle Williams, Carline Dorisca, and Ernest Duval were all fired on trumped-up charges. They were ordered reinstated by the administrative law judge who heard testimony and reviewed documents, and the NLRB upheld the judge's order.

Jean Aliza was "set up" by managers and fired early in the organizing effort, after a year-long "satisfactory" record suddenly became "unsatisfactory" based on warning notices he never saw.[180] Lude Duval was fired next for not having a CNA certificate, though she had three years of college toward an RN degree and had passed a CNA test administered by King David (by contrast, another employee, opposed to the union, who lacked a CNA certificate, was given alternate work until she obtained a certificate). Duval got her certificate a month after she was terminated, but King David refused to take her back.[181]

Marie Larose was fired after she refused a supervisor's peremptory order to take off a union button.[182] Michelle Williams was fired for having fourteen "call-ins" (calling in to say she would not come to work), while a leader of an anti-union employee group was untouched with twenty-two call-ins.[183] Management "concocted" a misconduct charge to get rid of Carline Dorisca.[184]

King David "was determined to rid itself of the most vocal union supporter from the beginning," said the administrative law judge's ruling, referring to Ernest

---

[178]See NLRB Decision and Order, *PVMI Associates, Inc. D/b/a King David Center et.al. and 1115 Nursing Home Hospital & Service Employees Union-Florida*, 328 NLRB No. 159 (August 6, 1999), p. 10.

[179]Ibid, p. 12.

[180]Ibid., p. 13.

[181]Ibid., p. 14.

[182]Ibid., pp. 14-15.

[183]Ibid., p. 21.

[184]Ibid., p. 21.

Duval. Duval told Human Rights Watch he told a company manager, "I'm happy I'm in this country because I'm free, I can choose, I choose for union," after the union won the NLRB election in 1994, where he was a union observer.[185] Just days later, Duval was fired on trumped-up misconduct charges "clearly for this enthusiastic support for the union," said the judge.[186]

Ernest Duval was still vocal about his union support when he spoke with Human Rights Watch in July 1999, but he was also frustrated. "I see the government protecting management," he said. "It's been four or five years now, and I've got bills to pay. Management has the time to do whatever they want."[187]

Duval and other union supporters were illegally fired in 1994 when workers voted in favor of union representation. On August 6, 1999, the NLRB upheld the administrative law judge's decision. Based on calculations of Duval's interim earnings during the years he was unlawfully dismissed from King David, he was entitled to $1,305 back pay and $493 interest for a total of $1,798. Jean Aliza, the first worker fired in the union organizing effort, was granted $1,207 back pay and $586 interest for a total of $1,793.[188]

For such modest financial liability, company management has succeeded in preventing workers' exercise of freedom of association. Even though King David workers had won their election, bargaining had ground to a halt. The remaining workers feared for their own jobs if they became active in bargaining or acted as union stewards. "I don't know the people at King David now," said Ernest Duval. "A lot of the older people who voted for the union have left. They hire all new people who hear a union gets you fired or they can't get raises because of the union."[189] Union representative Dale Ewart told Human Rights Watch, "[W]e can't even get a committee to the bargaining table. People are absolutely scared. Everything they see is a disincentive to get involved."[190]

Duval returned to the nursing home in December 1999. He was the only one of the unlawfully fired workers who returned. "The government told me to go back," he told Human Rights Watch. "They told me not to worry, my rights would be respected."[191] In March 2000 Duval left the workplace and filed a new unfair labor practice charge of discrimination for union activity. Duval alleged that

---

[185]Human Rights Watch interview, Palm Beach, Florida, July 24, 1999.
[186]NLRB Decision, p. 18.
[187]Human Rights Watch interview, Palm Beach, Florida, July 24, 1999.
[188]See NLRB Region 12, Draft Settlement Agreement, *Greenwood Rehabilitation Center (formerly King David Center)*, Cases 12-CA-16368 et.al., December 1999.
[189]Ibid.
[190]Human Rights Watch telephone interview, Miami, Florida, March 15, 2000.
[191]Human Rights Watch telephone interview, North Miami, Florida, March 20, 2000.

management assigned an employee to constantly watch him and report any potential infraction of work rules. "I don't feel safe," Duval told Human Rights Watch. "They threatened to fire me."[192]

Avante at Lake Worth: Leaders Fired for Speaking Creole

Thousands of Haitian immigrants have become certified nurse assistants in Florida nursing homes in recent years as they seek a foothold in the labor market and aspire both to provide for their families and advance in the health care field. The mostly Haitian-American workers at the Avante chain's nursing home in Lake Worth, Florida voted overwhelmingly in favor of union representation by the SEIU by a 56-16 vote in March 1999.

The March vote was a second election, following an earlier 77-24 tally in favor of representation in November 1998. Avante management had objected to the results of that first vote and gained a second election on the grounds that a Creole interpreter arrived late at the NLRB election.[193] In management's view, the delay in providing translation had deprived some Haitian workers of assistance with questions about the voting process. The NLRB had agreed and held the second election, where workers repeated their overwhelming vote in favor of union representation.

Avante challenged the second election now claiming, among other objections, that pre-election notices were not fully translated into Creole.[194] The NLRB dismissed all the company's new objections as unfounded, however, and ordered the company to bargain with the union. The company has appealed that order and launched a process of legal appeals that may last for several years.

But Avante management's concern for the rights of Creole-speaking employees appears to be selective. In December 1999, after promulgating a "No-Creole" rule forbidding Haitian-American workers from conversing in their native language, Avante fired Marie Pierre, Jean Reuter and Propheta Masse for allegedly violating the rule. All three of these CNAs were active in the union organizing

---

[192]Ibid. It must be noted that this new unfair labor practice charge is still at the allegation stage. It is cited here for Duval's perception of his treatment, and because it is consistent with the earlier finding by an administrative law judge that management "was determined to rid itself of the most vocal union supporter."

[193]In elections with significant numbers of workers who speak another language, the NLRB provides an interpreter to assist with procedural questions.

[194]See NLRB Region 12, "Hearing Officer's Report on Objections to Rerun Election with Findings and Recommendations," Case No. 12-RC-8275, May 21, 1999. The hearing officer overruled all the company's objections.

effort and in the continuing effort to hold their organization together while the company appealed the election results favoring union representation.

Marie Pierre had been a union observer at the elections. "After two elections they knew who are the leaders of the union," Pierre told Human Rights Watch.[195] She had worked at Avante for ten years when she was fired. Pierre helped lead the organizing effort because, as she put it, "[W]e couldn't take any more disrespect. We needed somebody to represent us. We know our job, we love our job, we love our patients, but management doesn't respect us."[196]

Jean Reuter, a six-year employee, told Human Rights Watch in a separate interview, "I was always outside at the union demonstrations. Inside Avante I always defended other workers. They came to me for help. I talked to the supervisor for them."[197] Like Pierre, Reuter expressed his motivation for organizing: "[W]e needed dignity and respect. They don't respect people."[198]

Avante management also appeared to be selective in formulating rules about non-English languages spoken by employees. According to Pierre and Reuter, most of the Haitian workers were supportive of the organizing effort. A smaller group of Spanish-speaking employees was opposed to the union, they said, and management did not issue any rule prohibiting or limiting employees from speaking Spanish with each other at work.[199]

Like the workers at King David who waited five years for a reinstatement order, and like other workers interviewed for this report in cases described below who have been out of work even longer after being unlawfully fired, Marie Pierre, Jean Reuter and Propheta Masse could be waiting several years for their firings to be resolved. In the meantime, in a workplace where employees twice voted emphatically in favor or union representation, their right to organize and bargain is frustrated and their key leaders are fired.

A Management View
For every case study cited in this report, Human Rights Watch made written requests for interviews with owners or managers of companies where workers sought to exercise the right to freedom of association. Of the Florida nursing home owners or managers asked for interviews, only one responded. This senior manager offered key insights into management's views on workers' self-organization in a

---

[195]Human Rights Watch telephone interview, Lantana, Florida, March 8, 2000.
[196]Ibid.
[197]Human Rights Watch telephone interview, Riviera Beach, Florida, March 8, 2000.
[198]Ibid.
[199]Human Rights Watch interviews, March 8, 2000.

telephone interview conducted September 7, 1999. He asked that neither he nor his company be identified.

The manager said that there is an important distinction between the nursing home industry and other service industries. The nursing home industry is the second most regulated industry in the country, he said, after nuclear energy. It is also heavily dependent on government reimbursement for its services. Government payments make up more than 75 percent of the industry's income. The industry's profit margins are only 1 to 2 percent if they make a profit at all.

"We are very pro-worker," the manager said, "but when a union comes in they [the union] can't do anything about the wage base or benefit base." He said that the biggest problem relates to state regulation. "Union facilities get poorer surveys from state regulators," he said, "because unions make it hard to get rid of bad employees." For example, he said, if a resident complains about mistreatment by a worker, "we are obliged to discharge that employee. The union makes it more difficult. They make it hard to fire employees who underperform. Unions defend the indefensible."[200]

Having a union "doesn't allow me to give bonuses subjectively to employees who do a really good job," said the manager, and "it's hard to make wage adjustments for certain groups without doing it for the rest." With a union, he added, "it's hard to get outside agency employees when we want to. We have to offer overtime to union workers." In all, he concluded, "the concern is more operational than financial."

Regarding union organizing efforts, this manager said, "It's all sales and marketing. The union comes in and promises everything. They promise the world—'I'll make everything better, all you have to do is vote for it.'" He said, "I do believe that most union reps are sincere and see it as a service," but added, "They promise what they can't deliver." He also criticized "a significant ethnic bent that they put in their marketing" by appealing to immigrant worker groups facing U.S.-born owners and managers.

"I'm bothered that the union can visit any employee's home," the manager said. "A couple of my people said they felt intimidated. The unions exploit some of their rights." He acknowledged that "delays typically do work to management's advantage," but added, "When the union gets in, the NLRB works to the union's advantage—they can file charges willy-nilly and tie you up in court."

---

[200]The official cited a personal experience of having to go through an arbitration proceeding in a union-represented facility in another state involving an employee who fell asleep while on duty. The arbitrator upheld the discharge. At the time of this interview, the manager's company was facing charges of unlawfully firing several workers for union activity.

Asked whether the right to form and join a union is a basic human right, the manager said, "I don't know. I'm not an expert. It's probably an important right. We as a pro-worker company support workers' rights." However, the official added, "In a capitalist economy the benefits that a union gives are more contrived than real. If you're a good worker, you can get a good job. I need to be competitive in terms of good workers."

"These people have very hard jobs," the manager told Human Rights Watch, speaking of CNAs in the nursing home industry. "The government has not done a good job to keep up reimbursement rates to keep wages up." Asked whether unions and employers in the industry could work together to press government for higher rates, he characterized this approach as "creating a health care crisis to force the government to capitulate—it happened in Connecticut." He concluded, "It's all right if they want to play chicken with the government, but not with my body."

The manager said that theoretically it might be a benefit for unions and managers in the nursing home industry to cooperate, but "in practice in Florida we don't have that kind of relationship with unions." The manager pointed to union campaign tactics giving information he saw as false and taking out full-page newspaper advertisements blasting company owners. "This doesn't engender a spirit of cooperation," he concluded.

San Francisco, California Hotels

You gave up your right to express your opinions.

—A San Francisco hotel manager to workers who chose union representation[201]

In 1980, Marriott Corporation agreed with the Hotel and Restaurant Employees union (HERE) to abide by a "card-check" for workers' choice of union representation at a new hotel the multinational hospitality company was building in San Francisco. Twenty years and a series of judges, mediators, and arbitrators later, all wrapped up in myriad unfair labor practices, the company's reneging on its agreement has never been redressed.

A "card-check" is an alternative method for determining majority sentiment among workers for union representation. Under a card-check agreement, an employer and a union set a period of time for workers to sign cards authorizing the union to represent them in collective bargaining. A typical agreement contains safeguards to ensure that cards are signed voluntarily. It also provides for a

---

[201] See NLRB Region 20, Settlement Agreement, *Marriott International, Inc.*, Cases 20-CA-28111 et.al., April 15, 1999.

"check," hence the name, by a respected, neutral person or organization verifying the authenticity of the cards and the signatures, and certifying whether a majority of workers have chosen representation. The card-check method is an accepted, legal alternative means for workers to choose collective bargaining.[202]

HERE and many hotel and restaurant companies have made card-check agreements a viable method of determining workers' sentiment. The card-check method has been applied at most new hotels and resorts in Las Vegas, allowing cleaners, bellpersons, cooks, servers and other workers to obtain good wages and benefits while avoiding labor strife.[203] Other unions and employers with relatively stable bargaining relationships have made card-check agreements an accepted means of testing majority sentiment in other workplaces of the company, including the Union of Needletrades, Industrial and Textile Employees (UNITE) with Levi Strauss, the Communications Workers of America (CWA) with AT&T, and the United Food and Commercial Workers (UFCW) with several regional supermarket chains.

In addition, in two of the important cases studied for this report (discussed in detail in *New Orleans, Louisiana Shipbuilding* and *Washington State Apple Industry* below), card-check agreements between unions and management resolved long, acrimonious disputes. These cases are worth noting briefly here as examples of the benefits of a card-check mechanism, if it is mutually agreed upon and satisfies workers and employers.

Apple workers seeking representation by the Teamsters union at the Stemilt Bros., Inc. packing and shipping facility in Wenatchee, Washington agreed with management in April 1999 on a card-check procedure to settle an unfair labor practice case. The settlement was reached near the end of a long hearing before an administrative law judge growing out of a 1998 NLRB election marred by threats, intimidation, and firings.[204]

Under the card-check agreement, Stemilt workers had four months to obtain signatures of a majority authorizing union representation.[205]   Both worker

---

[202]See *NLRB v. C&C Packing Co.*, 405 F.2d 935 (9th Cir. 1969).

[203]See, for example, Steven Greenhouse, "Labor Rolls On in Las Vegas, Where Hotel Union Is a National Model," *New York Times*, April 27, 1998, p. A10; Michelle Amber, "First Pact Between HERE, MGM Grand Calls for On-Site Child Care Facility," *Daily Labor Report* (Bureau of National Affairs, November 21, 1997), p. A-1.

[204] See NLRB Region 19, Order Consolidating Cases, Consolidated Complaints and Notice of Hearing, *Stemilt Growers, Inc.*, Case No. 19-CA-25403 et.al.

[205]See NLRB Region 19, Agreement, *Stemilt Growers, Inc. and International Brotherhood of Teamsters*, April 23, 1999.

representatives and Stemilt management agreed not to make any references to immigration, raids, the INS or deportation as part of their campaigns. While preserving the ability to communicate with its employees about its desire to have employees remain non-represented, the company agreed not to use an outside consultant. Workers agreed that Teamster employees would not engage in organizing activity on Stemilt property.[206] The parties agreed on safeguards for integrity of the cards, including the text of the card statement, non-coercion guarantees, even that signatures would be made in blue ink. They also agreed on an arbitrator and an expedited mechanism for resolving disputes over the card-check agreement.[207] In November 1999 the neutral arbitrator certified that a majority of Stemilt workers chose union representation. Bargaining got underway early in 2000.

At the Avondale shipyard in New Orleans, a bitter dispute was resolved when new owner Litton Industries, which purchased Avondale in 1999, agreed on a card-check procedure for determining whether a majority of workers desired union representation.[208] Although the agreement allowed a one-year period for the union to obtain signatures, a substantial majority signed cards within a few weeks. Litton accepted the outcome and began bargaining with the workers' union, putting an end to nearly a decade of turmoil and strife at the shipyard.[209]

In contrast to these examples, Marriott refused to honor its card-check agreement with Local 2 of HERE when the new San Francisco hotel opened for business in 1989. The company and the union had agreed earlier that a card check rather than an NLRB election would be used to determine workers' choice of representation, and that management would remain neutral while workers made their choice.[210]

Instead, management launched a campaign against union representation that is still being fought. HERE had to sue Marriott for breach of contract to enforce the card-check agreement. A district court ordered mediation, which led finally to a new card-check agreement in early 1996.

---

[206]Ibid.

[207]Ibid.

[208]See Keith Darce, "Deal Gives Union Good shot at Organizing Avondale Yard; New Managers Take Fresh Tack," *New Orleans Times-Picayune*, November 3, 1999, p. C1.

[209]See Keith Darce, "Avondale to Become Union Yard; Long Labor Dispute Is Over," *New Orleans Times-Picayune*, December 1, 1999, p. A1.

[210]The agreement is cited in *HERE Local 2 v. Marriott Corporation*, 961 F.2d. 1464 (9th Cir., 1992), p.3. This federal circuit court decision recounts the factual background used here.

An independent arbitrator was picked to verify the cards. In October 1996, the arbitrator certified that a majority of workers chose union representation.

Marriott then intensified its campaign against the union. A complaint issued by the NLRB found merit in unfair labor practice charges throughout 1997 and 1998 that managers:

- accused workers of being "union plants;"

- ordered workers not to talk about the union under pain of discipline;

- told workers that signing a union contract was against Marriott's company policy;

- prohibited workers from distributing union flyers in non-work areas on non-work time;

- picked up union flyers and threw them in the trash;

- told workers they would get no raises until the union was gone;

- told workers "you gave up your right to express your opinions as soon as you chose Local 2 as your representative;"

- granted raises to non-represented workers while withholding them from workers who chose union representation to punish them for choosing a union;

- held captive-audience meetings to discuss bargaining issues without union representatives present;

- fired key union activists because of their involvement with the union.[211]

Marriott reached a settlement with the NLRB with promises not to repeat the cited conduct and to pay union-represented workers the wage increases earlier granted to non-union workers. However, the company refused to settle the firings

---

[211]See NLRB Region 20, Settlement Agreement, *Marriott International, Inc.* The settlement agreement contains a standard non-admission clause that "the execution of this agreement does not constitute an admission by the Charged Party that it has violated the National Labor Relations Act, as amended."

of two workers active in the organizing and bargaining effort, and refused to settle another meritorious charge involving back pay for medical benefits denied to workers who chose union representation. Based on these refusals, the union has appealed the settlement to the NLRB in Washington, where the case was still pending at the time of this report.

Meanwhile, Marriott workers who chose union representation by a majority showing in the card-check method remain without a collective bargaining agreement. Sporadic negotiations resumed in 1999 after no bargaining took place for twenty months, but they have not yielded results. Key union leaders fired for exercising their right to freedom of association remain outside the workplace.

One of the workers fired because of his union support, Grover Sanchez, told Human Rights Watch, "It's unfair that the company can fire people and let them wait and wait."[212] In the meantime, Sanchez has found a job at the new W Hotel in San Francisco. Affiliated with the Starwood Hotel Co. group that includes Westin and Sheraton hotels, the W agreed in May 1999 to a card-check method for workers to choose representation by HERE Local 2. The card-check agreement guaranteed workers' choice and contained a procedure for resolving any disputes over cards' authenticity. Under the agreement, union advocates were granted access to the workplace to discuss worker organizing without affecting work operations. A local Catholic priest chosen jointly by HERE Local 2 and W Hotel management verified that a majority of workers chose representation. Workers and hotel management moved swiftly to completion of a collective bargaining agreement.

Sanchez explains, "With the contract, it's better. There's no favoritism. The worker is more respected. One feels more secure." However, said Sanchez, he will return to the Marriott if he finally wins a reinstatement order "because I would have high seniority and with the union it would be respected." Sanchez said he was one of the first workers hired at the Marriott when it opened for business in 1989.[213]

Marriott International, Inc. declined to comment or respond to questions from Human Rights Watch about the San Francisco Marriott dispute. Instead, a company official referred Human Rights Watch to a newspaper article for what he termed "insight into both parties' positions and the departure points."[214]

---

[212]Human Rights Watch telephone interview, San Francisco, California, January 12, 1999. Sanchez was fired early in 1998; his wait is still a short one compared with that of many other workers in this report.

[213]Ibid.

[214]See letter from Senior VP George J. Palladino to Human Rights Watch, February 10, 2000, on file with Human Rights Watch.

The article characterized the dispute as one "between two very different sets of workplace rules and cultures."[215] According to the article, Marriott "rejects ideas such as a seniority system and fixed job descriptions—both longtime practices in unionized hotels." In contrast, Local 2 "insists that traditional practices like seniority in assigning shifts are essential to a fair and dignified workplace." Both sides agree that "the dispute doesn't center on wages, which are about $1 per hour higher at the Marriott than at other union hotels."[216]

Marriott management stated that "they want us to implement work rules that we really believe would hurt our customers and are not in the best interest of our employees." A workers' representative replied that "we're not trying to take away their right to manage, but there's no reason to require cooks to mop floors."[217]

The article cited by Marriott management contrasted views of two workers. Room-service waiter Ramón Guevara was quoted as saying "he wants a union contract with seniority provisions to prevent favoritism by management," adding "'managers put personality into the (staffing) decisions. They penalize people who don't look as good or who don't speak as good English.'" Guevara also cited overtime policy as a problem, saying that Marriott managers arrange workers' schedules to avoid overtime pay requirements. "'I can work 10 days in a row and not get one single minute of overtime pay . . . You rarely get two days off in a row.'" Cook Kenny Minnis told the reporter, "'we're the highest-paid hotel in the city and we have a benefits package second to none. It's like a family. In this town, there's no better hotel to work for and be represented by.'"[218]

Referring to the 1980 card-check agreement between Marriott and HERE Local 2, the article concludes, "By now, the dispute between Marriott and Local 2 is almost as old as some of the hotel's workers . . . Local 2 and Marriott spent years in court fighting over the interpretation of that agreement. Finally, after a court ruling in its favor, Local 2 turned in union cards representing more than half of Marriott's workers in 1996. The two sides started bargaining for a contract."[219]

---

[215]See Hana DeWare, "Workplace rules at core of dispute between Marriott and hotel union," *San Francisco Chronicle*, February 18, 1999, p. B1. This article appeared before the NLRB found merit in workers' unfair labor practice charges and issued a complaint in the case.
[216]Ibid.
[217]Ibid.
[218]Ibid.
[219]Ibid.

Food Processing Workers

North Carolina Pork Processing
   It really hurt us that the people only heard one side.
   —A worker who sat through captive-audience meetings in a 1999 organizing
campaign

   Dominating the flat, sparsely populated terrain around it, where tobacco and
sweet potato farms are giving way to hog growing, Smithfield Foods' incongruously
immense hog-processing plant in Tar Heel, North Carolina draws more than 4,000
workers each day from the eastern half of the state. Smithfield is the largest pork
producer in the United States. Its Tar Heel plant is the largest hog-killing facility
in the country. Workers there slaughter, cut, pack and ship more than 25,000 hogs
a day.
   Not many workers stay long. Low wages and hard working conditions
contributed to a turnover of more than 20,000 employees at the plant between 1993
and 1997.[220] "Do you know what it's like to go home to your kids every day with
your arms aching and you're smelling like hog blood and guts?" said one worker
who stayed. "You don't want to pick them up, and they don't want you to. What
kind of a life is that for eight dollars an hour?"[221] He asked not to be identified,
since he is active in trying to form a union at the Smithfield plant and is fearful of
retaliation by company management.

   A Pattern of Abuse
   Smithfield workers have sought union representation from United Food and
Commercial Workers (UFCW) Local 204 since soon after the plant opened. Wages
are substantially lower than pay at other Smithfield locations, including some where
workers have formed UFCW local unions. According to NLRB complaints, ten

---

[220]See hearing transcript for February 11, 1999, pp. 4748-49, *The Smithfield Packing
Company, Inc. Tar Heel Division and United Food and Commercial Workers Union Local
204, AFL-CIO, CLC*, Cases Nos. 11-CA-15522/15634/ 15666/15750/15871/15986/16010/
16161/ 16423/16680/ 17636/ 17707/17763/ 17824, 1993-1998, on file at the Region 11
Office of the NLRB, Winston-Salem, North Carolina.
[221]Human Rights Watch telephone interview, White Oak, North Carolina, October 12, 1999.

workers were fired between 1993 and 1995 for union activity at the Smithfield plant, and five more organizing leaders were fired in 1997 and 1998.[222]

Two NLRB elections were held at the Tar Heel plant, one in 1994 and one in 1997. The union lost both but has filed objections to the latest election based on alleged management misconduct in both campaigns. Because the misconduct also involved unfair labor practice charges which the NLRB regional office found meritorious, the objections case has been consolidated with unfair labor practice cases in a single proceeding stemming from both organizing drives.

Besides firing key union activists, Smithfield management opposed workers' organizing efforts with interference, intimidation, coercion, threats, and discrimination. These unfair labor practices came so fast and furious that a hearing originally set for 1995 on complaints from the 1994 campaign did not take place until 1998-99 as new complaints were consolidated with earlier ones.

The NLRB complaints describe in detail Smithfield's offensive against union supporters. In dozens of instances cited in the complaints, Smithfield managers and supervisors:

- issued oral and written warnings and suspensions against union supporters;

- threatened to close the plant if a majority of workers voted for the union;

- threatened to deny pay raises if workers chose the union;

- threatened to deny promotions to union supporters;

- threatened to fire workers who supported the union;

- threatened to fire workers if they exercised the right to strike;

---

[222]The regional director of the NLRB issued complaints finding merit in workers' charges that they were fired for union activity. Smithfield challenged these complaints. All these cases are still in litigation and face the prospect of many months, even years, until a final determination is made. An unfair labor practice hearing on many consolidated complaints against Smithfield was held in late 1998 and early 1999 by an NLRB administrative law judge. His decision in the case is later in 2000. His decision can then be appealed to the NLRB in Washington, D.C. After that, the board's decision can be appealed to a federal court of appeals. The appeals court decision can then be appealed to the U.S. Supreme Court.

- threatened to force workers to strike if they chose the union;

- threatened that workers who went on strike would be blacklisted from employment at other companies;

- threatened to have workers arrested for distributing union flyers;

- confiscated union flyers from workers;

- asked workers to spy on other workers' union activity;

- grilled workers about other workers' union activities ;

- interrogated workers about their own union sentiments;

- indicated to workers that management was spying on their union activities;

- *did* spy on the activities of pro-union workers;

- applied a gag rule against union supporters while giving union opponents free rein;

- applied work rules strictly against union supporters but not against union opponents;

- offered benefits to workers if they would drop support for the union;

- assaulted and caused the arrest of an employee in retaliation for workers' engaging in union activity.

Testimonies: a Management-Recruited Worker and a Supervisor

Most of these violations occurred not once but repeatedly before, during, and after the two elections at Smithfield's Tar Heel plant. Some of the most compelling testimony to the NLRB about Smithfield's conduct came from a line worker active in management's campaign against workers' self-organization and from a supervisor who fired a union supporter.

Sanitation department employee Latasha Peterson testified that shortly before the August 1997 election she was recruited by managers to distribute anti-union material during work time and to report employees' reactions, noting those who spoke favorably of the union. Training in how to campaign against workers organizational efforts, and report-back meetings, took place while Peterson was "on the clock;" that is, supposed to be working.[223]

Peterson testified that she attended training sessions with company lawyers and consultants. Key workers in the company's campaign against workers' organizing efforts were called "the A-Team." Peterson said she also attended the company's captive-audience meetings where management warned workers of dire consequences of organizing and collective bargaining. Management stressed the company's right to take away pay and benefits in bargaining and to permanently replace workers if the union "pulled them out" on strike. Management also showed a series of anti-union videos.[224]

Following these meetings, "A-Team" members, as instructed by the company's consultants, engaged co-workers in conversations about the meetings and videos and made lists of workers and their reactions. They handed these lists to company personnel officials. Peterson said that she received overtime pay while working on management's campaign that amounted to double her normal weekly pay.[225]

Sherry Buffkin was a supervisor in Smithfield's laundry department during the 1997 election. She testified that company officials and consultants instructed her to probe the union sentiments of employees under her and report her findings to management.[226] Buffkin said supervisors were also told to apply disciplinary rules harshly against union supporters but not against union opponents and to deny overtime to union supporters but grant it to union opponents.

"We were told that we were no longer to give the leniency and leeway that we had given previously and to make sure employees knew that if the Union came in we would not do the things that we had done previously to help them such as being late and excusing it without writeups, things of that nature."[227] As for overtime opportunity, a benefit often desired by many employees to supplement their regular

---

[223]*In the Matter of Smithfield Packing Company, Inc.—Tar Heel Division and United Food and Commercial Workers Union Local 204, AFL-CIO* (hereafter Smithfield hearing transcript), November 4, 1998, pp. 1609-1620.
[224]Ibid., pp. 1621-1624.
[225]Ibid., pp. 1621-1631. Smithfield fired Latasha Peterson for alleged misconduct in February 1998. Management has claimed that her story is a false one motivated by the firing. Peterson replies that she testified against the company to make up for "manipulating my own people" (ibid., p. 1659).
[226]Ibid., p. 85.
[227]Ibid., p. 22.

wages, Buffkin said "overtime was subjective to the supervisor to allow the people who were pro-company at this time. There was always overtime but it was given to employees who were active in the company stance."[228] Conversely, said Buffkin, pro-union employees who usually declined overtime because of family needs "were instructed to work overtime."[229] Buffkin said top company officials and lawyers told supervisors to use these tactics.

Buffkin's account of what happened to Margo McMillan is a stark example of interference with workers' rights. McMillan, a laundry room attendant under Buffkin's supervision, was fired in 1997. According to Buffkin, when the chief company attorney learned of McMillan's support for the union, "He then looked me in the face and told me 'fire the bitch. I'll beat anything she or they throw at me in Court.'"[230] According to Buffkin's testimony, "I told him we could not do that. There was no disciplinary action in her file. I mean there was no grounds for it . . . Margo worked for me for years. I knew Margo. I knew her as an employee. I knew from dealing with her that she had family problems. She's got kids. She's got bills she's got to pay and I begged [management] not to do it. . . ."[231]

Smithfield Foods president Joseph Luter testified that he considered the NLRB and the union "one and the same" and that he considered NLRB complaints "to be a matter of—to be frivolous, outrageous." Luter said, "I do not know of one business person in this country that thinks that the NLRB is impartial and neutral on these matters. Not one. We all believe, particularly in the business community, that the NLRB is certainly pro-labor. . . ."[232] Luter did not respond to an August

---

[228]Ibid., pp. 89-90.

[229]Ibid., p. 90.

[230]Ibid., p. 34.

[231]Ibid., pp. 35-36. Sherry Buffkin signed a statement as Margo McMillan's supervisor stating grounds for termination. She later said that she signed the statement knowing it was false "because I had a job, I had a family and I know that you don't go against [the plant manager] or what I've been instructed to do by them. That's exactly where the statement come from." Ibid., p. 42. Buffkin was fired by Smithfield Foods in September 1998 for taking medication during work time. As with Latasha Peterson, management argues that Buffkin is a disgruntled ex-employee whose testimony is motivated by her firing. Buffkin stated at the hearing that she was fired because management became aware of her sympathies toward the union and her feelings of guilt about her conduct during the union organizing campaign. As a supervisor, Buffkin is excluded from coverage by the National Labor Relations Act and has no recourse for a dismissal based on union sympathy. She cannot be reinstated to work at Smithfield.

[232]Smithfield hearing transcript, February 24, 1999, pp. 5992, 5998, 6024-25.

1999 written request from Human Rights Watch to discuss the union organizing campaign and management's campaign against the union at the Tar Heel plant.

State and Local Authorities' Role

The 1997 union election campaign in Tar Heel involved not only abuses of workers' rights by management but also troubling actions by state and local authorities. Instead of fulfilling the affirmative responsibility of government authorities to protect workers' rights, state power was used to interfere with workers' freedom of association in violation of international human rights norms.

Smithfield's director of security, Daniel Priest, had been a local police officer and was still a deputy sheriff exercising police authority. Priest supervised a contingent of twenty-four full-time security guards at the Smithfield plant. In addition to the plant security force, local police officers were told to take instructions from Priest, who was authorized, in his words, to "handle all law enforcement type functions at the plant."[233]

According to union organizer Milton Jones, local police and sheriffs "turned up in force" during the pre-election campaign when union advocates attempted to distribute flyers to workers driving into the plant.[234] Priest testified to the NLRB that police officers were "patrolling around the plant, up and down 87 [the main road in front of the plant], which they would have been all week" prior to the election.[235] "It was hard seeing police cars lined up there every day when we went into the plant," one worker told Human Rights Watch. "It scared a lot of people against the union, especially the Mexican workers."[236] This worker asked not to be identified. There was no record of prior incidents justifying such a wide police involvement in the lead-up to the election, nor the palpable police presence during the voting process. In a departure from normal practice in an NLRB election, Smithfield management stationed security guards under instruction from company security chief Priest in the cafeteria where the 1997 voting took place.

Several dozen Smithfield managers and supervisors packed the small cafeteria where NLRB agents counted the ballots. When it became clear that the union was going to lose the election, these company officials began taunting the union representatives and workers who served as election observers for the union. Union organizers testified that the taunts included racial slurs (the main UFCW staff organizers and key shop floor organizing leaders were African-American). In

---

[233]Smithfield hearing transcript, February 16, 1999, pp. 5188.
[234]Human Rights Watch interview, Wilson, North Carolina, July 13, 1999.
[235]Smithfield hearing transcript, February 16, 1999, pp. 5172.
[236]Human Rights Watch telephone interview, White Oak, North Carolina, October 12, 1999.

testimony at the hearing before an administrative law judge, Smithfield president Joseph Luter characterized management conduct as rubbing "mud in their face, so to speak" and likened it to "during NFL football games where a player would taunt another player if they had a victory play."[237]

When final results were announced, the large management contingent, joined by security guards and by local police officers summoned by Priest, began pushing union supporters toward the door out of the cafeteria. In the confusion, police beat, maced, handcuffed and arrested Ray Shawn Ward, a worker active in the union campaign.[238]

Prisoners Working at Smithfield

North Carolina state officials were implicated in another element of the Smithfield case, involving prison inmates in a work-release program. According to union officials, approximately forty-five workers were bused into the plant each day from the Robeson Correctional Center, a state prison. They were bused into the plant premises without stopping to receive union flyers and boarded the bus at the same internal point so they could not receive flyers leaving the plant.

Smithfield management denied union advocates' request to communicate with these workers, who qualified as "employees" under the NLRA and were eligible to vote in the union election. However, management required these work-release employees to attend captive-audience meetings to hear its arguments against forming and joining a union.

On August 6, 1999 union representative Chad Young called the superintendent of the Robeson prison to request meetings with inmates working at the Smithfield plant. According to Young, the prison official said "no way . . . under no circumstances," and hung up the phone.[239] The following day, a union attorney made a formal request to the Office of the Attorney General requesting permission to visit these workers in the prison to discuss the union organizing effort.[240] The

---

[237]Smithfield hearing transcript, pp. 5978, 5995. Luter based his characterization on reports from local plant management.

[238]Police and company witnesses testified that Ward struck a police officer first. Charges and countercharges were later settled. Police officials said Ward admitted guilt; Ward argued that it was a reciprocal agreement not to prosecute and not to sue for wrongful arrest. The issue of what happened to Ray Shawn Ward is still before the administrative law judge of the NLRB, who is to rule on the unfair labor practice charge related to the incident.

[239]See letter of Carol L. Clifford to Dale Talbert, Esq., August 7, 1997, on file with Human Rights Watch.

[240]Ibid.

state attorney general's office did not respond to this request. The union was never able to communicate with the work-release employees.

Wilson, North Carolina: Same Company, Same Pattern

The experience of Smithfield Foods workers in North Carolina and their efforts to form and join a union do not begin and end in Tar Heel. Smithfield ships pork parts one hundred miles north to Wilson, North Carolina, where a Smithfield plant employs some 300 workers who produce bacon, sausages, hot dogs and other retail pork items.

Workers at this smaller Smithfield plant tried to form a UFCW local union in early and mid-1999. Many of the same tactics used in Tar Heel to thwart workers' organizing—firings, threats, interrogations, spying —were repeated in Wilson. Accounts by workers who spoke with Human Rights Watch were borne out by an NLRB investigation that produced a complaint in January 2000 detailing repeated unfair labor practices by Smithfield managers in Wilson:[241]

- threatening workers with plant closure if they voted in favor of collective bargaining;

- threatening stricter enforcement of disciplinary rules if workers supported a union;

- threatening that it would be futile to form and join a union;

- threatening loss of business and resulting loss of jobs if workers chose a union;

- interrogating workers about their organizing activities;

- spying on workers involved in organizing activity;

- prohibiting workers from discussing salaries with each other;

- firing five workers because of their support for forming and joining a union.

Recounting management's captive-audience meetings with workers, shipping department employee Robert Atkinson told Human Rights Watch, "It really hurt us

---

[241]These unfair labor practices are described in more detail in NLRB Region 11, Order Consolidating Cases, Complaint, and Notice of Hearing, *Smithfield Foods, Inc. and United Food & Commercial Workers*, Case No. 11-CA-18316 (January 21, 2000).

that the people only heard one side. It would be a lot fairer if the union could come in and talk to us. The company has a big advantage, making people come to meetings and showing videos. A lot of people don't come to union meetings. They're scared the company will know."[242]

As in Tar Heel, a large number of workers in Wilson were single mothers eligible for one or more government benefit programs—food stamps, child care subsidies, Medicaid. Workers interviewed by Human Rights Watch estimated the number of employees in this condition at 25-30 percent of the total, although an exact number is not ascertainable. Workers meeting with Human Rights Watch said that in the final days before the July 1999 election, company supervisors launched a targeted campaign to tell these workers that they would lose their benefits or never be eligible for government assistance again if the union came in and "pulled them out" on strike (the argument that a union "pulls out" workers is standard in management campaigns against workers' efforts to form and join a union, even though the UFCW's constitution, like those of most unions, requires a membership vote to authorize a strike). Wilson workers told Human Rights Watch that this tactic swayed many of the single mothers in the plant who need supplemental government benefits to make ends meet.[243]

Atkinson told Human Rights Watch that the plant manager called in workers one at a time to ask them what they thought about the union. "He asked me if I signed a card. I said yes but that I was going to vote against the union. I told him that because I wanted to keep my job."[244] Another Wilson plant worker, Shaniqua Moore, said, "I did everything under the sun for the union." In a one-on-one meeting, she said, the plant manager asked her why she was "so angry" with the company and said he could "make things better" if she worked with him.[245]

In captive-audience meetings, said Atkinson, "I saw about seven different videos on how the union just takes your dues, goes on strike, gets into fights and stuff."[246] Workers told Human Rights Watch that Wilson plant management used another common tactic in captive-audience meetings: separating active pro-union workers for a meeting apart from undecided coworkers to avoid disagreement with management's views.[247]

---

[242]Human Rights Watch interview, Wilson, North Carolina, July 13, 1999.
[243]Human Rights Watch interview with four workers, Wilson, North Carolina, July 13, 1999 (these workers asked not to be identified).
[244]Ibid.
[245]Ibid.
[246]Ibid.
[247]Ibid.

Latino Workers at Smithfield Plants

A separate set of issues in the union organizing campaigns in Tar Heel and Wilson arose from the sizeable presence of Latino workers in both plants. UFCW organizers estimated that 20 percent of the workers in the two plants were Latino. "We never asked, and we tried to tell them it didn't matter, but the truth is that most of them are probably undocumented," said union representative Jeff Greene.[248] Both UFCW staff organizers and workers interviewed by Human Rights Watch said that reaching out to Latino workers in the plants was "practically impossible" despite union efforts to involve Spanish-speaking organizers and attorneys to help in the campaign. "They just want to keep their heads down and not get noticed," said Greene. "This is North Carolina; it's not southern California or New York City where they have some community support."[249]

Human Rights Watch was also unable to speak directly with Latino workers at either plant despite calls and assurances of anonymity. However, one person, a U.S. citizen who had married a Central American immigrant working in the Wilson plant, told Human Rights Watch that, according to his wife, management segregated Latino workers for captive-audience meetings conducted by Spanish-speaking consultants in the weeks before the Wilson election. Union representatives said the same consultants had appeared earlier in the Tar Heel election campaign, meeting separately in captive-audience sessions with the hundreds of Hispanic workers there.

According to the husband, these consultants told Latino workers that the union was dominated by black workers and that the organizing drive was really an effort by African-Americans—the majority of employees at the plant—to get rid of Latino workers and take all the jobs for black people. He said Latino workers were told "the union will see to it that you get fired because you don't have good papers" and that "the company will not bother you about your papers as long as you vote against the union."[250]

The problem of immigrant workers' status in union organizing drives was discussed in Human Rights Watch interviews with African-American workers at the Smithfield plant who were active in the union effort. They expressed frustration about a "bloc vote" against the union by Latino workers. Said one worker, "It's not fair that management can take them all aside and fill them up with lies about us and

---

[248]Human Rights Watch interview, Wilson, North Carolina, July 14, 1999.
[249]Ibid.
[250]Human Rights Watch telephone interview, Wilson, North Carolina, August 17, 1999.

about the union, and we don't know what they said and can't explain what we believe."[251]

Government Takes Sides

Local government partisanship against workers' self-organization emerged when the mayor of Wilson and two other city officials passed out leaflets before the vote urging workers to reject union representation. The city officials were invited by management onto company premises—access denied to union advocates—to pass out flyers against workers' organizing. The flyer detailed earlier closings of the plant and attributed them to union activity, suggesting that the same fate would befall Smithfield workers in Wilson if they chose union representation. The flyer said, "[H]istory paints a bleak picture . . . Are you willing to risk your job and your future for a group of paid organizers? . . . If the plant did close, where would you go to work? . . . Unemployment in Wilson County is 11%."[252]

As in Tar Heel, the application of government presence and power on the side of employers seeking to prevent workers' forming and joining a union violates international humans rights norms. The central obligation of government is to protect workers' right to choose, not to take sides on behalf of the employer, throwing the weight of the state to one side and destroying any semblance of balance.

Detroit, Michigan Snack Foods

A lack of respect—that's why we organized.
—A Detroit food worker telling Human Rights Watch researchers what prompted a failed organizing drive

Lodged alongside a small chemical plant in a residential area in northwest Detroit, the Cabana Potato Chips division of Jenkins Foods supplies snack food products, mainly potato chips, to a regional market under various brand names. The company has been in business for over forty years and employs 120 workers.

Nearly all the plant's workers are African-American, and a majority are women. Many live in the modest homes surrounding the plant and walk to work,

---

[251]Ibid.
[252]See "An Open Letter to the Employees of Smithfield Packing," characterized as "A message from the Wilson County Right to Work Committee—fellow citizens concerned for your future" (on file with Human Rights Watch). The mayor of Wilson did not respond to a written request from Human Rights Watch for an interview about his actions in connection with the union election at the Smithfield plant.

recalling an earlier pattern of work and home life in this era of suburban industrial parks linked by interstate highways. Many workers do not own a car.

The starting wage at Cabana in late 1998 was $5.50 per hour, or $220 per week. Most workers in operator jobs earned between $6 and $7.25 per hour, $240-290 per week. A few workers in higher mechanical classifications made $9-10 per hour, up to $400 per week. If they wanted health insurance, it cost $38 per week for individual coverage and more than $80 per week for family coverage.[253] Workers had no pension plan or other retirement benefit and no sick pay for days of illness.

Most workers were not directly employed by Cabana. Instead, they were employed as "temps"—even those with years of service at the plant—by a shifting series of temporary employment agencies. In recent years, for example, the temporary agency that supplied Cabana with workers changed its name successively from "Creative Staff" to "Crown Temps" to "Total Temp Connection" to "Simplified Temps" to "Future Force Services."[254] Oddly, for an agency that was supposedly independent of Cabana, "Creative Staff" and its successors maintained a permanent office inside Cabana's plant.

With each change, workers were notified that they worked for the new agency from which they now received their paychecks. But over the years, they worked the same job under the same company management at Cabana. Some workers interviewed by Human Rights Watch had up to twelve years of work at Cabana. Because they were "temps," however, seniority did not count for much. They accrued no pension benefit. Workers reported that when some long-service Cabana employees sought to borrow money to purchase a car, the bank said they were ineligible for loans because they worked for a temporary agency.[255] While the names changed, agency owners and staff continued operating from the office in the Cabana plant.

Workers interviewed by Human Rights Watch believe that the temp agency structure is meant to assure they will not be eligible for unemployment benefits in case of layoff. Either they would not attain a "base year" with one employer (a standard requirement for eligibility) or, as some attested happened to them

---

[253]These payments are employees' share of health insurance premium costs. Total premium costs are higher.
[254]Human Rights Watch interview with Cabana workers, Detroit, Michigan, April 20, 1999. Workers interviewed ranged from one year to ten years' service with Cabana.
[255]Ibid.

personally, the temp agency would offer them a position in a far-off suburb, then deprive them of unemployment benefits because they refused a job offer.[256]

Among Cabana's 120 workers, a significant number were former welfare recipients in Michigan's "WorkFirst" mandatory welfare-to-work program. Human Rights Watch was not able to obtain a precise number of WorkFirst employees at Cabana. Interviewed workers characterized it as "a lot," but said that, on the job, it was a subject about which workers did not feel comfortable asking or telling one another. None of the workers interviewed indicated if he or she was in this category.[257]

The Organizing Drive

Cabana workers' move to exercise the right to freedom of association began with a spontaneous protest in September 1998, when the company failed to include Labor Day holiday pay in their paychecks. More than a dozen workers refused to leave the plant after their shift ended, going "upstairs" to demand holiday pay. They received payment for the holiday, but workers remained upset about this and other instances of what they perceived as arbitrary treatment by management, along with low wages, lack of benefits, health and safety problems, and what several workers in interviews with Human Rights Watch called "lack of respect" by management.

Cabana workers called Local 326 of the Bakery, Confectionary & Tobacco Workers union (BCT), which represents several thousand workers in food processing and related industries in Detroit and southeastern Michigan. In general, BCT collective bargaining agreements in other snack food companies provide wages substantially higher than those at Cabana, along with comprehensive medical, pension, vacation, holiday, and other benefits not enjoyed by Cabana workers.

Those Cabana workers most keenly interested in forming and joining a union began meeting with BCT local leaders Don Rogers and Mary Peterson, along with representatives of the national union and shop leaders from other BCT unions in the area. Workers told Human Rights Watch that "first we met secretly, then more out in the open," sometimes in their homes, sometimes at fast food outlets. Union

---

[256]Ibid. Workers who refuse a job offer can be denied unemployment insurance benefits. Employers gain when workers are denied benefits because unemployment insurance taxes are "experience-rated;" that is, taxes are higher for employers who lay off workers who are eligible for benefits.

[257]To respect confidentiality, Human Rights Watch did not press individual workers to reveal if they were WorkFirst employees. The company did not respond to requests from Human Rights Watch for interviews or other information on the number of WorkFirst employees and other issues.

adherents in the shop talked about the union with coworkers and invited them to meetings with union representatives away from the plant. Union organizers made visits to workers' homes if they could locate their addresses and if the workers let them in. All these are typical steps for workers seeking to organize and bargain collectively with their employer.

One Cabana worker was fired by management when the campaign first began, but a charge filed with the NLRB resulted in a settlement of the charge and reinstatement. By mid-November 1998, eighty-four workers—70 percent of Cabana's hourly force—signed cards joining the BCT and authorizing the union to represent them in bargaining. BCT representatives and shop floor leaders personally informed management that the union represented a majority of Cabana workers and requested recognition and bargaining. Management refused.[258] The workers then petitioned the NLRB to hold a secret-ballot election to determine the union's majority status.

The "Vote No" Campaign

The NLRB set an election date of January 14, 1999, about eight weeks after the petition was filed. On November 30, 1999, the union and company agreed with the NLRB on the composition of the bargaining unit and the workers eligible to vote, a total of 121 employees. The relationship between Cabana and Future Force, the temp agency at the time of election, did not delay the election in this case, as it could have had the employer chosen to make an issue of it. As NLRB regional director William C. Schaub, Jr. explained, "As both Jenkins Foods L.L.C. and Future Force Services Inc. signed an election agreement as Joint Employers, there were no novel issues or complications in setting up an election due to the involvement of a temporary employment agency."[259]

Cabana management immediately engaged three full-time consultants to direct a "vote no" campaign in the plant during the weeks before the election. According to workers interviewed by Human Rights Watch, the consultants developed a campaign with two main themes. One was the threat of closing the plant or "moving south" if a majority of workers voted for the union. A former Cabana supervisor told Human Rights Watch that the company owner and the owner's

---

[258]Under U.S. labor law, management can technically claim a "good-faith doubt" of the union's majority status even in the face of overwhelming evidence of majority support for the union. The union must then petition for a secret ballot election by the National Labor Relations Board.

[259]Letter to Human Rights Watch, May 4, 1999, on file with Human Rights Watch.

daughter, also a management official, repeated to the supervisor in separate conversations that they would "close the door" before dealing with a union.[260]

U.S. labor law prohibits open, direct threats to close a plant in retaliation for workers' choosing union representation. Such threats are considered a violation of Section 8(a)(1) of the NLRA, which says, "It shall be an unfair labor practice for an employer to interfere with, restrain, or coerce employees in the exercise of the rights guaranteed in section 7."[261] However, Section 8(c), the "employer free speech" clause adopted as part of the Taft-Hartley Act of 1947,[262] has been interpreted by the courts to allow a "prediction" of plant closing if it is "carefully phrased on the basis of objective fact to convey an employer's belief as to demonstrably probable consequences beyond his control."[263]

This fine distinction in the law is not always apparent to workers or, indeed, to anyone seeking common-sense guidance on what is allowed or prohibited. Unfortunately for workers' rights, federal courts have tended to give wide leeway to employers to "predict" dire consequences if workers form and join a union.

One prediction a court found to be "carefully phrased" was made by the owner of an Illinois restaurant where workers sought to form a union and bargain collectively. In a tape-recorded speech in a captive-audience meeting the owner stated, "If the union exists at [the company], [the company] will fail. The cancer will eat us up and we will fall by the wayside . . . I am not making a threat. I am stating a fact. . . . I only know from my mind, from my pocketbook, how I stand on this." The NLRB found this statement unlawful. A federal appeals court reversed the board, finding the employer's statement a lawful prediction that did not interfere with, restrain, or coerce employees in the exercise of the right to freedom of association.[264]

At an Illinois auto parts plant where workers began organizing, a supervisor told workers, "I hope you guys are ready to pack up and move to Mexico." Again,

---

[260]Human Rights Watch interview, April 21, 1999. The former supervisor asked not to be identified.

[261]Section 7 guarantees "the right to self-organization, to form, join, or assist labor organizations, to bargain collectively through representatives of their own choosing, and to engage in other concerted activities for the purpose of collective bargaining or other mutual aid or protection . . ."

[262]Section 8(c) of the NLRA states, "The expressing of any views, argument, or opinion, or the dissemination thereof, whether in written, printed, graphic, or visual form, shall not constitute or be evidence of an unfair labor practice under any of the provisions of this Act, if such expression contains no threat of reprisal or force or promise of benefit."

[263]See NLRB v. Gissel Packing Co., 395 U.S. 575 (1969).

[264]See NLRB v. Village IX, Inc., 723 F.2d 1360 (7th Cir. 1983).

the NLRB found that the statement was a plant closing threat. And again, the appeals court overturned the finding by the NLRB . The court said the statement was "a joke, not a threat,"[260] apparently not noting the irony of federal judges with lifetime job security deciding what is funny to unprotected auto workers.[261]

Another key theme at Cabana was the threat of permanent replacement if workers exercised the right to strike. For example, a company letter to employees said:

> In a strike employees:
> 1. Lose their wages.
> 2. Lose their company-paid benefits.
> 3. Cannot collect unemployment compensation.
> 4. Can be permanently replaced if the strike is for economic reasons (a strike over wages, benefits, or working conditions).
>
> Question: Do you mean that non-strikers could be hired to take my job in an economic strike?
> Answer: YES. Federal law gives the company the right to hire permanent replacements to continue to serve our customers.
> Question: Isn't the company required to fire the replacements when the strike is over?
> Answer: NO. The company is NOT required to fire the replacements by law. Strikers are only entitled to get their jobs back when and if openings occur.

---

[260]See *Hunter-Douglas, Inc. v. NLRB*, 804 F2d. 808 (7th Cir. 1986).

[261]These examples should not be taken to mean that courts always, or even in most cases, overrule the NLRB on employer threats. A majority of NLRB rulings are upheld by the courts. But the leeway afforded employers by court precedents means that the NLRB mostly prosecutes "slam dunk" cases where the employer's conduct is so outrageous that a finding of violation is likely to be upheld on appeal. Cases that are closer to the borderline, or within the bounds of lawful conduct even when a common sense observer would hear a clear threat, rarely proceed. As a dissenting judge noted in another case where the court of appeals overruled an NLRB finding that the employer had unlawfully threatened workers, "An employer can dress up his threats in a language of prediction. 'You will lose your job,' rather than 'I will fire you' (and fool the judges). He doesn't fool his employees. They know perfectly well what he means." See *NLRB v. Golub Corp.*, 388 F.2d 921 (2d Cir. 1967). The parenthetical remark is in the original citation.

Cabana management then reproduced a portion of the NLRB's Guide to Basic Law and Procedures underlining a sentence saying strikers can be replaced by their employer, then wrote below: *"Remember! 'But they can be replaced by their employer.'"* [267]

Cabana management held a series of captive-audience meetings to fend off the organizing drive. According to workers interviewed by Human Rights Watch, leaders of the organizing effort and active supporters were segregated in one group. Management gave them a perfunctory reading of a script prepared by the consultants and sent them back to work. The larger group of workers, most of whom had signed union cards but were not union leaders and were fearful of management reprisals, were gathered separately for longer, more intensive sessions stressing plant closings and permanent strike replacements.[268]

The solid majority in favor of union representation wilted in the face of management's opposition campaign. The union lost the NLRB election 68-44. This result is not unusual. Most often, workers wait until two-thirds of eligible voters have signed union cards before seeking an election, because experience shows a predictable fall-off in support after management's campaign against the union. Employer representatives attribute the drop-off to workers' changed opinion after hearing the facts from management.

When asked why the union did not raise objections to the election or pursue unfair labor practice charges about arguably unlawful plant-closing threats and pressures on WorkFirst employees, BCT local union president Don Rogers explained, "We just don't have the resources or staff time to put into legal cases that take years to resolve. We need to spend our time organizing and bargaining and handling grievances and arbitrations. Sometimes we have to walk away and just try again later."[269] Rogers added, "We would file for a worker who got fired. We wouldn't leave the worker hanging out there with no help."[270]

Rogers pointed to another common problem. "The workers are often scared to give affidavits or to testify. They figure they'll be on management's hit list if they do, that even if management doesn't fire them they'll get harassed or assigned to worse jobs or something else to make their lives miserable."[271] Rogers's observation

---

[267]Letter to employees of January 7, 1999 from company president (on file with Human Rights Watch; all emphases in original).

[268]Human Rights Watch interview, April 20, 1999.

[269]Under the NLRA, workers can seek another NLRB election after one year from the date of a previous election.

[270]Human Rights Watch interview, April 20, 1999.

[271]Ibid.

was echoed by union representatives in other Human Rights Watch case studies—pointing up the personal courage it takes for workers to go public in complicated legal proceedings that require sworn statements and testimony against employers who control their economic fate.

Welfare-to-Work Employees

The results at Cabana may simply reflect the generalized fear among employees just noted, or in some cases a genuine change of opinion. But another feature of the Cabana campaign may also have played a part. Workers in the WorkFirst welfare-to-work program could lose their food stamps, medical insurance, child care subsidies or other benefits available from the state if they became active in the union and went on strike. The special vulnerability of WorkFirst employees to the loss of vitally important benefits like medical insurance for their children could be a decisive factor in an NLRB election.

Welfare reform and related "workfare" programs are subjects of intense policy debate in the United States. But workfare workers' freedom of association is often low on the agenda.[272] In Michigan, a recipient of cash welfare assistance who joins a strike in the workplace ceases to be eligible for that cash assistance.[273] "Cash assistance" refers to Temporary Assistance for Needy Families (TANF), which replaced the Aid to Families with Dependent Children (AFDC) program under the 1996 welfare reform. It is federal money given as block grants to the states.

If a welfare-to-work employee in Michigan is fired for involvement in or sympathy with an organizing effort, the situation is equally bleak. A state official told Human Rights Watch that, to his knowledge, the eligibility manual contains "nothing specific that speaks to union organizing," and a review of the eligibility manual confirms this.[274] That is, if a welfare-to-work employee is in fact fired for organizing but the employer uses a pretext, such as incompetence, as the stated

---

[272]See, for example, Bettina Boxall, "How Fair Is Workfare?: Rapid expansion of programs raises new questions about the rights of participants," *Los Angeles Times*, March 9, 1997, p. B1; Steven Greenhouse, "Wages of Workfare," *New York Times*, July 7, 1997, p. B3.

[273]Human Rights Watch telephone interview with Alan Durkee, director, Office of Financial Assistance Programs, Family Independence Agency (FIA), Department of Social Services, State of Michigan, February 24, 2000; and "Strikers" section of the Program Eligibility Manual of the FIA, numbered PPB 1998-003, 4-1-98.

[274]Ibid.

reason for discharge, the state has no mechanism in place to protect the welfare status and benefits of the employee.[275]

A Michigan state official indicated that the NLRB would be the avenue of recourse for a welfare-to-work employee who suffers discriminatory reprisals for organizing activity.[276] But a favorable NLRB ruling several months or even years later does nothing to serve the immediate needs of the worker. According to the state official, a welfare-to-work employee losing a job under these circumstances is liable to lose benefits for one to two months before becoming eligible again.[277] The firing also becomes part of her case history, which defines whether she has been deserving of assistance by genuinely seeking to get and to hold a job. In Michigan, if a person "fails to comply" with welfare requirements a second or third time, some benefits may be withdrawn for six months or more, while others may be reduced.[278]

Similar rules apply in most states under federal rules imposing sanctions on individuals for noncompliance with work requirements.[279] States may create "good cause" exceptions for noncompliance with work requirements, including unjustified or unlawful discharge.[280] However, the issue of whether an employer dismissed a worker unlawfully or not is precisely the issue litigated before the NLRB, often requiring many months or even years before a determination is made. In any event, workers are likely too fearful to exercise organizing rights at the risk of losing vital benefits.

The unique status and vulnerability of welfare-to-work employees are only beginning to interest trade unions and legislators. The states have considerable

---

[275]Federal law requires that a grievance procedure be available to determine whether a welfare-to-work employee had "just cause" to fail to keep a job, but the just-cause provisions do not take firing for pro-union sympathy or activity into account. Failure to prove just cause leads to temporary loss of benefits. A narrow exception applies to a food stamps-only recipient: where a worker "must join, resign from, or refrain from joining a labor organization as an employment condition," food stamp benefits can be maintained if employment is not accepted. This exception is not applied for benefits besides food stamps. See "Failure to Meet Employment Requirements: FS-Only Cases," Program Eligibility Manual, FIA, PPB 1999-008, 10-1-99; "Failure to Meet Employment Requirements: FIP," Program Eligibility Manual, FIA, PPB 1999-008, 10-1-99.

[276]Human Rights Watch Durkee interview.

[277]Ibid.

[278] See "Failure to Meet Employment Requirements: FS-Only Cases" and "Failure to Meet Employment Requirements: FIP," Program Eligibility Manual, FIA.

[279]See 64 Federal Register 17776; 17793-97 (April 12, 1999).

[280]Ibid.

latitude in determining eligibility for benefits, and obscure rules like those noted above are little known even to advocates and activists, let alone to workers who are directly affected by them. What welfare-to-work employees do know is that their lives are precarious, and as they enter the national workforce by tens and hundreds of thousands, their vulnerability becomes a factor in workplace dynamics when they and coworkers exercise rights of organizing and collective bargaining.[281]

Manufacturing Workers

Baltimore, Maryland Packaging Industry
Five years later I've got nothing to show for it.
—A worker fired for organizing

Another company in a similar urban factory setting, with low-wage workers exercising their right to freedom of association, offers an example of even harsher anti-organizing tactics. In the mid-1990s, a new company called Precision Thermoforming and Packaging, Inc. (PTP) employed more than 500 workers in a federal "empowerment zone" in a Baltimore, Maryland neighborhood called "Pigtown."

The company received indirect state subsidies worth millions of dollars through a low-cost lease of manufacturing space in a converted warehouse bought by the state in 1994. PTP also received a federal subsidy of $3,000 for each employee it hired who lived inside the empowerment zone. It hired more than 250 such workers. Thanks to subsidies, the federal government's empowerment zone designation is worth a lot of money to employers who set up operations in a zone. But the government does not use this financial leverage for conditioning empowerment zone benefits on fair treatment of workers.

PTP ran a plastic packaging and shipping operation for flashlights, batteries, and computer diskettes. Major customers included Eveready Battery and America Online (AOL). AOL shipped millions of free diskettes to consumers from the PTP plant.

PTP's starting wage was $5 per hour. Most workers after passing probation and staying with the company could get incremental raises to $5.25-7.00 per hour. Health insurance cost employees $36 per week from their paychecks—a benefit most of them declined, since they made only $200-$280 per week. There was no pension plan.

---

[281]For a survey of rules affecting welfare-to-work employees, see National Employment Law Project, "Employment Rights of Workfare Participants and Displaced Workers" (2000).

In mid-1995, a group of PTP workers began an effort to form and join a union in the United Electrical, Radio and Machine Workers of America (UE). The UE represented employees at other Baltimore-area manufacturing plants with better wages and benefits. The UE also had a reputation for democracy and rank-and-file involvement that attracted PTP workers. A leader in the PTP campaign, Gilbert Gardner, had worked in a UE plant years earlier and had been active as a union steward. "I remember the UE was real democratic and close to the people," said Gardner. "When I saw how things were going at PTP, I called the UE for help."[282]

Abuses by Management

A complaint issued by the NLRB finding merit in unfair labor practice charges filed by the union tells what happened next.[283] PTP management fired Gilbert Gardner and eight other workers active in the union organizing effort. In addition to the firings, PTP managers and supervisors:

• threatened to close the plant if a majority of workers voted in favor of union representation;

• threatened to move work to Mexico;

• threatened to move the AOL production line to another country;

• threatened that Eveready Battery would pull its business from PTP;

• threatened to fire workers who attended union meetings;

• threatened to fire anyone who joined the union;

• threatened to replace American workers with foreigners if the union came in;

• threatened to transfer workers to dirtier, lower-paying jobs if they supported the union;

• told workers not to take union flyers from union organizers;

---

[282]Human Rights Watch interview, March 19, 1999.
[283]See NLRB Region 5, Consolidated Complaint and Notice of Hearing, *Precision Thermoforming and Packaging, Inc. and United Electrical, Radio and Machine Workers of America*, 5-CA-25642, 25699, 25802, 25805, 25853, April 7, 1997.

- told workers upper management was going to "get them" for supporting the union;

- asked employees to report to management on the activities of union supporters;

- stationed managers and security guards with walkie-talkies to spy on union handbilling and report on workers who accepted flyers;

- interrogated workers about their union sympathies and activities;

- denied wage increases and promotions to workers who supported the union.

"I'd say I was the one who got the union going," said Gardner, who began working at PTP in April 1993. "Then they fired me the day after I went to a hearing at the NLRB to set up the election," he told Human Rights Watch interviewers. "Earlier they wrote me up for smoking during working hours, which I did ever since I started. I would step outside when I caught up with my work to have a smoke with my supervisors. They never said anything about it until I started supporting the union."[284]

As for his firing, Gardner explained, "On the day after the hearing they demoted me from shipping to production associate, with a fifty-cent cut in pay. When I said I thought it was because of my union work, they fired me for threatening a supervisor."[285] When he was fired, Gardner made $6.25 per hour; management wanted to cut his pay to $5.75.

Union supporters lost the NLRB election by a vote of 226-168. Before the vote, 60 percent of the workers signed union cards to join the UE and authorize the union to represent them in collective bargaining.

The Immigrant Factor

Approximately 25 percent of the hourly workforce at PTP was composed of Vietnamese immigrant workers placed with the company by a social services

---

[284]Human Rights Watch interview, Baltimore, Maryland, March 19, 1999. In a separate proceeding, the Maryland unemployment compensation commission held a hearing on the circumstances of Gardner's dismissal. The commission found no evidence of misconduct, and awarded him unemployment benefits.
[285]Ibid.

agency in Silver Spring, Maryland, a suburb of Washington, D.C. thirty miles from Baltimore. Most of these workers were bused to the PTP plant each day.

"PTP has been a constant customer," Phu Le, a director of the agency, told a reporter. "They like having a lot of refugees, especially Asian."[286] Le's agency received $1400 from the U.S. Department of Health and Human Services for each Vietnamese immigrant placed at PTP. He placed nearly 150 people there in 1995.[287]

"We have come out of hell," said PTP worker Thi Nguyen, "so we are pleased with anything at all." Nguyen, his wife, and four adult children were placed at PTP by Le's agency in September 1995 while the union organizing effort was underway, just eighteen days after they had arrived in the United States. "It is important to work and not complain," Nguyen told a reporter.[288]

Accompanied by Gilbert Gardner, a Vietnamese-speaking union representative tried to visit Vietnamese workers in the suburban Washington apartment where they lived. According to Gardner, "None of them would let us in to talk to them. They were too scared. They didn't want to get in trouble with the company."[289]

Gilbert Gardner told Human Rights Watch that PTP management held separate captive-audience meetings for Vietnamese workers. On the afternoon before the election, the union held a rally at the plant gate for workers leaving the day shift and arriving on second shift. According to Gardner, managers told Vietnamese workers that African-American union supporters were "rioting" at the entrance, and made Vietnamese workers board their bus in the rear of the plant to leave through a rear gate where they could not see the union rally.[290]

Aftermath: Justice Delayed and Denied

UE's charges of massive unfair labor practices by PTP were upheld by the NLRB's regional director, who issued a wide-ranging complaint on management conduct described above. Company president William Hartley wrote a letter to the mayor of Baltimore complaining that "PTP is an employer who invested millions

---

[286]See Joe Matthews, " Opportunity and Disillusionment in Pigtown," *The Baltimore Sun*, November 7, 1996, p. 1A.
[287]Ibid.
[288]Ibid.
[289]Human Rights Watch interview, March 19, 1999.
[290]Human Rights Watch interview, March 19, 1999. Gardner told Human Rights Watch he saw Vietnamese workers being taken to separate captive-audience meetings, and was told by Vietnamese workers about management's "riot" claims.

of dollars in the empowerment zone, only to find itself subjected to a slanderous campaign by a renegade union aided by public officials."[291]

The NLRB found PTP's conduct so egregious that the regional director announced he would seek a *Gissel* bargaining order, an unusual remedy in U.S. labor law based on a 1969 Supreme Court decision.[292] Under the *Gissel* doctrine, a union that has obtained majority support from workers who sign cards joining the union and seeking bargaining can be certified as the bargaining agent even if it loses an election. The *Gissel* remedy is available when an employer's unfair labor practices have made the holding of a fair election unlikely or have undermined a union's majority and caused an election to be set aside. Many workers' organizing efforts match these conditions. However, an employer who resists a *Gissel* order can obtain years of delay by appealing the order to federal courts.

The Supreme Court in *Gissel* said that the bargaining order remedy is not limited to "exceptional" cases marked by "outrageous" and "pervasive" unfair labor practices. The court said that a bargaining order can also be applied "in less extraordinary cases marked by less pervasive practices which nonetheless still have the tendency to undermine majority strength and impede the election process." However, in practice, the NLRB and the federal courts have applied the *Gissel* remedy sparingly, effectively undermining the right of many workers to bargain collectively.

The NLRB also sought reinstatement and back pay ranging from $6,000 to $21,000 for workers fired for union activity, with Gilbert Gardner due to receive the highest amount. In March 1997, however, PTP shut its Baltimore plant and declared bankruptcy, citing a legal dispute with America On Line and AOL's failure to pay $2 million in accounts receivable. AOL countercharged that PTP committed postal fraud and overcharged AOL for mailing expenses.[293] With no employer to order to bargain with the UE, the NLRB fashioned a settlement of the unfair labor practice case before it went to hearing. Under the settlement, PTP acknowledged the actions outlined in the complaint, promised not to repeat them, and promised back pay to the fired workers in the amounts sought by the NLRB.

Since then, Gilbert Gardner and the other fired PTP workers have waited in vain to receive the first penny of back pay for their unlawful firings. "What kind

---

[291]See Matthews, "Opportunity and Disillusionment."

[292]See Complaint and Order of Hearing, *Precision Thermoforming and Packaging, Inc. and United Electrical, Radio and Machine Workers of America*, 5-CA-25642 et.al., August 8, 1996; *NLRB v. Gissel Packing Co.*, 395 U.S. 575 (1969).

[293]See Kevin L. McQuaid and Joe Matthews, "Baltimore employer of 600 to close," *Baltimore Sun Arundel Edition*, March 20, 1997, p. 1A.

of a system is this?", Gardner asks.   "PTP got millions of dollars from the government. They fired me and the other strong union people. They scared other people into voting against the union.   They settle a case promising to pay me $20,000. And five years later I've got nothing to show for it."[294]

With PTP out of business, Gilbert Gardner's first concern now is the back pay that is due him. The *Gissel* remedy is meaningless with no employer for Gardner and his coworkers to bargain with. However, had the NLRB been empowered to act quickly to initiate bargaining, workers might have been able to negotiate over severance pay, continued medical insurance, and other conditions in a bankruptcy-related closing, or indeed to offer steps to avoid closing.

Northbrook, Illinois Telecommunications Castings

When we won the election we thought, "Finally we can start making things better."

—A worker with no contract and no union, twelve years after winning an NLRB election

In the flush of an NLRB election victory, workers' hopes are high for a rapid move to the bargaining table to tackle the issues that gave rise to organizing. Some employers honor workers' choice and join a good-faith bargaining effort to solve problems in ways that meet workers' needs while respecting the needs of the business.   However, other employers view workers' election victories as just temporary setbacks in a long-term campaign to rid themselves of unions.   A governmental commission found that only about one-third of workers' unions are able to achieve a first collective bargaining agreement after winning an NLRB election.[295]

Under the NLRA, refusal to bargain in good faith is an unfair labor practice.[296] But as discussed earlier, good-faith bargaining does not require agreement to any proposal from a bargaining counterpart. Instead, the obligation simply requires meeting at reasonable intervals and exchanging proposals with "a sincere desire to reach an agreement."[297]   By appearing to do so, employers can avoid a finding by the NLRB or the courts of bad-faith bargaining.   If they slip up, the remedy is

---

[294]Human Rights Watch interview, March 19, 1999.

[295]Based on data covering 1986 through 1993. See U.S. Department of Labor and U.S. Department of Commerce, Commission on the Future of Labor-Management Relations, *Fact Finding Report* (May 1994), p. 74.

[296]NLRA Section 8(a)(5).

[297]See *NLRB v. Montgomery Ward & Co.*, 133 F.2d 676 (9th Cir. 1943).

merely an order to return to the bargaining table, where the cycle can repeat itself at little cost to the employer, who now knows from their decisions what the NLRB and the courts are looking for to indicate sincerity in bargaining.

What Happened at Acme

The bargaining history at one facility in suburban Chicago illustrates how delays and loopholes in the law can be exploited to punish workers for choosing representation and to avoid giving them the satisfaction of a collective agreement. Acme Die Casting, a division of Lovejoy Industries, makes a variety of small aluminum and zinc castings, mainly for the telecommunications industry.

Jorge "Nico" Valenzuela is still working at the suburban Chicago company, where he began in 1977. In October 1987, Valenzuela and coworkers Tony Aguilera, Arturo Ramirez and other Acme employees, most of them immigrants in Chicago's large Mexican-American community, voted in favor of representation by the United Electrical Workers union (UE). "We lost another election with a different union earlier," Valenzuela explained, "when the company promised to make things better. At first I didn't want to get involved again. But the UE seemed more democratic; it involved more workers in the leadership."[298] The company employed about 120 workers in 1987, when an NLRB election was held at the plant. Workers voted 69-39 in favor of union representation.

A natural leader, Nico Valenzuela became the head of the organizing committee and then the president of the shop union in 1987. Antonio Ramirez and Tony Aguilera also became leaders. "When we won the election we thought, 'Finally we can start making things better.' We elected a negotiating committee and asked management to start bargaining, " said Valenzuela. He and the other Acme workers did not know that years would go by before any bargaining would begin and that, when it did, bargaining would be futile.

After the election, the company filed objections to the election so unfounded that the NLRB dismissed them without a hearing. But Acme refused to accept the decision, leading the union to file refusal-to-bargain charges and a new round of labor board and court proceedings. While the NLRB and the courts pondered Acme's claims, workers tried to maintain their organizational activity. They mounted community support campaigns in Chicago's labor and Latino communities and traveled to Washington, D.C. to meet with members of Congress and NLRB officials.

In a letter-writing campaign to the NLRB, one Acme worker said, "We expected that after the election we would negotiate with the company and it would

---

[298]Human Rights Watch interview, July 8, 1999.

be all over. But we have received so many humiliations." Another wrote, "We won the election. We want our contract. We can't take the company's abuses any longer." A third wrote, "I don't think it's fair, this country being a free country where everybody has rights."[299]

Acme management launched a campaign of reprisals after the NLRB election. The vote took place on a Friday; on the following Monday, the company issued new rules reversing longstanding practices. For example, management told workers to ask permission to use the bathroom and stopped allowing coffee and soft drinks in work areas. The company cut off access to microwave ovens during lunch time. A wash-up period was eliminated. Under the new rules, management began issuing warning notices and suspensions.[300]

Valenzuela, the leader of the organizing drive and of the workers' negotiating committee, was a skilled mechanic popular throughout the plant. His job took him to all parts of the facility keeping machinery operating. After the election, management assigned him to a rote grinding job isolated from other workers and far below his skill level. This took him out of circulation among coworkers and served as a constant reminder that support for the union carried serious consequences. Since his pay was not cut, the NLRB did not treat the move as discrimination, saying management has the right to assign work.[301]

After workers voted for representation, management halted salary increases for over a year. A judge found that, while refusing to bargain with the union, the company president told a group of workers who requested a pay increase, "I told you guys not to bother with the union because that was going to happen, no raises . . . You want the union, go to the union."[302] However, when a smaller group of workers promising to decertify the union asked for pay increases, they were granted raises within two weeks. The administrative law judge who heard the evidence found that Acme's president fraudulently backdated a letter authorizing the pay

---

[299]Letters signed by Acme workers to NLRB General Counsel James K. Stevens, March 1988, on file with Human Rights Watch (Spanish originals translated by Human Rights Watch).

[300]These and other reprisals were the subject of numerous unfair labor practice complaints issued by the NLRB that were later settled by the company. See Acme Die Casting, *To the Employees of Acme Die Casting*, company memorandum announcing settlement and restoration of past practices, March 29, 1989 (on file with Human Rights Watch).

[301]Human Rights Watch interview with Terry Davis, UE representative, July 5, 1999.

[302]See *Acme Die Casting, a Division of Lovejoy Industries, Inc. v. NLRB*, 26 F.3d 162 (D.C. Cir. 1994).

increases to a date prior to the meeting with anti-union workers to make it appear that the decision was not motivated by bias against pro-union workers.[303]

Ten Years of Appeals and Fruitless Bargaining

In 1998, eleven years after the election, Acme ran out of appeals and had to pay $900,000 in cumulative back pay to workers unlawfully denied their pay increases.[304] But the back-pay case involved discriminatory retaliation against workers for forming and joining a union. It did not address the collective bargaining process. Negotiations had been going on intermittently since 1990 when the company exhausted appeals in the earlier refusal-to-bargain case.[305]

In negotiations after 1990, Acme was again found guilty of refusal to bargain in good faith. The company subcontracted work without either notifying the union or bargaining, a move the administrative law judge called "an example of subcontracting during negotiations over an initial contract by an employer who spent years trying to avoid any obligation to bargain at all."[306] Acme gave "merit" increases to certain high-paid employees who opposed the union while refusing to bargain on general salary increases with the union, which was seeking to improve the status of lower-paid workers.

To the company's argument that a bargaining "impasse" permitted such moves, the judge ruled that "the Respondent [Acme] has been guilty of repeated violations of Section 8(a)(5) of the Act going back to 1987 . . . In light of this history, it cannot claim benefit of any impasse in bargaining since its own intransigent and illegal behavior . . . would have contributed to any stalemate." The judge concluded that the company's violations "are repeated and pervasive and evidence on its part an attitude of total disregard for its statutory obligations."[307]

In an April 1993 decision, the administrative law judge ordered Acme to "cease and desist" from refusing to bargain and to return to the table and bargain in good faith. The NLRB upheld the judge's decision in September 1994. Thus admonished, Acme management shifted to a strategy of appearing to bargain by making proposals and counterproposals to the workers on minor subjects. However,

---

[303]Ibid. Under NLRB rules, no particular penalty attaches to such fraudulent behavior. It is just another piece of evidence of an unfair labor practice. No punitive measures against workers' rights violations are permitted under U.S. law. Remedies consist only of cease-and-desist orders, reinstatement orders, bargaining orders, and the like.

[304]See Francine Knowles, "Acme Die workers to get $900,000," *Chicago Sun-Times*, March 3, 1998.

[305]See *NLRB v. Lovejoy Industries, Inc.*, 904 F.2d 397 (7th Cir. 1990).

[306]See *Acme Die Casting and United Electrical Workers (UE)*, 315 NLRB 202 (1994).

[307]Ibid.

the company "made demands they knew would be suicidal for the union" in other areas, said UE representative Terry Davis. Acme proposed small wage increases and demanded enormous hikes in employee payments for health insurance that would far exceed any pay increase.[308] However, a careful employer can nearly always couch such demands as "hard bargaining," which is legal, as long as it makes proposals and counterproposals in other areas.

Bargaining went nowhere. In 1996, nearly a decade after he played a key role in helping coworkers win their election and serving on the workers' bargaining committee, Antonio Ramirez died. The loss of Ramirez's leadership was compounded, said Davis, when management took advantage of the supervisory exclusion in the NLRA to entice several activists from the bargaining unit by making them supervisors and giving them pay raises. Union chief steward Tony Aguilera was one unionist tapped for a supervisor's post.[309]

In March 1999, the UE sent a letter to Acme and to the NLRB disclaiming representation rights. Under NLRB rules, a certified union may inform the board in writing that it relinquishes representation.[310] Although rarely invoked, this step is the only one left to unions that have exhausted all possibilities of achieving a collective agreement even after the application of labor law remedies against prior unfair labor practices by employers. "At this rate," said union negotiator Davis, "the company would still have deal-killers on the table twenty-five years from now."[311]

A Manager Speaks

A top Acme official, while denying a request for an interview at the plant, told Human Rights Watch "[W]e worked long and hard for years to convince our employees that they're better off with us than with a union. The union did nothing but lie about us. People now believe they're better off with us than with a union."[312]

These were years when, under the law, the company was supposed to be bargaining in good faith with the workers with a sincere desire to reach an agreement. The manager's statement to Human Rights Watch shows how far from

---

[308] Human Rights Watch interview, Chicago, Illinois, July 5, 1999.
[309] Ibid.
[310] See NLRB, "NLRB Casehandling Manual," Part Two, section 11120.
[311] Ibid.
[312] Human Rights Watch telephone interview, July 8, 1999. The manager quoted did not agree to an interview but did, without prompting and without conditions, offer the statement cited here. Most company managers in other cases studied for this report refused to speak with Human Rights Watch.

sincere the company's bargaining was. Yet in the end, its methods prevailed against workers' right to bargain collectively. Acme outlasted the life of one organizer and the endurance of others, and the legal structure supposed to protect workers' rights proved no impediment to these tactics.

The Acme Die Casting case is a dramatic example of profound weakness in U.S. labor law and its inability to deal with a determinedly intransigent employer intent for over a decade on denying workers' right to bargain collectively. Over this time, authorities repeatedly found the employer guilty of interference, restraint, coercion, discrimination, and bargaining in bad faith; that is, without a sincere desire to reach an agreement. But the only remedy was an order to cease and desist such conduct. In effect, by repeated findings of unlawful behavior with no punitive remedies, the NLRB and the courts simply gave the employer a road map to minimally lawful-appearing conduct. In fact, as the Acme manager's statement makes clear, the company harbored no desire to reach an agreement. Instead, it acted to "convince" employees to abandon the union at the same time the company was supposed to be bargaining in good faith.

New Orleans, Louisiana Shipbuilding

[Y]ou better make sure these whiners, malcontents and slackers don't even come close to winning this election.

—Company president in a captive-audience meeting before a 1993 NLRB election

Seen from the Huey P. Long Memorial Bridge just up the Mississippi River from New Orleans, the cranes, drydocks and hulls of ships being built at the Avondale Industries, Inc. shipyard rise from the flat riverside plain like giant stalagmites. With more than 6,000 workers, Avondale Industries is Louisiana's largest private sector employer. It is also the site of one of the largest workers' organizing efforts in the United States during the 1990s.

Up close, sounds of surging motors and clanging metal envelop workers who build and repair ships for the U.S. Navy. The Navy is Avondale's biggest single customer, accounting for more than three-quarters of its business—$3 billion in Navy contract awards in the past decade. Avondale also makes oil tankers for petroleum firms. It is seeking to expand its base of private commercial customers, including cruise ship companies.

In August 1999, Avondale Industries was purchased by California-based Litton Industries. Along with Avondale assets, though, Litton inherited a longstanding labor dispute rife with a decade's worth of workers' rights violations.

"We didn't get a raise for almost ten years. The pension was a joke. People were getting hurt and killed. There was a lot of discrimination. The foremen treated you like dirt. We needed respect. We needed a union bad," said machinist Joseph Johnson, a leader in the movement to form a union at the yard in 1993. He had also been active in earlier unsuccessful organizing tries. When Johnson retired in 1996, after nearly thirty years of service at Avondale, his monthly pension was $270.[313]

In 1993, Johnson and others among the nearly 4,000 hourly paid Avondale workers launched an effort to form and join a union in the Metal Trades Council of the AFL-CIO.[314] The council represents workers at many large U.S. shipyards, gathering the specialized crafts of welders, pipefitters, machinists, electricians, painters and others to bargain collectively with shipbuilding employers. The union represents more than 10,000 workers at Litton Industries' Ingalls shipyard in Pascagoula, Mississippi, along the Gulf Coast some 200 miles east of New Orleans.

"Egregious Misconduct"

Avondale management unleashed a massive campaign to deter the workers' organizing effort. "They called in each craft to talk down the union" in captive-audience meetings, said sheet metal worker Bruce Lightall, who has worked at the plant since 1979. "They told us they'd shut the door if the union came in, that we'd lose Navy contracts."[315]

In a speech to assembled Avondale workers at a captive-audience meeting before the 1993 election, company president Albert L. Bossier, Jr. said:

> You know, those of you who are for Avondale already understand how serious this is. Those of you who are undecided need to think, and really think, about what this union is doing to Avondale . . . [T]hey want their dues money and if they don't get it they don't give a damn what happens to Avondale. Now those of you who are for this union I can   only conclude that you hate this company so much that you don't give a damn if the Union takes action to destroy us . . . If you really want to destroy Avondale you oughtta go and support and vote for the damn union. You know, those of you who don't want to destroy Avondale, you better make

---

[313]Human Rights Watch interview, New Orleans, Louisiana, May 11, 1999.
[314]The rest of the Avondale labor force is salaried supervisory, managerial, engineering and technical personnel not part of the bargaining unit sought by the Metal Trades Council.
[315]Human Rights Watch interview, May 11, 1999.

sure these whiners, malcontents and slackers don't   even come close to winning this election . . . Secure your future by rejecting this union and its bosses.[316]

The findings of an NLRB administrative law judge provide a more systematic description of Avondale management's violations of workers' freedom of association. The judge issued his 700-page decision in February 1998 after an unfair labor practice hearing that lasted from July 1994 to July 1996. The hearing required 165 days of hearings and resulted in a hearing transcript thousands of pages long.[317] The judge found that Avondale management:

- applied stricter enforcement of work rules against union supporters than against union opponents;

- transferred union supporters to more difficult and dirtier jobs;

- threatened to withhold wage increases if a majority of workers voted for the union;

- threatened to close the yard if a majority of workers voted for the union;

- interrogated and spied on union supporters;

- threatened to fire union supporters;

- fired twenty-eight union supporters.

---

[316]Quoted in NLRB, Decision of administrative law judge David L. Evans in *Avondale Industries, Inc. and New Orleans Metal Trades Council*, Cases 15-CA-12171-1 et.al., February 27, 1998. It should be noted that Bossier's statements were found by the judge not to contain unlawful threats or promises. The judge found Bossier's calling pro-union employees whiners, malcontents and slackers "only simple name-calling" (Ibid., p. 27). However, the judge did rely on Bossier's speech, which he termed "a diatribe toward prounion employees," as "raw evidence of animus toward the employees' protected activities" that supported other unfair labor practice findings, particularly those involving discriminatory discharges (Ibid., p. 51).
[317]Ibid.

These labor rights violations took place in a one-year period before and after the June 1993 NLRB election at Avondale. Years of legal proceedings followed the workers' election victory. In his 1998 decision, the judge ordered Avondale to reinstate fired workers and to pledge not to repeat the unlawful conduct.[318] Avondale did not comply with this order, and the cases remain on appeal.

The administrative law judge characterized Avondale's behavior as "egregious misconduct, demonstrating a general disregard for employees' fundamental rights." In these extreme circumstances, he ordered the extraordinary remedy of having company president Bossier read the NLRB's remedial notice to assembled employees (or, if Bossier refused, to be present while a board agent read the notice).[319] This remedy, too, was never implemented.

Defying the NLRB

In June 1993, despite management's tactics, a majority of Avondale workers voted in favor of bargaining collectively with the company. The original vote count was 1,804 favoring representation by the Metal Trades Council of the AFL-CIO, and 1,263 opposed to representation. After adjusting for challenged ballots, the union ultimately prevailed 1,950 to 1,632. Avondale management refused to accept the results and began a series of appeals to the NLRB. In April 1997—nearly four years after the election—the NLRB certified the results and ordered Avondale to bargain with the union. The company still refused, appealing the board's order to the federal courts.

Frank Johnson, an Avondale machinist with twenty-five years in the yard, told Human Rights Watch in May 1999, "After the election I thought we'd sit down after a week or so and start bargaining. Now it's six years later, and we're still waiting."[320] Echoing Johnson, Bruce Lightall said, "I thought we'd sit down after the election and negotiate a contract like reasonable people, to get some justice, respect, dignity. In time I found out how the law doesn't work for workers. It just helps the companies. They can appeal forever."[321] Pipefitter Harry Thompson, another leader of the organizing drive who has since retired from Avondale, put it even more bluntly, "The law stinks."[322]

---

[318]This is the standard NLRB remedy for unfair labor practices. Reinstated workers are entitled to back pay for time off the job, "mitigated" by subtracting all interim earnings the worker was able to obtain.
[319]Administrative Law Judge decision, February 27, 1998, pp. 106-107.
[320]Human Rights Watch interview, May 11, 1999.
[321]Human Rights Watch interview, May 11, 1999.
[322]Human Rights Watch interview, May 11, 1999.

In the separate unfair labor practice case involving threats, discrimination, and firings of twenty-eight workers, Avondale appealed the administrative law judge's 1998 decision to the NLRB in Washington. In the meantime, another massive unfair labor practice case labeled "Avondale II" has begun, consolidating NLRB complaints upholding union charges of a new round of threats, coercion, discrimination, firings of union supporters and other unlawful conduct by Avondale management taking place between 1994 and 1998. Several of these cases involve acts of retaliation against the union's health and safety activists and their efforts to publicize and halt the company's failure to obey occupational health and safety laws. Between 1990 and 1997, seven workers were killed in accidents at the Avondale yard, more than any other major shipyard in the country.[323]

On November 10, 1999 the NLRB upheld virtually all of the findings and orders of the administrative law judge in the "Avondale I" unfair labor practice case. The NLRB cited "the quantity and severity of the unfair labor practices committed" by Avondale and supported most of the judge's extraordinary remedies. However, the NLRB only required a senior company manager, not necessarily Albert Bossier, Jr.—now the ex-president of Avondale—to read the NLRB's order to assembled workers.[324] Avondale appealed the order.

A Fired Worker Speaks

A sandblaster and spray painter at the yard since beginning work in 1985, Donald Varnado is a worker fired in April 1993 who is still waiting for a final ruling in the "Avondale I" case. With the case now pending before a federal court in Washington, Varnado will have to wait years more.

"I was an activator, a supporter. I went to union meetings and talked to the guys. We needed more of a voice, more respect. The foremen and supervisors were always watching me and the other union guys, just looking to get rid of us," Varnado told Human Rights Watch.[325]

The administrative law judge who heard the evidence ruled that Varnado was fired for his union activity, ordering him—like twenty-seven other workers—reinstated with back pay minus interim earnings. While waiting for final

---

[323]See Frank Swoboda, "Avondale Faces Fine of $537,000 by OSHA," *Washington Post*, April 6, 1999, p. E2.

[324]See NLRB Decision and Order, *Avondale Industries, Inc. and New Orleans Metal Trade Council*, 329 NLRB No. 93 (November 10, 1999). Avondale's new owner, Litton Industries, has appealed the NLRB's decision.

[325]Human Rights Watch interview, New Orleans, Louisiana, May 11, 1999.

action, said Varnado, "It's been a struggle. I had one steady job in construction for a couple of years. The rest were on and off, contractor jobs with no benefits."

Like many precariously employed workers, Varnado had no health insurance during most of his years away from Avondale. "I had Avondale's family medical for $25 a week out of my pay, but I lost that coverage when they fired me," he explained. "Since then, I had a lot of medical expenses that I had to pay for me and my family."

"I hope I get some reward for all my suffering from Avondale," said Varnado. "But it's not about the money. It's about what the union can do for you to get some respect from the company."[326]

Government Subsidies Against Workers' Rights

During the years between the 1993 election and Litton Industries' acquisition of the company in 1999, the federal government effectively paid Avondale its legal expenses for violating workers' rights. The Department of the Navy reimbursed Avondale for more than $5 million in expenses for campaigning against workers' self-organization and resisting unfair labor practice charges. As Avondale's biggest customer, providing more than three-quarters of its business, the U.S. Navy has enormous influence over events at the company. "Why doesn't the U.S. government say 'You can't do this!'?" asked union supporter Bruce Lightall in an interview with Human Rights Watch.[327]

Responding to an inquiry from Human Rights Watch, a Navy representative explained, "The costs of legal services, including those associated with Avondale's NLRB and Court of Appeals litigation, are generally allowable as an indirect cost (as part of overhead rates) . . . Avondale's overhead costs for Fiscal Years 1993 through 1998 have included approximately $5.4 million for legal fees related to the labor dispute . . . [T]he total costs for legal services that may be reimbursed . . . have not yet been finally determined."[328]

This response did not address the underlying issue for human rights consideration. The federal government is supposed to be a guarantor of rights protection. It cannot weigh in on the side of a rights violator without becoming itself complicit in human rights abuses. Where the support involves public funds, the complicity is even more serious. Avondale worker Bruce Lightall put it

---

[326]Ibid.

[327]Human Rights Watch interview, New Orleans, Louisiana, May 11, 1999.

[328]See letter to Human Rights Watch from G.H. Jenkins, Jr., rear admiral, SC, U.S. Navy, Office of the Assistant Secretary for Research, Development and Acquisition, July 29, 1999, on file with Human Rights Watch.

succinctly, "We pay taxes. That's our money. They're making us pay to hang ourselves."[329]

Aftermath: Recognition from a New Employer

In July 1999, the United States Court of Appeals for the Fifth Circuit upheld Avondale's objections to the 1993 election, reversing the NLRB decision and ordering a new election.[330] The appeals court overturned the election because the voter lists used in the election contained the first initial, middle initial, and last name of the employee, rather than the full first name, middle initial, and last name of the employee. No NLRB election had ever been overturned on such grounds before. The court called the board's conduct of the election "unthinking adoption of 'standard practice.'"[331]

In a tone of scorn for the union and the federal agency charged with upholding the law, the court's ruling stated that the NLRB and the union, "parroting the hearing officer's allocation of responsibility . . . attempted to saddle Avondale with the blame for any failure in voter identification."[332] Just as astonishing in its one-sided view of the case, the court said full name voter lists should have been used because "electioneering was hostile and bitter," without any acknowledgment that the administrative law judge in the separate unfair labor practice case had already found Avondale guilty of massive threats, discrimination and firings in the period leading up to the election.

Despite this ruling, a rapid series of developments after the late 1999 sale of Avondale to Litton Industries brought the decade-long dispute over representation rights close to a conclusion. With a longstanding relationship with the Metal Trades Council at its other major shipbuilding locations, Litton agreed to a card-check method of certifying majority support for the union among Avondale workers.

Although the card-check agreement called for a one-year period in which the union could obtain cards signed by workers, a large majority signed cards within five weeks. A private arbitrator commissioned by the company and the union to

---

[329]Human Rights Watch interview, New Orleans, Louisiana, May 11, 1999.

[330]See *Avondale Industries, Inc. v. NLRB*, No. 97-60708, 1999 U.S. App. LEXIS 15036, July 7, 1999. It should be remembered that the case involving Avondale's objection to the election is separate from the unfair labor practice case involving threats, coercion, discrimination, firings and other company abuses. That case is still awaiting a decision by the NLRB in Washington on Avondale's appeal from the ruling of the administrative law judge.

[331]Ibid., p. 14.

[332]Ibid., p. 18.

certify results confirmed the union's majority status. Collective bargaining finally began early in 2000.[333]

Avondale workers demonstrated patience and determination during a decade-long attempt to form and join a union to bargain collectively. Litton Industries deserves credit, too, for moving quickly to resolve the dispute by acknowledging workers' free choice rather than interfering with that choice. But the new developments are not all favorable for workers. While it is willing to bargain with the workers' union, Litton has launched an appeal against the NLRB's November 1999 ruling upholding the administrative law judge's order to reinstate all fired workers.

Agreement to recognize a union based on voluntary card-signing is still exceptional in U.S. labor law and practice. It took an extraordinary turn of events and a willing employer for workers to achieve a goal that government authorities had so far failed to afford. It seems clear that without the sale to Litton, Avondale workers would have gone far into the new century before they could effectively exercise their right to freedom of association. And still, twenty-eight workers including Donald Varnado, who suffered the ultimate workplace reprisal as long as eight years ago for exercising their right to freedom of association, have a long wait ahead.

New York City Apparel Shops
We didn't know what our rights were, so we just accepted it.
—Antonia Arellano, a sweatshop worker who organized . . . for two weeks

The resurgence of sweatshops in America reflects a "race to the bottom" on labor rights and labor standards more often attributed to export processing zones in Third World countries. For workers in the United States, as is often the case in Central American or East Asian sweatshops, freedom of association is the first casualty.

Researching violations of workers' freedom of association in U.S. sweatshops posed a sharp challenge. Workers trapped in the sweatshop system are so victimized in every aspect of their working lives that an open exercise of the right to organize and associate is an extraordinary event. Most sweatshop workers are so burdened by the need to make it through another day that forming a union is beyond their energies. Moreover, as Human Rights Watch found in other, non-

---

[333]See Keith Darce, "Avondale To Become Union Yard: Long Labor Dispute Is Over," *New Orleans Times-Picayune*, December 1, 1999, p. A1.

sweatshop sector cases, immigrant workers' problems with authorization papers and fear of deportation also prevent efforts to organize in sweatshops.

Sweatshop workers turn to collective action as a last resort, usually when they realize that their employer has no intention of paying them even their subminimum wages for weeks of work already performed. Minimum wage violations, overtime pay violations, health and safety violations, sexual harassment and other problems in the garment industry are an accepted fact of working life, especially in the two largest urban regions in the country, New York and Los Angeles.

A 1994 report by the federal government's General Accounting Office found that sweatshops were widespread in the garment sector. The report noted declining resources for labor law enforcement by federal and state authorities and concluded, "In general, the description of today's sweatshops differs little from that at the turn of the century."[334]

One year after the release of that report, a shocking exposé of sweatshop labor in El Monte, California put a human face on the GAO's findings. Seventy-two workers from Thailand were discovered toiling in conditions akin to slavery. These workers were forced to work seventeen hours a day for seventy cents an hour. They had to eat and sleep where they worked, with ten workers in bedrooms built for two persons. Armed guards threatened to kill them if they tried to leave. They were not allowed to make unmonitored phone calls. Supervisors censored their letters home. They had to buy food and other necessities at inflated prices from their employer.[335] American consumers had become aware of conditions in Central American and other foreign sweatshops following network television exposure.[336] Now they saw similar conditions in their own front yard.

The Thai workers in El Monte made no attempt to form and join a union or to bargain collectively. Their concern was survival. In the same way, most sweatshop workers are afraid to complain about conditions or treatment. Because their work is underground and unauthorized, they accept exploitation in silence, fearful that filing complaints with labor law authorities or seeking to form and join a union will cost them their jobs and subject them to deportation.

---

[334]See U.S. General Accounting Office, "Prevalence of Sweatshops," GAO/HEHS-95-29, November 2, 1994.

[335]For an account of the El Monte case, see Julie Su, "El Monte Thai garment workers: slave sweatshops," in Andrew Ross, ed., *No Sweat: fashion, free trade, and the rights of garment workers* (New York, Verso Press, 1997).

[336]See 60 Minutes, "Hiring Rosa Martinez," CBS television broadcast, September 27, 199; Nightline, "Paying to Lose Our Jobs," ABC television broadcast, September 29-30, 1992.

Apparel manufacturing is a multibillion-dollar industry employing more than 700,000 workers in the United States. While most of them work in the formal sector of the economy for registered places of business, an unknown number—at least in the tens of thousands, and possibly more—work in an underground, off-the-books sector of the industry.

Nationally, there are fewer than 1,000 manufacturers serving a relative handful of well-known retail and private-label brand name companies, but more than 20,000 contractors and subcontractors, most of them small shops with fewer than thirty workers. It takes only a few thousand dollars to open a sewing shop consisting of little more than sewing machines and space rented by the month. It costs almost nothing to close one.

The garment sector is the biggest manufacturing industry in New York and Los Angeles, where in each region more than 100,000 workers labor in some 5,000 contracting and subcontracting sewing shops. Women who have recently migrated to the United States from Asia and Latin America are a significant majority of the workforce.   These small shops compete fiercely for business from the manufacturers. Violating wage and hour laws is the quickest and easiest way to gain a competitive advantage, particularly when workers are not likely to complain or to organize for improvements.

U.S. Labor Department studies in 1997 and 1998 indicated that nearly two-thirds of garment industry shops in New York violate minimum wage and overtime laws.[337] A comprehensive private study of the Los Angeles garment industry concluded in 1999 that "this important industry is plagued by substandard working conditions . . . There is widespread non-compliance with labor, health, and safety laws."[338]

Under current law, retailers and manufacturers who profit from sweatshops' race to the bottom on labor standards are not held responsible for labor law violations committed by contractors or subcontractors, including violations of workers' organizing rights. The large companies are insulated by the hierarchical structure of the industry and the reliance on one-job, quick-turnaround, unpredictable subcontracting arrangements that have largely displaced traditional longer-term, stable contracting relationships. One study of Los Angeles' 184 largest manufacturers found that they accounted for close to 3,000 overlapping sewing

---

[337]See Steven Greenhouse, "Two-Thirds of Garment Shops Break Wage Laws, U.S. Says," *New York Times*, October 17, 1997, p. A37.
[338]See Report, Los Angeles Jewish Commission on Sweatshops (January 1999); Patrick J. McDonnell, "Jewish Group Urges Reform of Sweatshops," *Los Angeles Times*, February 1, 1999, p. B1.

contracts, providing an enormous amount of control, but no direct responsibility for conditions, in factories that provided them with contracted labor.[339]

Human Rights Watch examined two cases of sweatshop workers' organizing efforts in New York City:

MK Collections

In 1997 a group of workers at a mid-town Manhattan sewing shop called MK Collections formed a union in UNITE, the principal labor organization in the apparel industry. UNITE maintains two workers' rights and service centers in New York, one in Manhattan and one in Brooklyn, to assist both union and non-union workers with wage claims, workers' compensation claims, health and safety complaints and other work-related problems. The union also provides educational programs in English as a second language, skills training, immigration rights, and citizenship.

Mario Ramírez told Human Rights Watch that workers acted because they were owed seven weeks' pay for work performed and "because the owners screamed at people."[340] He came to the UNITE workers' center to seek assistance. With the union's advice, Ramírez and a group of coworkers formed an organizing committee.

Eduardo Rodríguez, who like Ramírez came to New York from Puebla, Mexico, was another union adherent. "We would talk outside before work and at lunchtime, but never in big groups," he explained.[341] Rodríguez estimated union support at about forty workers, a solid majority of the sixty-five to seventy people working at MK Collections.

In January 1997, MK workers brought their organizing effort to a head with a work stoppage demanding back pay for work performed. At first, their movement bore fruit. Seven members of the organizing group signed a handwritten agreement with the owner recognizing UNITE, setting a just cause standard for disciplinary action, promising to maintain clean bathrooms, and—besides paying wages on time—to pay an additional $50 per week until full back pay was reached for each worker.

The agreement held up for only four months. The employer fired two committee members, who did not want to protest because of immigration fears. In

---

[339]See Richard P. Appelbaum, "Global Commodity Chains, Emigrant Communities, and Labor in the Globalized Economy," UC MEXUS Global Migration Conference, Riverside, California, October 24-25, 1997, cited in Report, Los Angeles Jewish Commission, p. 13.
[340]Human Rights Watch interview, New York City, June 15, 1999.
[341]Human Rights Watch interview, New York City, June 15, 1999.

early May 1997, the company closed down, claiming that a manufacturer had
canceled a production contract. According to Ramírez and Rodríguez, the owner
reopened at a new location and hired a new workforce just weeks later.[342]

Their experience left its mark on Ramírez and Rodríguez. "I've thought about
organizing in my new job," said Ramírez, who found other work in the garment
industry. "But I need to be guaranteed that I won't be fired."[343] Rodríguez, who
took a new job in a restaurant, said, "As long as there is no law to protect us better,
I don't think it is likely that I will organize again."[344]

YPS

According to UNITE representative Bertha Wilson, herself a former garment
worker, employees from a Manhattan sewing shop called YPS came to the union-
sponsored workers' center in 1997 because they were owed back wages, even
though YPS subcontracted production for brand-name companies like Lord &
Taylor, Ann Taylor, and Express.[345] One of the workers, Antonia Arellano, told
Human Rights Watch that workers were not being paid on time, that managers
mistreated workers, that drinking fountains did not work, and that workers got no
rest or lunch breaks. "We were aware that we were illegal," she said, "so we were
kind of like slaves."[346] She said that women workers were especially mistreated.
"One of the managers would touch the women," she said. "If they complained they
were fired. A few women were actually fired, and others just took it. We didn't
know what our rights were, so we just accepted things. Some people said, 'I'm just
here to work, so I'll ignore the rest.'" With four to five weeks' back pay owing to
workers, said Arellano, "The boss wanted to pay us with clothes. But how were we
going to sell them for money?"[347]

In November 1997, YPS employees stopped work and demanded union
recognition and four to six weeks of back pay. According to Bertha Wilson, the
owner said he would recognize the union as long as the union did not contact Ann
Taylor. In December, the owner signed an agreement calling for an end to sexual
harassment, a forty-five-minute lunch break, and incremental back-pay
disbursements each week.

---

[342]Ibid.
[343]Ibid.
[344]Ibid.
[345]Human Rights Watch interview, New York, June 15, 1999.
[346]Human Rights Watch interview, New York, June 15, 1999.
[347]Ibid.

The YPS agreement held up only for two weeks. The owner again halted back-pay disbursements, and employees stopped work. YPS shut its doors and went out of business. UNITE organized a workers' demonstration at the headquarters of brand-name companies that had contracted for work with YPS. Those companies agreed to make workers whole for lost wages, but by now workers had scattered to other locations. Many failed to collect their pay, fearing to come forward, said Wilson, because they were undocumented and were afraid of INS action.

Migrant Agricultural Workers

Washington State Apple Industry
You have thirty minutes to get back to work or you're all fired.
—An anti-union consultant to a group of striking farmworkers

The brown, treeless mountains framing the Yakima Valley of central Washington belie the rich soil below. Vineyards, hop fields, and orchards run uphill from the river as it cuts through the valley. This is the center of the states's multibillion-dollar agricultural industry and its crown jewels, the Fuji, Granny Smith, Golden and Red Delicious, and other apples filling fruit bowls in homes around the world.

Washington is the world's most prodigious grower of the popular fruit. Washington apples feed 60 percent of the domestic U.S. consumer market (New York state apples are second, far behind with 10 percent of the domestic market). Forty percent of Washington's apple crop goes overseas.

For more than 50,000 workers in the Washington apple industry, freedom of association is less bountiful. Workers who want to exercise rights to organize and bargain collectively to improve wages and conditions continue to be stymied by employer violations and by the government's failure to protect their rights.

Like all agricultural workers, Washington apple pickers are excluded from coverage by the National Labor Relations Act because they are not defined as "employees" meriting the law's protection.[348] As noted above, the United States argued to the U.N. in its report on compliance with the International Covenant on Civil and Political Rights that this exclusion "means only that they do not have access to the specific provisions of the NLRA . . . for enforcing their rights to organize and bargain collectively."[349] But farmworkers' lack of access to

---

[348]NLRA, Section 2.
[349]See U.S. Department of State, " Initial Report to the U.N. Human Rights Committee" (July 1994), p. 166.

enforcement authorities leaves employers a free hand to threaten and to carry out reprisals against workers who seek to form and join a union to bargain collectively.

At high harvest, more than 40,000 pickers work in apple orchards in Washington. Although the Supreme Court of Washington has recognized the right of an agricultural worker to join a union, a worker who is fired for doing so must file a private lawsuit to vindicate the right.[350] That is, a worker can seek redress only by getting a lawyer and bringing an expensive and risky private lawsuit. The employer will usually assert that the worker was fired for cause. Such a dispute has to be litigated in court.

Most farmworkers fired for organizing are not likely to take their cases to court. Many are migrants who speak no English. They have no money to pay lawyers. They have no time to find witnesses who can testify on their behalf or to prepare for examination and cross-examination in court to pursue their case. They usually have to look immediately for work elsewhere, or follow the harvest to the next crop.

Similarly, most private lawyers are not likely to take such cases. Finding witnesses is difficult. So is overcoming employer testimony about the worker's alleged misconduct, the usual pretext for a discriminatory discharge. The testimony of a confident, bilingual supervisor on the employer's behalf is more polished than that of a little-educated, frightened worker struggling to explain what happened through an interpreter. The possibility of punitive damages is small, so even if the case is won there is no payoff for the lawyer.

The costs associated with this, along with the fact that many of the workers are undocumented and want no brushes with the legal system, make the use of such lawsuits unrealistic. Employers know this. As a result, employers may violate apple workers' right to freedom of association with effective impunity.

The 15,000 workers in the "sheds" sector of the industry who sort, pack and ship apples are covered by the NLRA. However, they have encountered serious violations of their right to freedom of association by employers and consultants exploiting weaknesses in the law and ineffectual remedies for violations. The shed sector was once highly unionized, but strikes broken by replacement workers and closures of facilities where workers had chosen union representation effectively ended collective bargaining by the 1970s.

Many apple workers are employed year-round. In the orchards, they tend older trees and plant new trees. In the sheds, they sort and store apples in temperature-controlled areas and ship them to wholesale and retail outlets in the United States and to overseas markets. Most of these year-round workers have

---

[350]See *Bravo v. Dolssen Companies*, 125Wn.2d 745; 888 P.2d 147 (1995).

settled permanently in the area. Increasingly, seasonal apple workers are also settling in the area and working on other crops that come to harvest at different times, like cherries and asparagus.

In the past two decades the demographics in the Washington apple industry, like those of many other regions and industries throughout the United States, have shifted from a labor force made up mostly of U.S.-born citizens to one heavily populated by immigrants. A majority of workers now employed in the Washington apple industry—all the orchard workers, in fact, and a majority of workers in sheds—are immigrants from Mexico. Many have been here for many years and are now citizens or hold legal work authorization. Many others are undocumented. Coincidentally, Mexico is the largest foreign customer for Washington State apples. According to an industry newspaper, "Mexico has become the core of the U.S. apple industry's export strategy."[351]

Many apple workers live in poverty, often in squalid company housing or, when growers fail to provide housing (which is not a requirement), on the banks of nearby streams. Low wages, intermittent work, dangerous pesticides, hazardous working conditions and inadequate medical attention make the lives of Washington apple industry workers precarious. Under optimal conditions, apple pickers told Human Rights Watch, they can earn up to $10 or $12 an hour in the orchards. But optimal conditions are not always present in the few weeks of harvest time each autumn. Workers often make closer to the minimum wage, with $6 or $7 per hour. In the sheds, the average salary is less than $15,000 per year. The average wage in the Yakima and Wenatchee areas, the centers of apple-growing activity, is 30 percent below the statewide average. Over 20 percent of the Yakima County population, and more than 30 percent of its children, live below the poverty level.

The lack of housing for migrant workers reached scandalous proportions in 1999 when employers closed workers' barracks instead of complying with Department of Labor housing standards on such items as solid floors, enclosed areas for cooking and eating, refrigerators, stoves, lighting, and toilets. After the closures, thousands of workers lived in forests and on riverbanks in cars, tents and cardboard boxes.[352]

Overall, conditions here bear out the conclusions of a study prepared for the U.S. Department of Labor that found:

---

[351]See *The Packer*, September 8, 1997, p. 1.
[352]See Lynda V. Mapes, "Crisis in the Camps: Harvest without Housing," *The Seattle Times*, June 22, 1999, p. A1.

Most migrant farmworkers live a marginal existence, even after they stop migrating and settle in one location . . . The poor living and working conditions of migrant farmworkers are the result of farm labor practices that shift production costs to workers [and] reduce employer costs at the expense of worker earnings. As a result, migrant workers, their families and communities, rather than producers, tax-payers and consumers, bear the high costs of agriculture's endemic labor market instability.[353]

A high-ranking apple industry employer representative blamed migrant workers for not leaving the area after the harvest is done. "We do need people for a relatively short period of time. But when the apples are picked, they're picked." Asked whether this meant that farmworkers "should never be more than migrants, following harvests from Texas through California and Oregon to Washington," the growers' representative said, "Yes."[354]

Action under NAFTA

In 1998, conditions for workers in the Washington apple industry prompted one of the first complaints filed under the North American Agreement on Labor Cooperation (NAALC), the labor side agreement to NAFTA, involving workers' rights violations in the United States. Most earlier complaints filed under the 1993 agreement involved violations in Mexico.

The NAALC apple workers' submission was the broadest case filed under the NAALC, citing labor law violations and inadequate enforcement in areas encompassed in seven of the NAALC's eleven labor principles. Most earlier cases addressed only union organizing issues. The Washington apple industry complaint covered the right to organize, collective bargaining, minimum labor standards, non-discrimination in employment, job safety and health, workers' compensation, and migrant worker protection. The filing generated a burst of publicity calling attention to conditions of migrant workers and the opportunity for advocacy presented by the NAALC.[355]

---

[353]See U.S. Department of Labor, "Migrant Farmworkers: Pursuing Security in an Unstable Labor Market," *Research Report No. 5* (May 1994).

[354]See Don McManman, "Temporary workers put strain on schools, welfare," *Tri-City Herald*, September 21, 1997. p. 1.

[355]See, for example, Steven Greenhouse, "Mexicans Were Denied U.S. Rights, Suit Says," *New York Times*, May 28, 1998, p. A18; Ken Guggenheim, "U.S. unions find new tool," *Seattle Post-Intelligencer*, May 29, 1998, p. C1; Raúl Trejo Delarbre, "Casablanca Laboral," *La Crónica*, June 1, 1998; Evelyn Iritani, "Mexico Charges Upset Apple Cart in U.S.," *Los*

Mexico accepted the Washington apple case for review in August 1998. In December 1998, Mexico held its first-ever hearing on a NAALC complaint. It was not a public hearing in the quasi-legal style of the United States and Canada in their handling of NAALC cases, but rather an "informative session" under Mexico's procedural guidelines conducted in private in a roundtable setting. A delegation of workers from packing sheds and orchards in Washington attended the hearing and presented direct testimony about pesticide poisoning, discharge for union activity, minimum wage violations, discrimination in the workers' compensation system, discrimination against migrant workers, and other violations of workers' rights.

The hearing provoked widespread publicity in the news media of both the United States and Mexico.[356] In August 1999, Mexico's secretary of labor formally requested ministerial consultations with the U.S. secretary of labor in the apple workers' case. This development sparked a new round of publicity and related attention to the conditions of migrant workers in the industry.[357] As this report goes to press, a program of conferences and workshops was being fashioned by the secretaries of labor of the two countries.

Apple Pickers: the Consequences of Organizing

Washington apple pickers interviewed by Human Rights Watch gave detailed accounts of violations when they tried to exercise rights to freedom of association, organizing, and collective bargaining to address poor conditions. As noted above, these workers are not protected by federal labor law prohibiting discrimination for union activity (see Chapter VI., *Defenseless Workers: Exclusions in U.S. Labor Law* for more discussion of workers excluded from organizing protection). Without resources to bring individual lawsuits against employers, they have no redress if they are fired, and growers can spurn any request to bargain collectively.

Angeles Times, August 20, 1998, P. D1.

[356]See Molly Moore, "Mexican Farmhands Accuse U.S. Firms: Panel Hears Washington Apple Pickers," *Washington Post,* December 3, 1998, p. A36; Elizabeth Velasco, "Trabajadores agrícolas denuncian explotación en EU", *La Jornada,* December 3, 1998, p. 41; Arturo Gómez Salgado, "Denuncian migrantes violaciones laborales," *El Financiero,* December 3, 1998, p. 19.

[357]See, for example, Arthur C. Gorlick, "State's apple hands abused, Mexico says: Complaint could lead to special investigation and even sanctions," *Seattle Post-Intelligencer,* September 9, 1999, p. A1; Farm workers are the subsidy," lead editorial, *Seattle Post-Intelligencer,* September 19, 1999 (beginning: "Mexico's accusation that Washington tolerates abuse of farm workers will be debated . . . but there's no debating that some agricultural sectors owe their success to systematic exploitation of migrant workers.").

"I was a ranch foreman for a big apple grower," said Luis Castañeda, a young farmworker who began in the apple orchards in 1993. "I had about twenty guys under me. We were close. I tried to help them however I could, and they gave me good production."[358] When workers at the ranch began contacting the United Farm Workers of America (UFW) in 1997 for help in organizing to improve wages and conditions, said Castañeda, his employer brought in a California-based consultant to train foremen and supervisors in combating workers' self-organization. "He told us to tell workers that growers in California plowed under the crops and left them with no work when the union came in," said Castañeda. "He told us to fire the leaders, that getting rid of the leaders would end the organizing."[359]

Management fired Castañeda himself for being too close to the workers, he said. Taking work as a picker at other ranches, he became active in farmworker efforts to form and join unions through the UFW. "I've been fired twice since 1997," he said, "when I signed up union members and we tried to get better wages."[360]

Rogelio Alvarez told a similar story. In several years of apple ranch work, "I was always speaking up for the people," he said. At one ranch, "the managers let it go until I started talking about the union. First they put me in a new job working by myself, where I couldn't talk to anybody. When they found out I was bringing people to UFW meetings, they fired me."[361]

"We need the union for job security, a grievance procedure, seniority, respect, not just for higher wages," said Arnulfo Ramírez, another long-time farmworker in the valley. "But when I say this, the foreman threatens me. He says there are twenty people waiting to take my job."[362]

José Godines reported suffering another kind of discrimination. The starting time at the orchard where he worked in 1994 was 7:00 AM. The manager told workers that those who came early would be assigned to easy, low-lying trees where they could quickly fill their bins. Godines protested. Family needs made it difficult for him to come early. He tried to organize coworkers to come at the regular starting time, with easy picking to rotate equitably. Management retaliated by assigning him to the highest, most difficult trees. Godines fell from a ladder and broke his arm. He missed the rest of the season and was not rehired the next year.[363]

---

[358]Human Rights Watch interview, Sunnyside, Washington, November 6, 1999.
[359]Ibid.
[360]Ibid.
[361]Ibid.
[362]Ibid.
[363]Ibid.

Samuel Vallejo gave similar accounts. A Washington apple worker since 1983, he and coworkers protested a pay cut at one of the industry's largest ranches in 1993. When management learned that workers had contacted the UFW, Vallejo and three other leaders of the effort were fired. "The company spread my name around with other big companies not to get hired," he told Human Rights Watch.[364]

Intimidation of Striking Apple Pickers

José Nevare and his brother Vicente were involved in a widely publicized dispute at Auvil Fruit company, one of the largest apple growers in the state. Protesting the sudden firing of eight coworkers accused of bruising apples, 150 Auvil farmworkers stopped work on Labor Day in September 1997 and began picketing the entrance to the ranch. "The next day the company brought in the consultant that was telling them how to beat the union," said José Nevare.[365]

The consultant, California-based Stephen D. Highfill, specializes in telling agricultural employers how to defeat union organizing efforts.[366] He directed employer campaigns against workers' efforts to form unions in Yakima and Wenatchee, Washington throughout late 1997 and early 1998. In a videotape made by workers during the strike at Auvil and reviewed by Human Rights Watch, Highfill, a large, burly man, approaches the workers, taps his wristwatch, and shouts in Spanish, "You have thirty minutes to get back to work or you're all fired."

Local and state police officials responded to the strike at Auvil with a show of force. Twenty-six police cars from three counties and the state highway patrol carrying heavily armed officers massed at the ranch entrance where workers were peacefully picketing. Officers with high-powered rifles flanked the workers in a military-style deployment. "Our picket was totally peaceful," said Vicente Nevare, "but they acted like we were criminals."[367]

A convoy of police cars escorted trucks and vans full of replacement workers sent by other growers to break the Auvil workers' strike. The strike ended after four days. Twenty-eight workers were fired, assigned to lower-paying jobs, or evicted from company housing.

---

[364]Ibid.
[365]Ibid.
[366]Highfill described his work in detail in testimony in an unfair labor practice hearing before an administrative law judge of the NLRB. See NLRB, Official Report of Proceedings (transcript), *Stemilt Growers, Inc.*, Case No. 19-CA-25403 et.al., Vols. 16-17 (1999).
[367]Human Rights Watch interview, November 6, 1999.

UFW representative Guadalupe Gamboa protested the police action in a letter to the chief of the Washington State Patrol.[368] The state rejected his protest. An official report by the Washington State Patrol characterized the strikers' parking their cars partially on the lightly traveled county road as "unlawful behavior" and said "the chanting and enthusiastic cheering from the strikers were perceived by law enforcement officials to be threatening in nature."[369] On the videotape made by workers and reviewed by Human Rights Watch, workers chant "*El pueblo unido jamás será vencido*" (The people united will never be defeated) and "*Sí se puede*" (Yes, it can be done) enthusiastically, but with no words or action that could be even remotely construed as threatening.

The state report cites police perception of a "threat of violence should police attempt to arrest Gamboa for inciting riotous behavior among strikers" as grounds for armed intervention. "Based on their threat assessment," said the report, state troopers "should provide cover for the arresting officers from outer perimeter positions. They decided to carry their AR-15's while functioning as cover officers . . . at no time did the sergeants point their muzzles at anyone."[370] At no time did the police move to arrest Gamboa, either, he told Human Rights Watch. In his view, the police never intended an arrest because, in fact, no violence occurred or was threatened. He saw the police action as one meant to intimidate workers exercising the right to freedom of association.[371]

Gamboa also pointed to the show of force when police vehicles escorted trucks and vans filled with strikebreakers past the Auvil workers' picket line. Any chance of peacefully persuading potential strikebreakers to respect the picket line was lost, he explained, in the face of such "blitzkrieg" tactics. The Washington State Patrol's report said troopers had "minimal involvement" in escorting strikebreakers past the picket line. "The allegation that WSP 'led a caravan of strikebreakers' is inaccurate," the report concluded. "Their actions were limited to providing back-up security as two WSP units trailed behind the convoy."[372] The report was silent, however, on the role of local and county police who led the convoy.

---

[368]See letter to Annette Sandberg, Chief, Washington State Highway Patrol, September 2, 1997, on file with Human Rights Watch.

[369]See Washington State Highway Patrol, *Investigative Review*, September 18, 1997, on file with Human Rights Watch.

[370]Ibid.

[371]Human Rights Watch interview, November 5, 1999.

[372]See *Investigative Review*, September 18, 1997.

Shed Workers

Thousands of workers are employed in the warehouse or shed sector of the Washington apple industry. Many seasonal workers in the sheds are migrants from Mexico, and many year-round workers are resident Mexican and Mexican-Americans who have put down roots in the communities of the apple region. Many Anglo workers long resident in the region are also employed in the sheds.

Apple shed workers are not defined as agricultural workers. They are covered by the NLRA, which makes it an unfair labor practice to threaten, coerce, or discriminate against workers for union organizing activity. But when workers at two of the largest apple processing companies sought to form and join a union in 1997 and 1998, they suffered severe violations of the right to freedom of association.

As detailed in complaints issued by the NLRB and workers' and employers' testimony at the unfair labor practice hearings, management of Stemilt Bros. in Wenatchee and Washington Fruit Co. in Yakima responded to workers' organizing efforts with dismissals of key union leaders, threats that the INS would deport workers if they formed a union, threats to discharge and blacklist workers who supported the union, threats to close the plants if workers voted for union representation, and threats to permanently replace workers who exercised the right to strike.[373]

Here is how one worker described the company's tactics before a January 1998 NLRB election at Stemilt Bros. in Yakima:

> I had to attend many anti-union meetings at Stemilt after we filed for a union election. At almost all of them, a consultant hired by the company [Stephen D. Highfill] was there [with various managers]. At the meetings they talked a lot about dues and strikes, but they talked the most about the INS . . . [Highfill] said the Union gets rid of undocumented workers so that it can keep their dues and get initiation fees from new workers. . . . I assume that the company keeps talking about INS because they know a lot of workers on the night shift are undocumented—I would guess at least half.
>
> I myself started working at Stemilt as an undocumented worker in 1991. [In May 1994] I was advised that there was a problem with my

---

[373]See NLRB Region 19, Order Consolidating Cases, Consolidated Complaints and Notice of Hearing, *Stemilt Growers, Inc., Ag-Relate, Inc. and International Brotherhood of Teamsters,* Case Nos.19-CA-25403 et.al.; *Washington Fruit and International Brotherhood of Teamsters*, Case Nos. 25702 et.al. (1998).

papers and didn't return to work. Later, around August of 1994, someone told me that Stemilt was taking back those of us who had left work because of problems with our papers if we came back with new papers . . . I applied for work with a new name and social security number and was given work in the same department with the same supervisors.

When I started work again, I realized that many of the same people were working again, but with different names . . . The reason I bring this up is because it shows that before we started organizing Stemilt didn't mind if we didn't have papers. It is only now that we have started organizing that they have started looking for problems with people's papers, like they did with [names omitted]. And it is only now that they have started threatening us with INS raids . . . They know that we are afraid to even talk about this because we don't want to risk ourselves or anyone else losing their jobs or being deported, so it is a very powerful threat . . . The fact that . . . the consultant was always talking about how the union was going to cause the INS to come made many workers very afraid. I know this because many of the workers would talk to me about how afraid they were about what the consultant said.[374]

Not just workers' testimony, but also the testimony of consultant Stephen D. Highfill in the unfair labor practice hearing on these complaints paints a vivid picture of the management's tactics against workers' self-organization. Highfill said he held captive-audience meetings with hundreds of workers in groups of twenty to twenty-five at a time.[375]

Highfill testified that he and colleagues from his consulting firm told employees that there was an agreement between the U.S. Department of Labor and the INS that no raids would be conducted in a workplace where an NLRB election was pending, but that "the only time this accord applies is during the pre-election period" and as soon as the election was over "they're going to do their business as usual"—meaning the INS could conduct raids.[376] Then they told workers that if the union won the election, the union would gain a $100 initiation fee from each new

---

[374]Stemilt worker affidavit to NLRB, on file with Human Rights Watch. The worker adds "I am married to a U.S. citizen. I became a lawful permanent resident here in the United States in about September of 1997."
[375]Highfill's testimony is contained in NLRB, Official Report of Proceedings (transcript), *Stemilt Growers, Inc.*, Case No. 19-CA-25403 et.al., Vols. 16-17 (1999).
[376]Ibid., p. 2886.

worker hired to replace a worker removed in a raid—"the only ones that appear to have any monetary gain at all, are those who collected an initiation fee . . ."[377] [i.e., the union].

In another tactic used in a captive-audience meeting, Highfill presented a Hispanic woman associated with his firm who claimed to be a former worker involved in a strike in Watsonville, California, some years earlier. According to Highfill, the woman "mentioned that after the strike that she'd been involved in, there had been a raid on that place . . . a full-blown raid . . . where they showed with the enforce (sic) and just took employees . . . grabbed people as they went in and out . . . a number of people were taken away who were new hires as well as some of the old hands."[378]

Highfill also testified that the same woman told workers that because of her union support she "had been blacklisted by area employers and she found it hard to get a job."[379] Meanwhile, according to Highfill's testimony, a second Hispanic woman associated with Highfill's consulting group also claimed to have been a union activist in California "for over 20 years, and when she attempted to find work outside the place where she had been employed as a union employee, she felt that she was being blacklisted. . . ."[380]

On prospects for collective bargaining, Highfill testified that he told Stemilt workers in the same series of captive-audience meetings:

> Very often, people have the idea that—that when you win an election, you—just right after that, you get a contract. But that the process itself can be a matter of just a couple of days or it can be months and sometimes years . . . the process can go on and on . . . And there are times, under those circumstances, when wages can be frozen and benefits can be frozen, you just never know . . . somebody asked if it went on forever and I remember we cited a company in—in California where it's been going on since '76. . . . We told them there have been circumstances under which—there have been times when wages were lowered . . . We told them that there have been occasions when people wound up making less than minimum wage.
>
> Q. Did you give them some specific examples?
> A. No.

---

[377]Ibid., p. 2987.
[378]Ibid., pp. 2877, 3007.
[379]Ibid., p. 2875.
[380]Ibid., p. 2878.

Just before the election, Highfill's consulting firm issued a flyer titled "An Important Piece of Advice" that said:

> ... none of the swindlers that the union has hired in this campaign has lived here before. They came here for only one thing—the money. If [Stemilt's owner] said that he could work with the union, it is because he could not say anything else under the law . . . remember that the growers are not wedded to Stemilt—they can put their fruit wherever they like if Stemilt had to charge them more . . . If the employers want the Teamsters like you want to be infected with AIDS, it is for the same reason—<u>a possibly catastrophic result.</u>[381]

In January 1998, although a majority of workers in each location had signed union cards, the Teamsters union lost NLRB elections at Stemilt and Washington Fruit. Stephen D. Highfill directed the employers' campaigns against workers' organizing attempts. The union filed unfair labor practice charges in both cases, and the NLRB regional office issued complaints detailing widespread violations of the law.

In Stemilt, the company agreed in August 1999 to settle the case and to accept the results of a card-check verification of worker sentiment in a process overseen by the judge. In October, the judge certified that a majority of Stemilt workers desired union representation, and bargaining had begun on a contract at Stemilt as this report goes to press.

Washington Fruit has refused similar settlement proposals by the union and the NLRB. The unfair labor practice hearing in that case concluded in November 1999, and the parties are awaiting the decision of the administrative law judge. His ruling can be appealed to the NLRB in Washington, and after that further appeals to federal courts are available.

North Carolina Farmworkers and the H-2A Program

H-2A workers are unlikely to complain about worker protection violations, fearing they will lose their jobs or will not be hired in the future.
—U.S. General Accounting Office, 1997

More than 10,000 workers in North Carolina's burgeoning agriculture industry hold H-2A visas legally authorizing them to work temporarily in the United States.

---

[381]Undated company flyer, "Un Consejo Importante," on file with Human Rights Watch. Translation by Human Rights Watch, emphasis in original.

But they share with undocumented migrant workers an acute fear of retaliation and deportation if they exercise the right to organize and bargain collectively. Reflecting other important aspects of freedom of association, the prospect of seeking legal counsel or taking legal action to vindicate their rights inspires similar fears.

This report focuses on workers' freedom of association. It does not dwell on conditions that give rise to workers' acting in association. But workers' exercise of freedom of association does not take place in a vacuum. Workers act in response to concrete needs and often harsh conditions. In North Carolina's fields, high heat, short pay, long hours, little drinking water, sparse toilet facilities, dilapidated housing, unsafe pesticides, and other realities of agricultural labor prompt a natural response of workers' coming together to make things better.[382]

Some North Carolina farmworkers seek to form and join a union. Some seek legal counsel to try to vindicate their rights through the courts. But they do so in the face of huge obstacles. From the time H-2A workers arrive in North Carolina, growers' association officials harangue them about dangerous "enemies:" union organizers and Legal Services attorneys devoted to farmworker rights advocacy. H-2A workers' standard employment contract with growers denies them basic rights of tenancy to receive visitors. The U.S. Department of Labor approves the ban, and local police enforce it.

H-2A workers in the United States have a special status among migrant farmworkers. They come to the United States openly and legally. They are covered by wage laws, workers' compensation, and other standards. They ought to have fewer problems, compared with undocumented migrant workers, exercising the right to freedom of association.

But valid papers are no guarantee of protection for H-2A migrant workers' freedom of association. As agricultural workers, they are not covered by the NLRA's anti-discrimination provision meant to protect the right to organize. If they try to form and join a union, the grower for whom they work can cancel their work contract, putting them "out of status" and liable to deportation. In effect, H-2A workers are caught in the antithesis of a free labor system, unable to exercise rights of association but also unable to move to another employer to seek better terms. This case demonstrates that any movement to strengthen workers' freedom of association in the United States will have to address the special problems of H-2A workers.

---

[382]For recent, extensive treatment of the plight of migrant agricultural workers in the United States, see Daniel Rothenberg, *With These Hands: The Hidden World of Migrant Farmworkers Today* (New York: Harcourt Brace, 1999).

Government Responsibility

The H-2A program is named after a section of immigration law which allows agricultural employers to hire temporary foreign workers when not enough U.S. farmworkers are available.[383] The program is administered by federal and state authorities, creating a direct government responsibility to see that international human rights norms are respected.

H-2A workers can remain in the United States until completion of their employment contracts with sponsoring employers. When they finish, workers must return to their home country—usually Mexico—hoping to be recalled to work the following year.

Being recalled often depends on being submissive. Human Rights Watch found widespread fear and evidence of blacklisting against workers who speak up about conditions, who seek assistance from Legal Services attorneys, or who become active in the Farm Labor Organizing Committee (FLOC).

Human Rights Watch also found evidence of a campaign of intimidation from the time they first enter the United States to discourage any exercise of freedom of association by H-2A workers. Most pointedly, growers' officials lead workers through a ritual akin to book-burning by making them collectively trash "Know Your Rights" manuals from Legal Services attorneys and take instead employee handbooks issued by growers.[384]

About 26,000 foreign migrant workers with H-2A visas entered the United States legally in 1999. More than 10,000 of them went to North Carolina, making growers there the leading employers of H-2A workers in the United States.[385] North Carolina's H-2A workers are mostly Mexican, single young men, who harvest

---

[383]See Secs. 101(a)(15)(H)(ii)(a) and 218 of the Immigration and Nationality Act (INA), as amended by the Immigration Reform and Control Act of 1986; U.S. Department of Labor, Office of Audit, "Consolidation of Labor's Enforcement Responsibilities for the H-2A Program Could Better Protect U.S. Agricultural Workers," March 31, 1998, p. 4.

[384]See affidavit of Juan Carlos Vieyra Ornelas, intern with Farm Worker Project of Benson, North Carolina, (hereafter Vieyra affidavit), August 10, 1999, on file with Human Rights Watch.

[385]Sandy Smith-Nonini, "Uprooting *La Injusticia*," Institute for Southern Studies, March 1999, pp. 5, 7 (hereafter Smith-Nonini, "Uprooting,"; Leah Beth Ward, "N.C. Growers' Trade in Foreign Farm Workers Draws Scrutiny," *Charlotte Observer*, October 30, 1999, p. 1 (hereafter Ward, "Growers' Trade").

tobacco, sweet potatoes, cucumbers, bell peppers, apples, peaches, melons, and various other seasonal crops from April until November.[386]

At home "there's no work," workers told Human Rights Watch as their main reason for emigrating.[387] Many of the workers come from rural villages in Mexico. Some spoke Spanish with difficulty, as in their village at home people mainly speak Misteco, a local Indian language. In most cases earnings in U.S. dollars from their H-2A employment are the only source of income for their families and for their communities.

While not protecting the right to organize and bargain collectively, the H-2A program on paper provides benefits not afforded to undocumented workers. Workers in the H-2A program are supposed to earn at least the U.S. minimum wage of $5.15 per hour or a higher H-2A progran rate, which is based on farmworkers' average wages at the local and state levels. Besides a wage guarantee, the program requires free housing that meets Department of Labor standards, free transportation to and from Mexico, and coverage under state workers' compensation programs for work-related injuries and illnesses. H-2A workers are entitled to legal representation by federally funded Legal Services attorneys. However, H-2A workers are specifically excluded from the principal federal labor law for agricultural workers, known as AWPA.[388] Among other gaps, this exclusion means that H-2A workers seeking recourse for violations of their work contracts may not go to federal court but instead must go to local state courts, where many worker advocates believe growers exert significant influence.

Even the H-2A program's modest benefits are precarious. Workers interviewed by university researchers, Legal Services attorneys, church-based delegations and reporters have said that they often are underpaid compared with promised piecework earnings. They described cramped, unsanitary housing that fails to comply with space, flooring, and sanitation standards. They said that they have to pay large fees to local recruiters in Mexico; and that they are afraid to file

---

[386]Human Rights Watch interview, Lori Elmer and Alice Tejada, staff attorneys of Legal Services of North Carolina, Farmworker Unit , Raleigh, North Carolina, July 13, 1999 (hereafter "Elmer-Tejada interview"); Ward, "Growers' Trade."

[387]Human Rights Watch interview with migrant H-2A workers, near Mt. Olive, N.C., July 14, 1999.

[388]See Migrant and Seasonal Agricultural Worker Protection Act, 29 U.S.C. §1802 (10)(B)(ii).

workers' compensation claims or seek legal help for any other problem because they will be sent home and never recalled to work in the United States.[389]

H-2A Entrepreneurship

Growers are required to file paperwork and comply with procedural steps, like advertising for U.S. workers, to be eligible to secure H-2A workers. In 1989, to facilitate the employment of H-2A workers by assisting with the administrative details of the program, Craig Stanford Eury, Jr. founded the North Carolina Growers Association (NCGA). Eury was a former state labor department official familiar with H-2A requirements.[390]

The overwhelming majority of the approximately 10,000 H-2A workers in North Carolina are employed by the 1,050 members of the NCGA. These growers pay a fee to the NCGA for securing H-2A workers.[391] In an interview with Human Rights Watch, NCGA head Eury called the H-2A program "the Cadillac of guest worker programs," citing "transportation, insurance, housing and housing inspections" and adding that he "can't figure out what more advocates want."[392]

Many farmworker advocates, however, find serious flaws in the H-2A program that violate workers' freedom of association."[393] H-2A workers are forced to remain with their sponsoring employers for the duration of an agricultural season. They cannot leave their employers if conditions are intolerable or if their rights are violated without losing their legal status. At the same time, employers can terminate workers at will. Dismissal revokes their authorized work status, and they must immediately return to their country of origin. In sum, the H-2A program generates a climate in which the H-2A workers "labor under the realistic fear that

---

[389]Elmer-Tejada interview; Smith-Nonini, "Uprooting"; Ward, "Growers' Trade"; see also National Farm Worker Ministry, "Harvesting for Mt. Olive: A National Farm Worker Ministry Delegation Report," (July 29, 1999), p. 10 (on file with Human Rights Watch; hereafter "NFWM Report"). The ministry is a national coalition of church-based farmworker advocates headquartered in Chicago, and the delegation was headed by a representative of the North Carolina Council of Churches.

[390]See Esther Schrader, "Widening the Field of workers: North Carolina man is among leaders seeking to expand program that lets U.S. farms hire foreign employees on temporary visas. But officials who oversee it cite problems," *Los Angeles Times*, August 26, 1999, p. A1.

[391]Ward, "Growers' Trade."

[392]Human Rights Watch telephone interview, Vass, North Carolina, May 8, 1999.

[393]See, for example, "The H-2A Program in a Nutshell," Farmworker Justice Fund, Inc., November 1999.

if they stand up for their rights, join a union, or do not work at the limits of human endurance, they will be fired and deported immediately."[394]

Organizing Among Pickle Workers

Approximately half of the 10,000 H-2A workers in North Carolina harvest cucumbers processed by the Mt. Olive Pickle Company in Mount Olive, North Carolina. The Mt. Olive company was founded in 1926 and is the fourth-largest pickle producer in the United States. It is the largest independent pickle company (that is, not owned by a conglomerate) and markets the number one brand of pickles in the southeast and the second-ranking brand of non-refrigerated pickles in the country.[395]

Separate from the migrant workers who pick cucumbers for growers that supply Mt. Olive, the company employs directly some 500 full-time year-round employees and over 800 employees during peak processing season. The company uses five local grading stations in North Carolina to contract with about fifty local cucumber farmers to provide the company with cucumbers. Mt. Olive contracts with these growers for delivery of a specified number of bushels, at a specified purchase price, grown in compliance with Mt. Olive's requirements and standards.[396] These growers, in turn, employ thousands of cucumber pickers during the harvest. Most of the growers are members of the NCGA.

In May 1997 FLOC announced a union organizing drive to obtain better working conditions for the estimated 5,000 workers who harvest cucumbers for growers that supply Mt. Olive. FLOC is an Ohio-based migrant farmworkers' union created and led by current and former farmworkers and affiliated with the AFL-CIO.[397] FLOC argues that processors like Mt. Olive protect their product's quality by influencing the way farmers cultivate and harvest cucumbers, so they should also use their influence to affect the way farmworkers are treated.

Mt. Olive has not agreed to recognize and bargain with FLOC, saying "We believe union representation on the farm is a decision for the farmer and the farm worker—a decision we will honor but not influence."[398] Mt. Olive has explained

---

[394]Ibid.

[395]Human Rights Watch interview, Bill Bryan, CEO of Mt. Olive Pickle Company, Mt. Olive, North Carolina, June 11, 1999; *Our Pickled History*, http://www.mtolivepickles.com/history.html (visited 10/23/99).

[396]Ibid.

[397]See Farmworker Justice Fund (Washington, D.C.), "FLOC Organizing Carolina Pickles," *Farmworker Justice News*, Summer 1997.

[398]See Mt. Olive Pickle Co., "FLOC Position Statement," at the company's web site, http://www. mtolivepickles.com (last visited March 9, 2000).

that "since Mt. Olive Pickle company does not employ farmworkers. . . . it is unfair and inappropriate for us to interfere by trying to influence the decisions of farmers and/or the workers they employ."[399] The company contends that "Mt. Olive Pickle Company is targeted solely because we have a well-known name in North Carolina, and we declined FLOC's demand to assist in unionizing farm workers."[400] Company president Bill Bryan told Human Rights Watch "We do not have integrated operations. If we put too much burden on the growers, they can go to other crops. We do not have economic leverage over the growers."[401]

A decade ago, FLOC reached a landmark three-party agreement with Campbell's Soup company and Ohio tomato growers for a contract covering terms and conditions for farmworkers who supply Campbell's tomato products.[402] The union is trying to replicate the Campbell's model with Mt. Olive by building a broad support coalition within North Carolina.[403]

There is no evidence that Mt. Olive Pickle Co. has directly interfered with farmworkers' organizing among its growers. The central question from a human rights perspective, however, is whether the economic benefits derived by Mt. Olive from the denial of workers' freedom of association at farms that supply the company create a moral responsibility, absent a legal one, to use its influence to promote respect for farmworkers' associational rights.

FLOC maintains that farmworkers' organizing rights are frustrated when large, centralized food processing firms refuse to meet workers in a bargaining relationship to improve wages and conditions in field operations that supply the large firms. Organizing individual-grower-by-individual-grower is practically impossible with a mobile labor force rotating through short crop cycles. To provide stability in an enduring employment relationship—even one marked by migrant labor that returns each year from Mexico—FLOC argues that large food processing firms should be open to new collective bargaining models that include workers, growers, and processing companies. The broader public policy question is whether

---

[399]Ibid.
[400]Ibid.
[401]Human Rights Watch telephone interview, Mount Olive, North Carolina, March 6, 2000.
[402]Human Rights Watch telephone interview, Baldemar Velásquez, Toledo, Ohio, March 23, 1999; See Craig Whitlock, "Union targets pickle plants: Mount Olive migrant workers focus of organizing," *News & Observer* (Raleigh, N.C.), May 29, 1997, 1A; Ned Glascock, "Rally calls for union on farms," *News & Observer*, June 27,1998.A full account of FLOC's Campbell's Soups campaign can be found as a case study at the University of Pennsylvania's Wharton School of Business at http://rider.wharton.upenn.edu/~ethics/cases/soup.htm.
[403]See, e.g., Patrick O'Neill, "Bishop takes up fight, calls pickers' cause just," *National Catholic Reporter*, July 17, 1998, 1.

such an obligation should be created by law if, in fact, it is the only practical way to give effect to workers' right to freedom of association in the agricultural setting.

Fencing Out Workers' Advocates

Among growers there is broad resistance to workers' organizing efforts in North Carolina agriculture. Both the NCGA and its member growers have undercut workers' associational activity with the union as well as with other workers' rights advocates, such as attorneys from the farmworker unit of Legal Services.

During a June 1999 visit to North Carolina, a delegation from the National Farm Worker Ministry, a church-based group, confirmed that cucumber growers in the state customarily refuse to grant union organizers and Legal Services representatives access to the farmworker camps located on their property. They often erect "No Trespassing" signs around the farmworkers' living quarters and require all visitors to be approved and accompanied by the growers.[404]

The employment contract that is standard for H-2A workers in North Carolina contains a clause restricting workers' access to legal advisors or union organizers. The clause says, "No tenancy in such housing is created; employer retains possession and control of the housing premises at all times. . . ."[405] Tenancy would give workers the right to have visitors of their own choosing, including union representatives, legal advisors, medical outreach personnel, religious counselors, and others. Despite this clear breach of the principle of freedom of association, the U.S. Department of Labor has approved the NCGA's contract containing this clause.[406] Similarly, the "Work Rules" issued by the NCGA states that "[T]he employer reserves the right to exclude any person(s) from visiting housing premises."[407]

The contract is known as the Agricultural Work Agreement, and it is standard for all NCGA members. In a letter of March 25, 1999 to Lori Elmer of Legal Services, Stan Eury stated that the new language of paragraph 6 adds a waiver provision establishing that "Any eligible individual wishing to exempt themselves from this tenancy condition can exempt themselves from this requirement by filing a request of waiver in writing with the North Carolina Growers Association prior to inhabiting the housing facility and beginning work." A farmworker in Mexico would have to be able to read and understand a dense legal contract and then muster the courage to write a "request of waiver" to avoid its restrictions, something that in practice is simply not going to happen.

---

[404]See NFWM Report, p. 2.
[405]NCGA Agricultural Work Agreement, on file with Human Rights Watch.
[406]Under H2-A regulations, all work contracts must be approved by the Department of Labor.
[407]NCGA "Work Rules," paragraph 12 (Vass, North Carolina, rev. 1/27/97).

NCGA official Eury said that "the tenancy clause . . . is designed to protect the rights, privacy, and privileges" of the farmworkers residing in the labor camps.[408] He further stated that although the farmworkers employed by the NCGA members do not enjoy a right of tenancy in their employer-provided housing, nonetheless "our employees are not being denied the right to freely associate with persons of their choosing at their employer-provided housing. We welcome all true friends and advocates of farm workers to our camps who do not come in the disguise of self righteousness, while intending malicious harm."[409]

FLOC union organizer Vicente Rosales told Human Rights Watch that he and two other FLOC representatives visited the farmworker camp of an NCGA member employer. The employer was "annoyed by our arrival . . . [and] threatened us that if we did not leave, she would call the police, and she told us that we were on her property and that if we wanted to speak with her, we should call her beforehand so that she could be ready for us and that she would also have to be present during the interviews with the workers."[410]

On August 13, 1998, FLOC national president Baldemar Velásquez and three other FLOC organizers visited a labor camp operated by another member of the NCGA. About one hour after FLOC advocates entered the premises, two police officers arrived and broke up the meeting they were holding with approximately twenty residents of the camp.[411] After FLOC organizers refused to leave the premises voluntarily, the officers arrested them on charges of trespass, based on the tenancy clause in paragraph 6 of NCGA's standard agricultural work agreement.[412] Although the case was later dismissed, the local sheriff told FLOC organizers that he would continue to arrest anyone accused by North Carolina growers of trespassing.[413]

FLOC organizers also told Human Rights Watch that even when they successfully enter farmworkers' camps and speak at length with workers, they find

---

[408]Letter from Stan Eury, president of the NCGA, to Lori Elmer, staff attorney of Legal Services, March 25, 1999, p. 5.

[409]Ibid., p. 2.

[410]Human Rights Watch interview, Vicente Rosales, FLOC organizer, June 30, 1999.

[411]See Sandy Smith-Nonini, "Uprooting La Injusticia," Institute for Southern Studies, March 1999, at 29; Letter from Robert J. Willis, attorney for FLOC, to Stan Eury, president of the NCGA, June 1, 1999, p. 1.

[412]Letter from Robert J. Willis, attorney for FLOC, to Stan Eury, president of the NCGA, June 1, 1999, p. 1.

[413]Ibid.

those workers "visibly afraid" of union organizers.[414] One farmworker told a delegation from the National Farm Worker Ministry that the workers "had been told many things about the union—one thing was that the union was trying to get rid of the H-2A workers because they do not qualify for a union contract."[415] When Human Rights Watch asked NCGA's Eury to comment on the FLOC organizing drive, he stated, "The union is attempting to line their own pockets at the expense of the workers. We give the workers everything that the union says it wants."[416]

Denying the Right to Legal Assistance

Lori Elmer and Alice Tejada of Legal Services told Human Rights Watch that in June 1998, when they visited an NCGA member's labor camp, they received treatment similar to that received by FLOC organizers. In June 1998, the staff attorneys received a call from a farmworker client at the camp. When they arrived in response to the call, they were invited to enter the premises by other farmworker residents. The grower called the sheriff, however, whose deputies arrived and instructed the attorneys to leave and threatened them with arrest if they failed to obey.[417]

When asked to comment on the incident, NCGA official Eury told Human Rights Watch that "it was an individual farmer who had been sued by Legal Services who didn't think it was right for them to go door to door soliciting complaints. He asked his workers if they wanted the people there. They said no. So the owner kicked them out. We did not deny access to Legal Services or the union."[418]

In a March 25, 1999 letter to Lori Elmer, Stan Eury asserted that "no NCGA member has ever denied you, or any other attorney the right to meet with a client."[419] He added:

---

[414] Human Rights Watch interview, Baldemar Velásquez, president of FLOC, Matt Emmick, Farmworker Ministries, Ramiro Sasrabia, FLOC organizer, Faison, North Carolina, June 9, 1999.

[415] See "NFWM Report," p.10.

[416] Human Rights Watch interview, Stan Eury, president of the NCGA, Vass, North Carolina, June 10, 1999.

[417] Human Rights Watch interview, Lori Elmer and Alice Tejada, staff attorneys of Legal Services, Raleigh, North Carolina, July 13, 1999.

[418] Human Rights Watch interview, Stan Eury, president of the NCGA, June 10, 1999.

[419] Letter from Stan Eury, president of the NCGA, to Lori Elmer, staff attorney of Legal Services, March 25, 1999, pp. 2-3.

> Everyone knows, in reality, that your visits do not result from
> specific requests or outreach activities, but rather are a systematic
> attempt on your unit's part to destroy the H-2A program by
> soliciting law suits and encouraging fraudulent workers
> compensation claims from our impressionable employees . . . It
> has become increasingly apparent that instead of trying to do
> meaningful things to improve the lives of farm workers, like the
> staff and members of the NCGA, you focus most of your energy
> and resources on trying to cause problems for the most compliant
> agricultural producers in the nation![420]

The National Farm Worker Ministry delegation also encountered growers'
antipathy toward unmonitored visitors in the camps. When the ministry delegation
visited the camp of one of Mt. Olive's growers in June 1999, they found that "the
grower, who knew in advance that we would be coming, stayed with us throughout
the entire visit, except for a brief interval. We were told that we were free to visit
his workers, but only if we checked with him first."[421] During the Farm Worker
Ministry delegation's visit, "the grower monopolized the conversation, answering
questions that had been addressed to the workers."[422]

One month later, Human Rights Watch met the same pattern. When Human
Rights Watch researchers arrived at a labor camp near Mount Olive, a bilingual
Mexican supervisor with a cell phone asked, "Are you with Legal Services? Are
you from the union?" Only after negative responses were Human Rights Watch
researchers permitted to speak with workers, but under close monitoring by the
supervisor.[423]

The supervisor remained with Human Rights Watch researchers as workers
responded to questions about working conditions and associational rights. All
responses were positive until one Human Rights Watch researcher asked to see the
housing conditions. The supervisor accompanied this researcher into the barrack-
style housing, offering a window of opportunity for workers to speak with another
Human Rights Watch researcher outside the supervisor's presence. "They don't let
us talk to Legal Services or the union," one worker whispered. "They would fire
us if we called them or talked to them."[424]

---

[420]Ibid.
[421]See "NFWM Report," p. 3.
[422]Ibid., p. 4.
[423]Human Rights Watch interview, near Mt. Olive, N.C., July 15, 1999.
[424]Ibid.

Trashing Books

NCGA's hostility to Legal Services is a focal point in orientation sessions and the accompanying materials provided to newly arrived H-2A workers. Juan Carlos Vieyra Ornelas, an intern with the Farm Worker Project of Benson, North Carolina, stated in a sworn affidavit that when he attended the NCGA orientation for 500 newly arrived H-2A workers from Mexico in Vass, North Carolina, in mid-1999, Jay Hill of the NCGA "spoke at length about the Farmworker Unit of Legal Services of North Carolina . . . He told the workers that Legal Services was their 'enemy.' He told the workers they should avoid Legal Services. He told the workers to contact only the NCGA, and not Legal Services, if they had any problems."[425]

Vieyra Ornelas further stated, "Mr. Hill then held up a copy of the 'Know Your Rights' booklet produced by Legal Services. He ordered workers to toss the 'Know Your Rights' booklet into the trash can. He told the workers that after throwing away the 'Know Your Rights' booklet, they could have a copy of the NCGA Employee Handbook."[426] Following Hill's admonition, workers discarded their booklets *en masse*.

The handbook that NCGA gives to workers after they discard their "Know Your Rights" booklets is titled "Understanding the Work Contract" and warns:

> FLS [Farmworker Legal Services] has a hidden motive when they approach you. They say that they are your friends and they are concerned about your rights and well being, but in reality their motive is to destroy the program which brings you to North Carolina legally . . . FLS discourage the growers with excessive suits which are for the most part without merit. The history of FLS shows that the workers who have talked with them have harmed themselves. Don't be fooled and allow them to take away your jobs.[427]

"Understanding the Work Contract" accuses Farmworker Legal Services of eliminating the H-2A programs in Idaho, West Virginia, Maryland, and Florida. It states that the 10,000 H-2A workers in Florida were "left with no hope of working

---

[425]Vieyra affidavit, p. 1.
[426]Ibid.
[427]North Carolina Growers' Association, Inc., "Understanding the Work Contract," pp. 12-13.

again in the United States" and calls the Florida H-2A workers "witnesses of the danger of speaking to FLS."[428]

Mary Lee Hall, managing attorney in the Farmworker Unit of Legal Services of North Carolina, wrote to Eury about reports from H-2A workers that NCGA officials told workers "if they keep our booklets or if they are ever seen with one of our booklets, they will be fired or have serious problems with the Association. Jay Hill conveys this message to the workers and then watches as they, feeling compelled not to give NCGA a reason to fire or retaliate against them, throw the booklets in a trash can provided by NCGA."[429]

Eury responded by asserting, "Our worker orientation includes information about the Legal Services attack on our program and the H-2A workers that have lost their jobs in Florida and West Virginia and other areas as a direct result of Legal Services attacks on the H-2A program. Our workers freely choose whether or not to associate themselves with you. Many workers choose to trash your propaganda after they learn the truth about your motives . . . Your shameless representations that you want to help H-2A workers are reprehensible."[430]

Eury's NCGA highlights its hostility to legal services by posting a large banner across an entire wall at its Vass, N.C. orientation site for newly-arrived H-2A workers. The banner proclaims *"Servicios Legales Quieren Destruir El Programa H2-A"* ("Legal Services Want to Destroy the H-2A Program"), and declares underneath this banner "Don't be a puppet of Legal Services," "Don't believe what Legal Services tells you about the NCGA," and other admonitions against legal services.[431]

---

[428]Ibid. Florida H-2A workers employed in the sugar cane industry were replaced by mechanized harvesting equipment. Here and in other states cited, growers argued that aggressive legal advocacy forced them to leave the H-2A program and move to mechanical harvesting. More often, growers moved to employ undocumented workers who have no access to legal services. Farmworker advocates respond that growers abandoned H-2A workers rather than comply with the law. For more on the Florida events, see Robert McCabe, "Firms Cutting Cutters," *Fort Lauderdale Sun-Sentinel*, April 28, 1993, p.1D; for Idaho, see Warren Cornwall, "Businesses seek help in immigration roulette," *Idaho Falls Post Register*, May 19, 1997, p. A1.

[429]Letter from Mary Lee Hall, managing attorney of Legal Services, to Stan Eury, president of the NCGA., July 2, 1999.

[430]Letter from Stan Eury, president of the NCGA, to Mary Lee Hall, managing attorney of Legal Services, July 6, 1999.

[431]A photograph of the banner and admonitions is on file with Human Rights Watch; Human Rights Watch translation of text.

Blacklisting

On paper, H-2A workers can seek help from Legal Services and file claims for redress for violations of H-2A program requirements (but not for violation of the right to form and join trade unions, since they are excluded from NLRA protection). However, in this atmosphere of grower hostility to Legal Services, farmworkers are reluctant to pursue legal claims that they may have against growers. In December 1997, the U.S. General Accounting Office (GAO) reported that "'H-2A workers . . . are unlikely to complain about worker protection violations fearing they will lose their jobs or will not be hired in the future.'"[432] The fear of blacklisting is well-founded, according to a 1999 Carnegie Endowment study, which based its findings on interviews conducted in Mexico with current Mexican H-2A workers. The Carnegie study found that "[b]lacklisting of H-2A workers appears to be widespread, is highly organized, and occurs at all stages of the recruitment and employment process. Workers report that the period of blacklisting now lasts three years, up from one year earlier in the decade."[433]

Mary Lee Hall of Legal Services, speaking from the experience of conversations with hundreds of farmworkers, confirms that the existence of a blacklisting system against workers who complain "is known to every H-2A worker, and I have yet to meet one who did not take this threat seriously."[434] The National Farm Worker Ministry delegation also reports being told by farmworkers that "[a]nyone who had dared to speak up in the past had been blacklisted . . . Word is spread of any H-2A workers who have spoken up about their working or living conditions, and those workers are sent back to Mexico and do not get rehired."[435]

Legal Services attorneys and others involved with H-2A workers and the H-2A recruiting process have reported concrete instances of blacklisting. Ventura Gutierrez, a labor organizer in California, told Human Rights Watch that he went to an H-2A recruiting office in Tlaxcala, Michoacan, Mexico, and saw a list of names posted on the wall, entitled "*lista negra*" (Spanish for "black list"), indicating which workers were not to be recruited as H-2A farmworkers. Gutierrez reported that a woman named Juana writes on a blackboard the names of people who are

---

[432]Ward, "Growers' Trade," p. 30.

[433]See Demetrios G. Papademetriou and Monica S. Heppel, *Balancing Acts: Toward a fair bargain on seasonal agricultural workers,* International Migration Policy Program, Carnegie Endowment for International Peace (1999), p. 13.

[434]Letter from Mary Lee Hall, managing attorney, Legal Services, to Stay Eury, president of the NCGA, July 2, 1999, p. 3.

[435]See "NFWM Report," pp. 4-5.

"blacklisted and therefore shouldn't get visas. Workers have to pay to get off the blacklist."[436]

Contingent Workers
We're in the orange ghetto.
—A Microsoft "permatemp" involved in worker organizing

Temporary work, part-time jobs, contracted and subcontracted employment, on-call employment, day labor and other forms of atypical, nonstandard, contingent, and often precarious work have shifted the ground workers stand on in the past decade. Nearly one-third of the U.S. labor force, or some forty million workers, are in what the Bureau of Labor Statistics calls alternative work arrangements. The widespread denial of associational rights for workers in these new forms of employment relations and the failure of authorities to protect them raise serious concerns under international human rights standards.

American labor law covering workers' freedom of association lags behind the reality these workers face. U.S. law presumes a stable employment relationship between a worker and a clearly identified employer. The paradigm was set in the 1930s, 1940s and 1950s with passage of the 1935 Wagner Act,[437] the 1947 Taft-Hartley Act,[438] and the 1959 Landrum-Griffin Act.[439]

While regular full-time work for one employer is still the norm for most workers in the United States, millions of others—and their number is growing—fit a variety of atypical molds. The largest group, some eighteen million, are regular part-time workers. About thirteen million are independent contractors and temporary, leased workers.[440] Employment in temporary agencies doubled between

---

[436]Human Rights Watch telephone interview, Ventura Gutierrez of the Farmworker Network, California, July 19, 1999.

[437]National Labor Relations Act, 29 U.S.C. §§ 151-69. See Chapter III., *The U.S. Legal Framework for Workers' Freedom of Association.* above for a full description.

[438]Labor Management Relations Act, 29 U.S.C. §§ 141-97. See Chapter III., *The U.S. Legal Framework for Workers' Freedom of Association.*

[439]Labor-Management Reporting and Disclosure Act, 29 U.S.C. §§ 401-531. See Chapter III., *The U.S. Legal Framework for Workers' Freedom of Association.*

[440]See Lawrence Mishel, Jared Bernstein, and John Schmitt, *The State of Working America* (Ithaca, New York, Cornell University Press, 1998), 243 (based on Bureau of Labor Statistics, 1995 and 1997 contingent work supplements to the Current Population Survey, the basic BLS guide to labor market data).

1982 and 1989 and doubled again between 1989 and 1997 to some three million workers.[441]

Many nonstandard workers prefer their arrangements to full-time work with one employer. For many, alternative work arrangements fit their family, education, and lifestyle needs where regular full-time work would create conflicts. Flexible work arrangements can also provide a helpful dynamism in the larger economy, with the ability to rapidly shift human resources to their most productive uses.

But workers pay a price for these alternatives. Health insurance for workers and their families, for example, is usually tied to full-time or near-full-time employment. Two-thirds of all regular full-time workers have both health insurance and pension benefits through their employer. Just one-third of workers in alternative arrangements have these benefits; less than 5 percent of those who work for temporary agencies enjoy them.[442] Moreover, as the federal government's Dunlop Commission found:

Whether voluntary or involuntary, part-time workers are lower paid per hour than full-time workers; have higher turnover rates; are disproportionally young and female; and are more likely to work for employers who do not offer pensions or health insurance. Perhaps seven million part-timers work fewer than 1000 hours per year and are exempt from Employee Retirement Income Security Act (ERISA) and Family and Medical Leave Act (FMLA) benefits. Unemployment insurance state earnings and requirements to be available for full-time work exclude most part-timers from UI benefits.[443]

Nothing in these kinds of contingent work arrangements inherently violates workers' freedom of association. Concerns about lack of health insurance or pensions, precarious job security and other problems of atypical workers are matters of social and economic policy. They might be implicated in a human rights report on social and economic rights. They might prompt recommendations for reforms like pro-rated benefits for part-time workers or universal health care for all workers.

---

[441]Ibid., pp. 246, 249.
[442]See, e.g., Nina Munk, "The Price of Freedom: In the much-romanticized free-agent nation, workers are liberated from routines, dress codes and office politics. As well as benefits, vacations and regular paychecks," *New York Times Magazine*, March 5, 2000, p. 50.
[443]See U.S. Department of Labor, U.S. Department of Commerce, Commission on the Future of Worker-Management Relations, *Fact Finding Report* (May 1994), 21.

But atypical work cannot be said to violate workers' freedom of association in and of itself.

At the same time, problems associated with contingent employment often inspire workers to try to address them through collective action. Here is where the human rights issue involving freedom of association emerges. Workers engaged in nonstandard employment relationships often face employer violations of labor laws and regulation and legal impediments when they exercise the right to freedom of association. Either they are not "employees" as defined in labor laws, or the proprietor of the place where they work is not their "employer" under the law. Some employers take advantage of these loopholes.

A prominent example of blocked freedom of association for workers in nonstandard employment is found in the office cleaning industry. Tens of thousands of workers are employed by janitorial service agencies in all parts of the United States. Most of the workers are immigrants making the minimum wage or slightly more, with few benefits. Many cleaning workers have attempted to form and join unions in recent years through a "Justice for Janitors" campaign mounted by the Service Employees International Union (SEIU).

But where workers successfully organize their cleaning agency, building owners often retaliate by cutting off the service contract with the agency. Workers are left without a job and without a union, expressly because they exercised the right to freedom of association. Yet labor law remedies that are supposed to protect this right do not reach the building owners who punished the workers, because the owners are not the "employer" against whom unfair labor practice charges can be laid.[444]

Exclusion from labor law protection affects both workers at the absolute bottom of the labor market and workers near the top. At the bottom, many workers made to take public works jobs under various state and city "workfare" programs are defined as "trainees," not employees. While some steps have been taken to apply the Fair Labor Standards Act to such workers, they are not covered by the NLRA. They have no protection against retaliation for exercising rights of association.[445]

---

[444]See Harry Bernstein, "While Building Owners' Profits Soar, Janitors Get Poorer," Los Angeles Times, August 15, 1989, Part 4, p.1; Stuart Silverstein, "Janitors' Union Vows To Turn Up Organizing Heat," Los Angeles Times, March 26, 1997, p. D1.

[445]See Joel Dresang, "Demonstrators Protest W-2 Training System: Community group says it wants 'real' jobs, wages for program participants," Milwaukee Journal-Sentinel, November 7, 1997, p. 3; Verena Dobnick, "Judge Rules Real Work Merits Real Pay; Says Training Cheated Homeless," Bergen County Record, March 20, 1998, p. A10.

Workfare workers' lack of protection pits them against ordinary workers. By 1997, workfare participants made up 75 percent of the New York City Parks Department labor force, and almost one-third of city sanitation workers were in the state's workfare program, called the Work Experience Program (WEP).[446] WEP workers have frequently protested working conditions and have sought greater protections, and organized workers have expressed concerns that good jobs are being eliminated to make room for exploited WEP workers, and that over time this will depress wages more widely. Some welfare recipients have even been recruited to serve as strikebreakers.[447]

A classic example involves Hattie Hargrove, a fifty-year-old custodial worker who was laid off by the Mineola (Long Island, New York) County Department of Social Services in 1992. Unable to find other work, she went on welfare. In 1993 she returned to her former job, but as a WEP worker earning not her former salary but $53.50 in cash assistance and $263 in food stamps per month. "I'd be making more money, and I'd have benefits instead of Medicaid," Hargrove told a reporter. "I know I would feel better because I'd be getting a paycheck and people wouldn't look down on me like I was crazy anymore."[448]

High-Tech Computer Programmers

The dilemma regarding freedom of association is stark for workers at temporary employment agencies, even at the high end of the economic ladder. They are defined as employees of the agency, not of the place of employment where they work. Therefore, if they want to exercise the right of association to organize and bargain collectively, they have to organize with other workers of the agency. Temporary agency employees usually have no contact and no opportunity to communicate with each other because they are spread among different work sites. Meanwhile, those temporary agency workers who work for long periods at one place, often called "perma-temps," have none of the rights, benefits or protections afforded to regular employees, including the right to form and join a union to deal with the employer.[449]

---

[446]See Melissa Healy, "N.Y. 'Workfare' Not So Fair After All, Some Say," *Los Angeles Times*, July 5, 1997, p. 1.

[447]See Nina Bernstein, "Fliers Given to Welfare Recipients Seek Workers to Cover a Strike," *New York Times*, April 8, 2000, p. A11.

[448]Ibid.

[449]For a description of an embryonic effort at association by temporary workers, see Steven Greenhouse, "Temporary Workers Seeking Code of Conduct for Job Agencies, New York Times, January 31, 2000, p. B1.

A recent, dramatic example of temporary agency workers' dilemma is found at the cutting edge of the new economy. Microsoft Corporation's elegant "campus" in Redmond, Washington indeed gives the appearance of a tranquil college setting. Graceful buildings are set among gentle slopes and winding brooks. Young people (mostly men) toss frisbees and play softball on broad lawns and fields. They gather in windowed cafeterias for lunch and snacks. Free video game machines are abundant. Shuttle buses with free candy baskets move employees around the site.

More than 20,000 workers are employed at Microsoft's Redmond campus and other nearby facilities. But 6,000 of them are not employed by Microsoft. Instead, they are employed by many temporary agencies supplying high-tech workers to Microsoft and other area companies. Many have worked for several years at Microsoft. They have come to be known as perma-temps, temporary employees working for long periods, often side-by-side in teams with regular, full-time employees (often referred to as "FTEs." in U.S. labor parlance).

Microsoft FTEs enjoy health insurance, pension plans, paid vacations and, most lucratively with the rising value of technology stocks in recent years, share ownership in the company. Perma-temps have none of that. They receive a generous hourly pay, usually $25-35 per hour, and nothing more. They have to pay $300 per month for family medical insurance. They often work fifty hours a week but are not entitled to overtime pay after forty hours because they are excluded from coverage by the Fair Labor Standards Act as highly skilled technical employees.

"It's an unbelievable erosion of what I expected from a company like Microsoft," said Marcus Courtney, a young Montanan who became a Microsoft perma-temp in 1996. "We do the same work, but for second-class status—no health, no pension, no vacation, no stock. We're in the orange ghetto," he said, referring to the orange ID cards that distinguish temporary employees from blue-carded FTEs.[450]

"Here's a common situation—tell me how you would feel," said Jeff Nachtigal, another Microsoft perma-temp. "You work on a project for months in a team of ten people, five perma-temps and five FTEs. You do the same things. You become friends. You're all part of the team. Then at the end of a project meeting, the FTEs plan a 'morale' event paid for by Microsoft, a dinner at the nicest restaurant in town. But only for them. The rest of us just sit there."[451]

"We needed to do something," said Courtney. He and other perma-temps formed the Washington Alliance of Technology Workers (WashTech) in early

---

[450]Human Rights Watch interview, Seattle, Washington, November 4, 1999.
[451]Ibid.

1998, with help from the Communications Workers of America (CWA). The CWA is the union of AT&T workers and others in the high-technology sector.[452]

WashTech is in the early stages of an effort to organize Microsoft perma-temps. "We've got a long way to go," Courtney concedes. "We're starting by establishing WashTech as a reliable source of information for high-tech workers in the area." Courtney said he told CWA organizers, "We have to do it differently here. The old-style union tactics of house visits and leaflets blasting management won't be enough."

But WashTech has a "Catch-22"-type problem. By defining perma-temps as contractors employed by various temporary agencies, Microsoft avoids being their employer for purposes of the National Labor Relations Act's protection of the right to organize. Meanwhile, the agencies tell temps that in order to form a union management will deal with, they have to organize other employees of the agency, not just those working at Microsoft.

Placed by an agency at Microsoft since May 1998, Barbara Judd worked in a perma-temp group of eighteen workers involved in a project developing a tax preparation software package. The only Microsoft FTEs in the project were their supervisors and managers.

Judd has an MBA and worked for years as a financial analyst. "I spent nine years with one company as a regular full-time worker," she said, "with health insurance, a pension, and paid vacations. I always thought of temporary work as something to fill in for people who are out, or as a probation to see if you can do the job, then become a full-timer." Judd said, "Microsoft brought in a bunch of skilled, experienced people to develop this new product. They told us how important it was to the company. We came from four different temp agencies. We thought we'd go blue [convert from temporary to regular FTE status] once it was launched. Now they've told us we'll stay orange for at least two more years."[453]

In early 1999 Microsoft announced it was going to require agencies supplying workers to the firm to provide more benefits for temporary workers. But when Judd asked her agency about the move, "They told me, 'We're grandfathered. We don't have to add benefits.' We were already upset about job titles and pay grade being out of line, both with each other and with other employees. And now this."[454]

Judd and her coworkers formed a union. Sixteen of the eighteen perma-temps in the group joined WashTech. "First we asked our Microsoft managers to bargain with us," she said. Management refused. A spokesman for Microsoft told the press

---

[452]Full disclosure: staff associates of Human Rights Watch voted in favor of representation by a New York-based local union of CWA in an NLRB election in October 1999.
[453]Human Rights Watch interview, Seattle, Washington, November 4, 1999.
[454]Ibid.

that "'bargaining units are a matter between employers and employees' and Microsoft is not the employer of the workers.'"[455]

The group turned to their agencies, but agency managers refused to talk to them. One manager told the press that "'the company does not believe the group 'is an appropriate bargaining unit under the federal labor laws.'"[456] According to Judd, one manager told her, "'If you keep it up, we're going to sic Microsoft's lawyers on you.'"[457]

When the workers sought to distribute WashTech information at work, their Microsoft managers issued a "non-solicitation and non-distribution policy for Contingent Staff [perma-temps] . . . to help maintain Microsoft project site efficiency and security."[458] That instruction was followed by another e-mail message: "Just a reminder that distribution of materials that are not related to Microsoft business purposes is PROHIBITED."[459] But when asked if an employee's solicitation for a school fundraiser was covered by the ban, a manager responded, "That was not the purpose of my talking about the distribution of materials."[460]

Attempts to be recognized by the temp agencies were equally unavailing. "'We don't have to talk to you, and we won't' is what they told us," said Barbara Judd. "They told us we had to get all the temps from all four agencies that worked at other companies besides Microsoft. We had no way to know who they were or how to reach them. Besides, they had nothing to do with our problems at Microsoft."[461]

Frustration of these workers' freedom of association was subtle, not raw. Marcus Courtney, Jeff Nachtigal, Barbara Judd and other Microsoft permatemps

---

[455]See Leslie Helm, "Technology: 16 Microsoft Temps Organize into Bargaining Unit; Labor: Group Hoping for Improved Benefits Signs a Petition Seeking Representation by Local Union," *Los Angeles Times*, June 4, 1999, p. C3.

[456]Ibid.

[457]ibid.

[458]Microsoft e-mail to all temporary workers, June 30, 1999, on file with Human Rights Watch.

[459]Microsoft e-mail of September 17, 1999 (capitalized in original), on file with Human Rights Watch.

[460]Microsoft exchange of e-mails, September 17, 1999, on file with Human Rights Watch. Discriminatory application of a work rule against distribution of worker organizing materials as distinct from other materials could give rise to an unfair labor practice charge. No charge was filed in this matter.

[461]Judd interview.

were not fired for leadership or activity in WashTech.[462] But their situation was still precarious. In February 2000, Microsoft announced a new policy effective July 1, 2000 limiting temporary workers to one year's employment at a time and requiring a one-hundred-day break between each individual's assignment at the company. Under this policy, perma-temps would have to take one hundred days off beginning July 1, 2000 unless they are hired as full-time employees. After one hundred days off, said a Microsoft manager, they would have to reapply for temporary work or request new jobs at a different company through their temporary employment agencies.[463]

Barbara Judd's permatemp post at Microsoft ended in March 2000 when the company announced it was abandoning the tax preparation software project that she and her coworkers developed.[464] "We are discontinuing our development effort on the TaxSaver product," a manager told workers. "We will be announcing a partnership with H&R Block tomorrow morning."[465]

"We received two days notice" of being laid off, Judd told Human Rights Watch. Some workers moved to another tax preparation software company, but Judd decided to look for full-time employment. "I believe the temporary worker industry is making a profit at the expense of workers, and I don't want to be a part of that system," she said. "Workers who take temp jobs do not realize there is a larger impact than just the absence of benefits. You essentially lose the ability to organize . . . [T]he legal system is just not set up to deal with these long-term temp [perma-temp] issues."[466]

A cynic, or more generously a pragmatist, might say that Human Rights Watch's sympathy and attention should be saved for downtrodden workers like those in other case studies in this report, not devoted to skilled workers who can command a premium in the new, high-tech economy. But the right to freedom of association is fundamental. It is not tied to economic status. All workers have this right and should enjoy its exercise and protection. Indeed, medical doctors might well soon be another case study if their definition as independent contractors bars

---

[462]See Nan Netherton, "Contingent Workers: Microsoft Changes Policy on Use of Temporary Employees," *Daily Labor Report*, Bureau of National Affairs, February 23, 2000, p. A-7.

[463]See John Cook, "Microsoft Limits Amount of Time Temps Can Work; New Policy Could End Its 'Permatemp' Problem," *Seattle Post-Intelligencer*, February 19, 2000, p. B3.

[464]See Paul Andrews, "Microsoft drops TaxSaver software; Workers on project call decision a shock," *Seattle Times*, March 24, 2000, p. D3.

[465]See Microsoft, "Partnering in the tax preparation category," e-mail to financial products group, March 22, 2000, on file with Human Rights Watch.

[466]Human Rights Watch telephone interview, April 25, 2000.

them from negotiating with powerful HMOs about pay and practice conditions, including medical decision-making.[467]

Express Package Delivery Workers

Another example of the frustration of contract workers' freedom of association can be found in the package shipping business. Airborne Express is a nationwide package delivery company. Airborne employs directly, as its employees, about 18,000 workers represented by the Teamsters union. These workers have a national collective bargaining agreement with Airborne providing good wages and comprehensive benefits—health insurance, pensions, vacations.   But about 15,000 other workers are employed in Airborne's underside. They work at nearly 300 Airborne subcontractors, with less than half the salary of regular Airborne employees and no benefits. To all appearances, though, they are Airborne employees. They wear Airborne uniforms and drive Airborne trucks. They report to work at Airborne buildings and watch Airborne training videos. They use Airborne's billing and records system. The contractors they work for serve Airborne as exclusive company contractors with a low-paid workforce.[468]

In November 1994, sixty workers at Airborne contractors in Rhode Island called Expressman Courier and Interstate Parcel formed a union and sought to bargain collectively with their companies. Airborne canceled the subcontracts, closed the companies, and fired all the workers. Shortly afterward, Airborne reopened the sites under new names and new contracts with the same managers, this time called Agents Transportation and Professional Delivery. These companies rehired former Expressman and Interstate workers, but only those they considered opposed to the union. They refused to rehire worker leaders and members active in the union. "They took all the non-union guys. The rest of us were out in the cold," said Peter Shaw, one of the leaders.[469] The NLRB regional office backed up the workers' discrimination charge after an investigation, finding merit and issuing

---

[467]See Amy Goldstein, "AMA Votes to Unionize Doctors: Group Acts in Response to Managed Care's Effect on rights, Duties of Physicians," *Washington Post*, June 24, 1999, p. A1; Charles Ornstein, "Seeking Treatment: Doctors' Groups Look for Ways to Stay Financially Afloat," *Dallas Morning News*, October 31, 1999 (noting "current antitrust law views independent physicians as small businessmen and regards collective bargaining as collusion").

[468]Airborne representatives did not respond to requests from Human Rights Watch for interviews or further information about the cases described here.

[469]See Bill Dermody, "Teamsters Says Airborne Is Playing a Shell Game," *Journal of Commerce*, May 17, 1997.

a complaint against Airborne and the contractors.[470] The complaint awaits a decision by an administrative law judge.

With some variation, the scenario repeated itself in other locations. Workers at an Airborne contractor in Wisconsin called EEI formed a union in 1994. EEI commenced bargaining but refused to make an economic offer because, in the words of an NLRB complaint, "Airborne controls the revenue available to EEI."[471] At a contractor in Ohio called Boone Cartage, workers formed a union in December 1997. As at the Wisconsin site, Boone claimed its hands were tied because Airborne controlled its revenues. Boone said if it raised workers' pay, Airborne would cancel its contract. Airborne, on the other hand, argued that Boone was an independent contractor and disclaimed any responsibility to bargain with Airborne workers at Boone.[472]

Dan Lamb, an Airborne contract worker at Boone, went on a forty-day hunger strike in mid-1998 to protest Airborne's refusal to deal with the workers' union. Lamb made $8 per hour, compared with regular Airborne workers' salary of $18 per hour. Lamb got no pension and had to pay for family health insurance by having $340 dollars per month deducted from his paycheck. "We've got to plant good seeds," said Lamb. "We've been planting bad seeds. Somebody's got to turn the tide."[473]

Asked about Lamb's protest, an Airborne spokesman said, "This is not an Airborne issue. It's Boone Cartage's issue. He's their employee. We don't determine his wages."[474] Airborne threatened Lamb with legal action if he kept Airborne's name on his protest signs. Airborne refused to bargain with workers at Boone.[475] This case is also before an NLRB administrative law judge.

---

[470]See NLRB Region 1, Order Consolidating Cases, Consolidated Complaint and Notice of Hearing, *Airborne Freight Company et.al. and Teamsters Local 251*, Cases 1-CA-32742, 32767, March 27, 1997.

[471]See NLRB Region 30, Order Consolidating Cases, Consolidated Complaint and Notice of Hearing, Airborne Express, Enterprise Express and Teamsters Local 344, Cases 30-CA-12786, 12963 (June 7, 1996).

[472]See NLRB Region 9, Order Consolidating Cases, Consolidated Compliant and Notice of Hearing, *Airborne Express and Boone Cartage and Teamsters Local 957*, Cases 9-CA-36244, 36272 1,-2,-3, December 31, 1998.

[473] See Kirsten Wicker, "Going Hungry: Airborne Express worker goes on a hunger strike to protest low wages," *Dayton Voice*, July 23, 1998, 1.

[474]See Glenn Burkins, "A hunger striker says he won't eat until his employer signs a union contract," *Wall Street Journal*, July 21, 1998, 1.

[475]See NLRB Region 9 Complaint and Notice of Hearing,; Glenn Burkins, "A hunger striker says . . ."

In another case, Airborne did not wait. Management at First Choice Delivery, an Airborne subcontractor in New York, fired two leaders of an effort to form a union in 1995. One of them, Gary Livingston, had a 1993 letter of commendation from Airborne president Robert G. Brazzen. "We really appreciate all your efforts in extending superior service to our Airborne Express customers," the letter said.[476]

Airborne's status as a "joint employer" with its subcontractors is now being litigated in a half-dozen separate cases at the NLRB. It could take years for these cases to be decided. It is already more than five years since workers in Rhode Island and Wisconsin formed and joined their union and since worker leaders were fired. And this is a case where the legal "indicia" of joint employer status are quite strong, as with the open use of Airborne uniforms and trucks by subcontractors, for example. Many other companies find it easy to maintain the appearance of an arms-length contractor-subcontractor relationship by avoiding such superficial indications of a controlling relationship. This way, the large company effectively maintains control over the subcontractor and the ability to cancel a contract where workers exercise their right to freedom of association.

---

[476]See Marc Carey, "Worker in union drive finds back against wall," *Albany Times Union*, April 8, 1995.

VI. LEGAL OBSTACLES TO U.S. WORKERS' EXERCISE OF FREEDOM OF ASSOCIATION

Defenseless Workers: Exclusions in U.S. Labor Law

Everyone has the right to form and to join trade unions for the protection of his interests.

—Universal Declaration of Human Rights (1948)

"Exclusions" from labor law protection affect tens of millions of workers in the United States ranging from farmworkers to college professors. Big chunks of the labor force are defenseless against employer reprisals if they try to exercise freedom of association. If they protest abusive working conditions, employers can fire them with impunity. If they seek to bargain collectively, employers can ignore them. Protection of the right to organize and bargain collectively, a bedrock requirement of international labor rights norms, is denied these workers.

The 1935 Wagner Act, the original NLRA, excluded agricultural workers and domestic workers from its coverage. In the 1947 Taft-Hartley Act, independent contractors and low-level supervisors were added to the list of exclusions in the NLRA. These exclusions run counter to international human rights standards compelling broad protection of workers' freedom of association and relevant comparative international practice.

The Universal Declaration of Human Rights states, "*Everyone* has the right to freedom of peaceful assembly and association . . . *Everyone* has the right to form and to join trade unions for the protection of his interests."[477] The International Covenant on Civil and Political Rights says, "*Everyone* shall have the right to freedom of association with others, including the right to form and join trade unions for the protection of his interests."[478] The International Covenant on Economic, Social and Cultural Rights urges guarantees for "the right of *everyone* to form trade unions and join the trade union of his choice . . . for the promotion and protection of his economic and social interests."[479]

As noted earlier in Chapter III., the United States ratified the ICCPR in 1992 and did not enter any reservations, declarations, or understandings with respect to Article 22 on freedom of association. The United States signed, but has not ratified,

---

[477]UDHR Articles 20, 23 (emphasis added here and in following references). As is known, the possessive pronoun is gender-specific in English, unlike most other languages. When these instruments were crafted, usually with French as the foundation, "his" in the English translation applied to men and women.

[478]ICCPR Article 22.

[479]ICESCR Article 8.

the ICESCR. Signature constitutes a preliminary and general endorsement of the covenant, and creates an obligation to refrain from acts that would defeat the objectives of the covenant, or to take measures to undermine it.

Under ILO Convention No. 87, "*Workers . . . without distinction whatsoever* shall have the right to establish and . . . join organisations of their own choosing."[480] ILO Convention No. 98 says, "*Workers* shall enjoy adequate protection against acts of anti-union discrimination. . . ."[481] More than 100 countries have ratified these two freedom of association conventions, reflecting a solid international consensus. Although the United States has not ratified them, it is bound by them by virtue of its membership in the ILO itself, since these conventions are taken to be of a constitutional nature over and above other conventions.[482]

Under the ILO's 1998 Declaration on Fundamental Principles and Rights at Work, championed by the United States, all member countries have an obligation, whether or not they have ratified conventions 87 and 98, "to respect, to promote, and to realise the principles concerning the fundamental rights which are the subject of those Conventions, namely: (a) freedom of association and the effective recognition of the right to collective bargaining. . . ."[483]

On its face, U.S. law is equally comprehensive. The Norris-LaGuardia Act of 1932 excluded no category of worker and stated, "[I]t is necessary that he have full freedom of association, self-organization, and designation of representatives of his own choosing, to negotiate the terms and conditions of his employment, and that he shall be free from the interference, restraint, or coercion of employers of labor. . . ."[484] Section 7 of the NLRA stipulates: "Employees shall have the right to self-organization [and] to bargain collectively through representatives of their own choosing. . . ." The NLRB was created to enforce these rights.

However, Congress created enormous exclusions of workers from the legal protection of these rights in the final version of the 1935 Wagner Act and in the 1947 Taft-Hartley amendments to the Wagner Act. Under Section 2 of the NLRA as it now reads, "The term 'employee' . . . shall not include any individual employed as an agricultural laborer, or in the domestic service of any family or person at his

---

[480] ILO Convention No. 87 Concerning Freedom of Association and Protection of the Right to Organise.

[481] ILO Convention No. 98 Concerning the Application of the Principle of the Right to Organise and to Bargain Collectively.

[482] See ILO Resolution, Official Bulletin, Vol LVII, p. 152 (1974).

[483] ILO Declaration on Fundamental Principles and Rights at Work and Its Follow-Up (1998).

[484] Norris-LaGuardia Act, 47 Stat. 70 (1932), 29 U.S.C. §§ 101-15 (1988).

home, . . . or any individual having the status of an independent contractor, or any individual employed as a supervisor. . . ."[485]

Under these clauses and related court decisions, workers in all walks of life are excluded from labor law protection. Their employers can fire them with impunity for engaging in concerted activity, including trying to form a union, to bargain collectively, or to strike. They have no labor board or unfair labor practice mechanism they can turn to for redress. These workers include many or all farmworkers, household employees, taxi drivers, college professors, delivery truck drivers, engineers, product sellers and distributors, doctors, nurses, newspaper employees, Indian casino employees, employees labeled "supervisors" and "managers" who may have minimal supervisory or managerial responsibility, and others.

Agricultural Workers

More than three million workers in the United States are excluded from federal law protecting the right to organize because they are "employed as an agricultural laborer."[486] Agricultural workers' exclusion under the NLRA was not the result of any argument that warned of undesirable consequences of their coverage under the law. Congress was focusing on industrial strife in the nation's manufacturing sectors and thought of agricultural employment as one or two "hired hands" helping a small family farmer. Although farmworkers were covered in the original drafts of the bill, the exclusion was added without much debate or dissent. There were no hearings devoted to farmworkers' problems.[487]

Human Rights Watch's research for this report reconfirmed what many previous studies, reports, documentary films and other investigations have found—that farmworkers confront low wages, bad housing, poor health care, workplace hazards, unfair treatment and other abusive conditions on a massive scale.[488] Their suffering could begin to be addressed by effective exercise of freedom of association and the right to organize and bargain collectively. Indeed,

---

[485]NLRA Section 2.

[486]Agricultural workers are covered by the Migrant and Seasonal Agricultural Workers Protection Act (AWPA) for certain working conditions, but this law does not protect the right to organize and bargain collectively, as it would conflict with the NLRA's exclusion of agricultural workers from coverage.

[487]See Michael H. LeRoy and Wallace Hendricks, *Should "Agricultural Laborers" Continue To Be Excluded from the National Labor Relations Act?*, 48 Emory Law Journal 489 (Spring 1999) (hereafter "'Agricultural Laborers'") for an extensive discussion of the legislative history of the agricultural exclusion under the NLRA.

[488]See, for example, Daniel Rothenberg, *With These Hands* (1999).

solving such problems through self-organization and bargaining with employers is the purpose of the NLRA.

Even if the "hired hand" model of farm labor prevailed in the 1930s, it has long since given way to large-scale corporate farming and massive movement of farmworkers by the tens of thousands through the harvest cycles of American agriculture. The continued denial of protection for farmworkers is both an anachronism and a case of U.S. labor law violating international human rights standards requiring protection of all workers' right to freedom of association.

Farmworkers in some states are covered by state laws regulating at least some aspects of organization and collective bargaining.[489] California and Arizona, in particular, have created labor boards to handle unfair labor practices, including discriminatory discharge cases. Given the size of these states' agricultural labor force, this softens the overall national effect of the agricultural exclusion under the NLRA. However, farmworker union organizers report that many of the problems that plague the NLRB system, such as employer threats, discriminatory discharges, years of delay, and weak remedies, also afflict California's Agricultural Labor Relations Act and Agricultural Labor Relations Board under state law. They see the Arizona law as openly favoring growers.[490]

In other states, notably Florida, New Jersey, and Washington, court decisions have affirmed farmworkers' right to organize.[491] However, in these and other states with court-created associational rights, there is still no administrative redress enforced by public authorities. Workers must file individual private lawsuits which, as noted above in the Washington State apple workers' case, they are reluctant to do and private attorneys are reluctant to undertake.

In these few states where protection of the right to organize exists under court-made law, the difficulty of mounting a successful lawsuit to vindicate the right makes such protection wholly inadequate. In the vast majority of U.S. states,

---

[489]These include New Jersey, Massachusetts, Wisconsin, Oregon, Kansas, South Dakota, Arizona and California. See LeRoy and Hendricks, "'Agricultural Laborers,'" p. 493.

[490]Human Rights Watch interview with Guadalupe Gamboa, United Farm Workers of America representative, Sunnyside, Washington, November 6, 1999; see S. Lynne, Walker, "ALRB has become foe, Chavez says," *San Diego Union-Tribune*, May 26, 1987, p. A-7; Russ Hemphill, "Politicians Rush to Honor Chavez; But Reject Farm Workers' Rights He Sought," *Phoenix Gazette*, November 9, 1993, p. B1. Since this Human Rights Watch report focuses on national law and practice, it does not examine workers' rights under these state laws or further evaluate criticisms of these laws. for more discussion, see LeRoy and Hendricks, "'Agricultural Laborers.'"

[491]See *COTA v. Molinelli*, 552 A.2d. 1003 (N.J. 1989); *Bravo v. Dolssen Companies*, 125Wn.2d 745; 888 P.2d 147 (1995).

farmworkers are completely defenseless. They have neither an unfair labor practice claim nor a lawsuit available for recourse when employers fires them for exercising freedom of association.

Domestic Workers

When it crafted the NLRA in 1935, Congress made a judgment that organizing and collective bargaining did not fit the intimate relationship between a householder and a domestic employee. Like the farmer's hired hand, the domestic worker was perceived by Congress as outside the scope of legislation addressing industrial strife. The reality sixty-five years later is that domestic workers are vulnerable to human rights abuse, and there is a pressing need to provide them the right to organize for their own protection.

Thousands of domestic workers have been brought into the United States by officials of multinational corporations, international organizations, and other elites residing in the United States. Several factors have created a dramatically increasing need for child care and a growing, largely unregulated, labor market for in-home child care, both "on the books" and "off the books." One is the surge of two-income households and single-parent homes in the United States. Another is the emergence of an even more affluent upper class able to afford domestic help. The dispersal of the extended family has made fewer relatives available for child care. In many areas, immigrant women fill this need.

The "graying" of the U.S. population has created parallel growth in elder care in the home. Much of this is provided by agencies who assign workers as "independent contractors" (see below), but many also are hired directly by a family to provide care. In all these settings, many of the child care and elder care providers are immigrant women.

Most European countries have developed special labor law regimes for domestic workers addressing their right of association and providing ways to standardize pay and working conditions through collective representation. But the United States clings to the exclusion of domestic workers from protection of the right to act in association with one another.

In the United States, more than 800,000 officially reported "private household workers" held jobs as domestic employees in 1998. Nearly 30 percent were foreign migrant workers, and the vast majority were women.[492] These figures are surely an

---

[492]U.S. Bureau of Labor Statistics, unpublished tabulations from 1998-1999 population survey, on file with Human Rights Watch. Of the 847,000 "private household workers": 1) approximately 1,000 are launderers and ironers; 2) approximately 4,000 are cooks; 3) approximately 14, 000 are housekeepers and butlers, defined as those who "hire, supervise,

undercounting: an unknown number of workers also labored as domestics "off the books"—U.S. citizens, workers with non-immigrant or temporary visas, workers with permanent visas or "green cards," and undocumented workers. In all, likely more than one million workers in the United States are maids, cooks, babysitters, cleaners, gardeners, and other domestic employees.

Domestic workers perform devalued household tasks.[493] In her role, the domestic worker is often correspondingly devalued. In the most egregious cases of exploitation, employers feel free to create living and working conditions equivalent to indentured servitude. Numerous cases have surfaced of live-in migrant domestic workers—both documented and undocumented—working over one hundred hours per week, from early morning until late at night six or seven days a week with no holidays, receiving compensation far below the national minimum wage if they are paid at all.[494]

Many domestic workers who have spoken out about their plight say that abusive employers deny them basic telephone privileges, prohibit them from leaving employers' homes unaccompanied, and forbid them to associate or communicate

---

and coordinate the household staff to keep the household running smoothly;" 4) approximately 278,000 are child care workers, including babysitters, nannies, infant nurses, and governesses; and 5)approximately 549,000 are "private household cleaners and servants," defined as those whose duties may include dusting and polishing furniture; sweeping, mopping, and waxing floors; vacuuming; cleaning ovens, refrigerators, and bathrooms; washing dishes; polishing silver; changing and making beds; washing, folding, and ironing clothes; washing windows; looking after children or elderly persons; cooking; feeding pets; answering the telephone and doorbell; and taking clothes to the cleaners, doing grocery shopping, and running other errands. U.S. Bureau of Labor Statistics, *1998-1999 Occupational Outlook Handbook,* http://stats.bls.gov/oco/ocos175.htm (visited 9/17/99).

[493]See Bridget Anderson, *"Just Like One of the Family"? Migrant Domestic Workers in the European Union* (unpublished thesis, 1998), p. 34, on file with Human Rights Watch.

[494]See, *e.g.,* Somini Sengupta, "An Immigrant's Legal Oddysey: In Suing employer, Maid fights Diplomatic Immunity," *New York Times,* January 12, 2000, p. B1; Tom Robbins, "Protecting Exploited Domestics," *New York Daily News,* August 9, 1999, p. 15; Kala Dwarakanath, "Fighting worker exploitation," *India in New York,* May 29, 1998, p. 16; Human Rights Watch telephone interview with Celia Rivas, attorney, Spanish Catholic Center, Gaithersburg, Maryland, November 29, 1999; Human Rights Watch telephone interview with Edward Leavy, attorney, Washington, D.C., November 19, 1999; Human Rights Watch telephone interviews with Steven Smitson, attorney, CASA of Maryland, Inc., Silver Spring, Maryland, November 4, 1999 and November 22, 1999.

with friends and neighbors.[495] To prevent domestic workers from leaving exploitative employment situations, employers confiscate the workers' passports and threaten them with deportation if they flee.[496] In the most severe cases of abuse, migrant domestic workers—both live-in and day workers—have reported instances of sexual assault, physical abuse, and rape.[497]

Shamela Begum, a Bangladeshi woman, came to New York with a special visa in December 1998 to be employed as a domestic worker by a couple in which the husband was a Bahraini diplomat at the United Nations.[498] Begum said that when she arrived in the U.S., her employers immediately confiscated her passport and refused to return it.[499] According to Begum, until August 30, 1999, when she was freed through the help of New York City police and local advocates, she labored from approximately 6:00 a.m. until 10:00 p.m. seven days a week caring for the couple's children and performing household duties for the family.[500] Begum said that she was paid only $100 per month for the first eight months of her work, money which was not given to her directly but was instead sent to her husband in Bangladesh, and that she was never paid for the remaining duration of her employment.[501]

Shamela Begum recounted that during her approximately nine months with the couple, she was allowed to leave their high-rise apartment on Manhattan's East Side only twice—both times to accompany the wife to the market.[502] Furthermore, she

---

[495]See, e.g., Jessica Shattuck, "Nahar Alam: fighting for the rights of domestic workers," *Mother Jones*, September 1, 1998, p. 22; Sonia Shah, "Help for Immigrant Women," *The Progressive*, June 1, 1998, p. 14; Human Rights Watch Leavy, Smitson interviews.

[496]See, e.g., Alex Tizon, "An Illegal Aliens' Tale--Caught in a Web of Fraud and Dreams," *The Seattle Times*, August 1, 1999, p. A1; Dwarakanath, "Fighting worker exploitation," *India in New York*; Human Rights Watch Leavy, Smitson interviews.

[497]Human Rights Watch Rivas, Smitson interviews; Margaret Ramirez, "Adding Injury to Insult: Domestic workers say they are humiliated, even hurt," *Newsday*, March 15, 1998, p. A36; Pamela Constable, "Housekeeper Wins Suit Against Boss," *The Washington Post*, June 10, 1997, p. E5.

[498]Complaint, *Shamela Begum v. Mohammed Saleh and Khatun Saleh*, Civ. No. 99-11834, (SDNY, December 7, 1999), para. 1; Letter from David Wohabe, attorney for Defendants Mohammed and Khatun Saleh, to the Honorable Richard M. Berman, United States District Judge, Southern District of New York, January 18, 2000, p. 1; Somini Sengupta, "In Suing Employer, Immigrant Fights Diplomatic Immunity," *New York Times*, January 12, 2000, p. A23.

[499]Complaint, *Shamela Begum v. Mohammed Saleh and Khatun Saleh*, ¶ 10.

[500]Ibid., paras. 1, 11, 19.

[501]Ibid., para. 12.

[502]Ibid., para. 14; Sengupta, "In Suing Employer . . .".

contended that when the couple vacationed, she was left alone, confined to their apartment with little or no food and no money to buy food.[503] According to Begum, throughout her time with the couple, not only was she imprisoned in their apartment and occasionally denied food, but she was also frequently verbally abused and humiliated by them and, on several occasions, was the victim of assault and battery by the wife.[504]

At nine months, Shamela Begum's suffering was relatively brief. Yeshehareg Teferra, an Ethiopian woman, worked in Silver Spring, Maryland, for eight years for an Ethiopian staff member of the International Monetary Fund. She worked seven days a week, thirteen hours a day with no days off during the eight years. She received total compensation of $1,060 during that time—the equivalent of three cents an hour.[505] Teferra said she was ordered not to speak with people outside the family; was required to ask permission prior to leaving the apartment; and was slapped, choked, and verbally abused when she complained of her treatment.[506]

Hilda Dos Santos was held as a "live-in slave" for nearly twenty years in a suburb of Washington, D.C. by an employer from her native Brazil. She was never paid a salary, was physically assaulted, and was denied medical care for a stomach tumor the size of a soccer ball. Her plight only came to light when neighbors acted at the sight of her tumor, and resulting publicity led to a successful prosecution.[507] Dos Santos's case illustrates the difficulty of uncovering such abuses. After twenty years of servitude, she was granted temporary legal status to testify against her employer but was then subject to deportation. An unknown number of similar victims remain silent because exposure means deportation for them, too.[508]

---

[503] Ibid., para. 13.

[504] Ibid. In June 2000 the case was settled out of court. See Somini Sengupta, "Settlement Reached in Maid's Suit Against Diplomat," *New York Times*, June 15, 2000, p. B2.

[505] See "Order Adopting Report and Recommendation," Deborah K. Chasanow, U.S. District Judge, September 14, 1999, and "Report and Recommendation, William Connelly, U.S. Magistrate Judge, August 19, 1999, *Yeshehareg Teffera v. Dawit Makonnen*, Civil No. DKC 98-3420, United States District Court for the District of Maryland.

[506] William Branigin, "A Life of Exhaustion, Beatings and Isolation," *The Washington Post*, January 5, 1999, p. A6.

[507] See Ruben Castañeda, "Man Found Guilty in Slave Case; Md. Couple Brought Woman From Brazil," *Washington Post*, February 11, 2000, p. B1.

[508] Ibid. Subsequent editorial comment noted that "the sad fact is that no one can say for sure how many other cases like hers may exist . . . more than 30,000 domestic workers were brought into the country during the 1990s on special work visas, and uncounted others came to work illegally. If these workers—isolated in homes, often unable to speak English and fearful of deportation—encounter abuse or exploitation, help can seem completely out of reach." (See "Slavery in the Suburbs," Editorial, *Washington Post*, February 13, 2000, p.

Domestic Workers' Initiatives in the United States

Whether or not they are enforced, minimum wage laws, overtime laws, and child labor laws apply to most domestic workers in the United States. But if they attempt to form and join a union, or exercise any freedom of association even without the intent of forming a union, they can be summarily threatened, intimidated, or fired with impunity by their employer because of their exclusion from coverage by the NLRA. In contrast, unions of domestic workers have formed in a number of European Union (EU) countries, including France, the United Kingdom, Italy, Spain, and Greece.[509]

Despite their exclusion from laws protecting the right to organize, some domestic workers in the United States have established local cooperatives and support and advocacy agencies. They seek to improve wages and working conditions of domestic workers by uniting them and educating them about their rights.[510] Human Rights Watch spoke with two such groups, Workers' Awaaz (Workers' Voice) and the Unidad Cooperativa de Limpieza de Casa (Unity Cooperative of Housecleaners), both based on Long Island in New York.

Workers' Awaaz was founded in June 1997 as an advocacy group run by and for South Asian women workers, primarily domestics, in Long Island City.[511] The group has one paid staff person and consists of approximately fifty members,

---

B6).

[509]Human Rights Watch telephone interview with representative, French Democratic Confederation of Workers (CFDT), Paris, France, December 14, 1999. The CFDT representative said that domestic workers in France negotiated a collective agreement in 1992—the *Convention Collective Nationale des Employés de Maison* (National Collective Agreement of Household Employees)—with the French national federation of employers of domestic workers. The collective agreement covers all domestic workers in France, both union and non-union members, and sets forth explicit terms and conditions with which the employer of a domestic worker must comply. If the collective agreement is breached, a domestic worker may report to a French labor inspector, request that the breach be documented, and take the case to court. Protections for domestic workers such as those set forth in the French collective agreement may soon apply to domestic workers throughout the European Union. A public campaign in support of a draft EU rule establishing minimum rights for domestic workers was launched in October 1999. Unions representing domestic workers are now engaging in a vigorous EU-wide campaign to garner support for the charter.

[510]See Dwarakanath, "Fighting worker exploitation."

[511]See Shah, "Help for Immigrant Women."

roughly fifteen of whom are actively involved in organizing and implementing the activities of Workers' Awaaz.[512]

Workers' Awaaz reaches out to local domestic employees and advocates for their rights in a variety of ways. Its active members set up tables on streets in neighborhoods where a large number of migrant domestic workers live; cooperate with other workers' groups and women's groups to expose the exploitative working conditions of many domestic workers; mount publicity campaigns by placing ads in local newspapers to educate domestic workers about their rights and to put employers who break the law on notice that they might face lawsuits; picket employers known to exploit domestic workers; refer domestic workers with legal claims against their employers to attorneys willing to represent them;[513] and join forces with other workers' rights organizations to reach out to injured domestic workers to expose the connection between long hours and health problems.[514]

The Unidad Cooperativa de Limpieza de Casa, which meets on alternate Sundays at the Workplace Project in Hempstead, New York,[515] began functioning in January 1999, after approximately six months of preparation and planning.[516] Like other migrant domestic worker cooperatives that have formed across the country in the 1990s, the Unidad Cooperativa is made up primarily of day workers, who have joined forces in response to abusive employment conditions in employers' homes and exploitative terms imposed by employment agencies.

According to Nadia Marín-Molina, executive director of the Workplace Project, employment agencies often charge domestic workers illegal application fees and illegally exorbitant agency placement fees and fail to abide by the

---

[512]Human Rights Watch telephone interview with Shabhano Aliani, co-founder and current volunteer and board member of Workers' Awaaz, November 29, 1999.

[513]In 1997, an ACLU attorney, Michael Wishnie, reached a settlement in Workers' Awaaz's first court case filed against an exploitative employer, obtaining $20,000 in back pay for the domestic worker. See Shattuck, "Nahar Alam. . . ."

[514]Ibid.

[515]The Workplace Project is a not-for-profit organization that uses grassroots organizing, legal action, and community education to seek just working conditions for Latino immigrants on Long Island. Lucia Hwang, "Workplace Project Helps Latino Laborers Help Themselves," *Newsday*, October 12, 1998, p. 27; Robert Gearty, "Fighting for Workers' Rights," *New York Daily News*, August 2, 1998, p. 2.

[516]Human Rights Watch telephone interview with Nadia-Marín Molina, executive director, Workplace Project, November 22, 1999.

minimum wage and hour terms of the Fair Labor Standards Act.[517] Marín-Molina described to Human Rights Watch the case of one domestic worker who sought the assistance of the Workplace Project after being forced by her employment agency to clean eleven homes in one day, from 6:00 a.m. until 10:00 p.m., for which she received $50.[518] The goal of the cooperative is to ensure that the domestic workers receive a fair wage, undertake only legitimate housecleaning tasks, and have input with regard to when and for whom they labor.[519]

According to Marín-Molina, the domestic workers "did not see the promise of organizing" because they "feared blacklisting and retaliation" from their employment agencies if they became workers "known to cause problems"[520] Marín-Molina noted that through the cooperative, the domestic workers have developed an indirect means of organizing against employment agencies by creating other employment alternatives.[521]   But as long as these workers are excluded from coverage by laws protecting their right to organize, their efforts can only affect conditions for that tiny percentage of domestics who manage to bypass the temporary agencies and day labor employers.

Independent Contractors

The 1947 Taft-Hartley Act added exclusions of independent contractors and supervisors to the 1935 Wagner Act's exclusion of agricultural and domestic workers. Under the Taft-Hartley exclusions, employers can appear to delegate a degree of autonomy to employees that they wish to transform into "independent contractors, restructuring their pay as "miscellaneous income" rather than taxable wages. Such maneuvering allows employers to escape many legal and financial obligations—Social Security and other payroll taxes, workers' compensation liability, minimum wage and overtime requirements, and others. Employers can also deny contractors the health insurance, pensions and other benefits that are available to employees.

Not least, employers become free to fire workers classified as independent contractors with legal impunity if they seek to organize. They can also refuse to

---

[517]*See* Katti Gray, "A United Front: A year-old co-op strives to give Hispanic maids a voice in their workplace," *Newsday*, September 21, 1999, p. B6; Ramirez, "Adding Injury to Insult ."

[518]Human Rights Watch Marín-Molina interview.

[519]Ibid.

[520]Ibid.

[521]Ibid.

bargain with workers, even a majority, who are seen as contractors rather than employees.[522]

Congressional and administrative hearings have produced evidence that many employers deliberately misclassify workers as independent contractors, confident that fear of lost income and the stress of legal action will prevent workers from challenging the decision.[523] One study estimated that the number of misclassified workers will exceed five million by the year 2005.[524] But U.S. labor law still rests on a model of workers holding permanent jobs with a single employer, rather than adapting to new systems of contracting and subcontracting business relationships.

The Dunlop Commission's 1994 report cited earlier noted what it called "abuses and trends" associated with contracting out for labor:[525]

- Many public and private employers have subcontracted activities to enterprises that use the same workers part-time performing the same tasks at lower benefits and wage rates.

- In trucking, agriculture, and construction the device of owner-operator has expanded rapidly.[526]

- Homework and subcontracting have expanded in a number of sewing industries.

---

[522]See *Dial-A-Mattress Operating Corporation,* 326 NLRB No. 75 (1998).

[523]See *Independent Contractor Status: Hearing Before the House Comm. on Small Business,* 104th Cong. (1995); Testimony of David F. Stobaugh, "An Employee By Another Name Is Still An Employee," U.S. Department of Labor, ERISA Advisory Council on Employee Welfare and Pension Benefit Plans, September 8, 1999 (on file with Human Rights Watch).

[524] Ibid., containing Coopers & Lybrand, *Projection of the Loss in Federal Tax Revenues Due to Misclassification of Workers* (1994), pp. 58-59.

[525]See U.S. Department of Labor, U.S. Department of Commerce, Commission on the Future of Worker-Management Relations, *Fact Finding Report* (May 1994), pp. 93-94.

[526]This refers to the practice whereby an employer terminates the employment relationship and requires workers to become self-employed operators performing the same work as previously, but bearing all the costs and risks of ownership. Workers must provide for their own health insurance, retirement benefits, etc., and are no longer allowed to form and join a union. If such "owner-operators" form an association to seek better wages and conditions, they can be prosecuted under anti-trust laws.

- These developments at times result in the avoidance of Social Security taxes, workers' compensation, unemployment insurance and benefits such as health insurance and pensions.

- These arrangements often attract new immigrants, minorities and women in the labor force who have few options.

Misclassification of workers as independent contractors and the resulting legal impediments to freedom of association run the length and depth of the economy. In some cities, building owners have subcontracted cleaning operations to businesses that then turn around and franchise parts of the work to different groups of workers, often those in ethnic immigrant enclaves. As franchisees, these workers are considered independent contractors who cannot bargain for better terms and conditions.[527]

Many limousine and taxicab drivers are defined as independent contractors, even though they work full-time (indeed, often excessive hours) for a taxi company that owns the medallion or charter, the cars, the dispatching system, and other attributes of an employer. As independent contractors, taxi drivers are excluded from coverage by labor laws that are supposed to protect the right to organize. If they try to form and join a union, they can be fired with impunity by the taxicab company.[528]

Equally vulnerable are truck drivers who transport cargo from the nation's shipping ports to nearby warehouses for transfer to long-haul delivery trucks. Some 50,000 workers perform this labor. These workers used to be union employees making good wages, benefits and pensions before the deregulation of the trucking industry in the late 1970s. Nearly all of them are now reclassified as independent contractors rather than employees of the cargo firms, even though they are still completely dependent on those firms for their work and their pay. They are paid by the load and often spend hours of unpaid time waiting for cargo to be loaded onto their trucks. As one leading industry periodical puts it, port truck drivers "are the collective low man on the [trucking] industry totem pole."[529]

Many of these workers are immigrants who scrape together enough money to buy a truck and haul goods from the dock to the warehouse. They often have to do their own loading and unloading. Many say that when they settle accounts for

---

[527]Commission Report., p. 93; see also Evelyn Iritani, "Franchise Hopes Turn to Frustration," *Seattle Post-Intelligencer*, November 19, 1991, p. A1.

[528]See Daphne Eviatar, "Trying to Drive Home Their Point: Workers Complain of Unfair Conditions," *New York Newsday*, December 12, 1999, p. A3.

[529]See "Organizing Drivers," editorial, *Journal of Commerce*, October 25, 1999.

expenses, income from the cargo firms, and time spent on the job, they earn barely more than the minimum wage.[530]   One researcher found that "most non-union truckload employees give away their loading and unloading time and waste many unpaid hours—even unpaid days—waiting to load or unload, waiting for dispatch, and waiting on equipment."[531] As one worker put it, "We are like slaves. We are like slaves to the big companies."[532]

While these workers are classified as independent contractors exempt from labor law coverage, many of them in fact have to sign exclusive contracts with trucking firms prohibiting them from selling their services to higher bidders. When companies shift employees to independent contractor status, workers are suddenly more vulnerable to costs they did not face before. For example, truck drivers injured on the job used to be covered by workers' compensation protection as employees. But as independent contractors, they must carry their own insurance, a benefit many forego as too expensive. Meanwhile, trucking firms escape any obligations to maintain workers' compensation insurance for injured drivers.[533]

Cargo firms have reacted to truckers' efforts to improve pay and conditions by renewed organizing and bargaining with refusals to bargain, blacklisting, and discrimination against organizing leaders. Excluded from coverage by the NLRA, these workers have no recourse. Employers even threaten to sue the workers under antitrust laws, accusing them of price-fixing for their services.[534]

Supervisors

In the Taft-Hartley Act of 1947, Congress also added supervisors to the list of workers excluded from protection of the right to organize and bargain

---

[530]See Stuart Silverstein and Jeff Leeds, "Independent Truckers, Union Form a Convoy: A high-stakes, long-shot campaign to organize would, if successful, write a new page in labor history, but many roadblocks remain," *Los Angeles Times*, May 11, 1996, p. D1 (hereafter "Convoy").

[531]See Michael H. Belzer, "Paying the Toll: Economic Deregulation of the Trucking Industry" (Washington, D.C., Economic Policy Institute 1994), p. 1. Belzer points out that such practices "contribute to inefficiency and low productivity, since the carriers who employ these low-cost workers have little incentive to improve their management practices (Ibid).

[532]Quoted in Patrick Harrington, "18 Wheels, $7 an Hour," *Seattle Times*, May 23, 1999, p. 1.

[533]See, for example, Stuart Silverstein, "Undaunted by Setbacks, Truckers Look to Union: Drivers' struggle to organize reflects passion, problems of Southland immigrant workers." *Los Angeles Times*, February 17, 1997, p. A1.

[534]See Silverstein and Leeds, "Convoy."

collectively. Overseeing even a small portion of just one other employee's time is sufficient to establish supervisory status and exclude a worker from labor law protection.[535]

Defenders of the new exclusion argued that employees with disciplinary authority over other workers must owe total allegiance to the employer; otherwise, an untenable conflict of interest would result. Critics have responded that the exclusion of supervisors, especially low-level supervisors who themselves often suffer low pay and poor working conditions, is part of a "divide-and-conquer" strategy to weaken workers' bargaining power.[536]

The supervisory exclusion has had notable impact on workers' freedom of association in the burgeoning health care sector. In an important 1994 decision, the Supreme Court ruled that licensed practical nurses (LPNs) who oversee the work of nurses' aides are supervisors and are unprotected by the NLRA.[537] Under the court's ruling, the LPNs could be fired with impunity for protesting their working conditions or seeking to form and join a union.

Nearly one million workers in the United States are LPNs. They are on the bottom rung of the nursing ladder, just above nurses' aides. They are themselves often low-paid, overloaded with patients, and burdened with long hours. These working conditions might be improved through self-organization and collective bargaining. However, health care employers can use the Supreme Court's decision to block LPN organizing and organizing by other health care workers. With an intricate system of state-based licensing of nurses, aides, therapists, technicians and other workers in various grades and classifications defining specific tasks that workers are allowed to perform or prohibited from performing, the health care industry is in a position to create layers of supervisory responsibility that can frustrate and delay workers' organizing efforts.[538]

---

[535]See *New Jersey Famous Amos Chocolate Chip Cookie Corp.*, 236 NLRB 1093 (1978).

[536]See, for example, George Feldman, *Workplace Power and Collective Activity: The Supervisory and Managerial Exclusions in Labor Law*, 37 Arizona Law Review 525 (1995).

[537]See *NLRB v. Health Care & Retirement Corp. of America*, 114 S. Ct. 1778 (1994); Peter Blackman, "Challenge to Labor: Employers Hope to Capitalize on High Court ruling," *New York Law Journal*, August 18, 1994, p. 5.

[538]Bargaining unit controversies have affected worker organizing in the health care field for many years. For an extensive description and analysis of these problems based on empirical research supported by the W.E. Upjohn Institute, see Michael H. LeRoy, Joshua L. Schwarz and Karen S. Koziara, "The Law and Economics of Collective Bargaining for Hospitals: An Empirical Public Policy Analysis of Bargaining Unit Determinations," 9 *Yale Journal of Regulation* 1 (Winter 1992).

Issues arising under the Supreme Court's decision continue to generate litigation and controversy. In an effort to protect nurses who seek to exercise the right to organize, the NLRB has sought to apply *Health Care & Retirement Corp.* narrowly, not applying the decision against nurses' whose supervisory duties are incidental. Some courts of appeals have supported the board's approach.[539] Other circuit courts are unsympathetic and continue to exclude nurses from coverage by the NLRA if they perform any supervisory function. In one recent decision, a federal appeals court overruled the NLRB and nullified an election in which a group of nurses voted 17-4 in favor of representation. The court said that thirteen of the nurses were supervisors.[540]

Managers

In 1974, the Supreme Court expanded the supervisory exclusion in the NLRA to include "managers." In *NLRB v. Bell Aerospace*, the court found that a group of buyers in the company's purchasing and procurement department were managers excluded from the NLRA's protection. The buyers had no supervisory responsibility and did not manage the enterprise in the common-sense meaning normally associated with "management." However, the court said that they "effectuate management policies" and were thus unprotected by the law.[541]

The Supreme Court used similar logic to define university faculty members in private universities as managers because of their collegial governance of academic life.[542] Although college professors have issues of pay, benefits, workload, fair treatment and other working conditions like any employed persons, some 300,000 of them lack any protection under labor law when they seek to act collectively to address the problems. And even if some professors might be protected by tenure rules from dismissal for organizing, a university administration can rebuff requests by a faculty organization to negotiate over terms and conditions of employment.

Other Exclusions

Tens of thousands of workers employed at Indian gambling casinos—and likely soon hundreds of thousands, given such casinos' rate of growth—are excluded from NLRB protection. These workers are not excluded because they

---

[539]See NLRB, "Guideline Memorandum on Charge Nurse Supervisory Issues," Memorandum OM-99-44, August 24, 1999); *NLRB v. GranCare Inc.*, No. 97-3431 (7th Cir., March 3, 1999).

[540]See *Schnurmacher Nursing Home v. NLRB*, 2d Cir., No. 98-4388 (l), June 6, 2000.

[541]See *NLRB v. Bell Aerospace Co.*, 416 U.S. 267 (1974)

[542]See *NLRB v. Yeshiva University*, 444 U.S. 672 (1980).

meet the "employee" exclusion but because their employers, sovereign Indian nations, are excluded from NLRA jurisdiction under Section 2 as a "political subdivision."[543] Based on a Supreme Court ruling interpreting the law, tens of thousands of employees of religious institutions are also excluded from protection, even those whose work has no relation to the religious mission of their institutions.[544] Tens of thousands of teaching assistants in universities are also excluded from protection of the right to freedom of association, based on the argument that they are students, not workers, even though they confront workers' problems like salaries, benefits, hours of work, treatment by managers, etc.[545]

Public Employees

Under international standards, the rights afforded "everyone" or "workers without distinction" apply to most public employees, too. International instruments make limited exceptions, mainly affecting police and military forces and government policymakers. The ICCPR's Article 22, for example, says "[t]his article shall not prevent the imposition of lawful restrictions on members of the armed forces and of the police in the exercise of this right."[546] The ICESCR makes the same exception, and adds "[members] . . . of the administration of the state."[547] ILO Convention 98 says "[t]his Convention does not deal with the position of public servants engaged in the administration of the State."[548]

These latter exceptions have been taken to apply to higher-level political appointees, not rank-and-file civil servants. Thus, most public employees come within international human rights standards for organizing and bargaining collectively. Not so under U.S. law. In this respect, the United States stands apart

---

[543]For a thorough history and analysis of the issue of tribal employers' exclusion from the NLRA, see Helen M. Kemp, "Fallen Timber: A Proposal for the National Labor Relations Board to Assert Jurisdiction over Indian-Controlled Businesses on Tribal Reservations," 17 *Western New England Law Review* 1 (1995).

[544]See *NLRB v. Catholic Bishop of Chicago*, 440 U.S. 490 (1979).

[545]See *Leland Stanford, Jr. University*, 214 NLRB 621 (1974). The NLRB is reconsidering the Stanford rule excluding graduate teaching assistants from the NLRA's protection, but has not made a final determination to change it. See NLRB Decision and Order, *Yale University and Graduate Employees and Students Organization (GESO)*, Case 34-CA-7347 (November 29, 1999; Courtney Leatherman, "Decision in Yale Case Leaves Graduate Students and University Both Claiming Victory," *The Chronicle of Higher Education*, December 10, 1999, p. A20.

[546]ICCPR Article 22(2).

[547]ICESCR Article 8(2).

[548]ILO Convention 98, Article 6.

from other developed nations and affords less protection even than many poorer, developing countries.

In many U.S. states public employees are denied the right to bargain collectively. North Carolina law specifically prohibits collective bargaining between any state, county or municipal agency and any organization of governmental employees.[549] Although it created an exception for local fire and police departments, Texas law declares it to be against public policy for any other state, county or municipal officials to enter into a collective bargaining agreement with a labor organization.[550]

Virginia holds collective bargaining "contrary to the public policy of Virginia." Indeed, the state Supreme Court ordered a local school board to renounce an agreement with a teachers' organization, something the teachers and the school board had willingly, voluntarily undertaken together.[551] Federal government employees, while allowed to form unions, are denied the right to bargain collectively over salaries and benefits. They may only bargain over non-economic terms and conditions.[552]

Public employees enjoy a type of protection against dismissal for associational activities not available to private sector workers. The First and Fourteenth Amendments of the U.S. Constitution protect public employees' right of association.[553] Civil service rules also guard against arbitrary or unjust dismissals. The problem for public workers in states where collective bargaining is prohibited is not so much fear of dismissal for organizing but the futility of an effort to organize. The employer—the state, county, or municipal government—can simply ignore them and their organization.

Public employee unions have had to deal with the roadblock to collective bargaining by engaging in political action—in effect, bargaining with state legislatures. Some have achieved substantial results, and some are still struggling,

---

[549]See N.C. General Statutes §§95-98 (1985). The constitutionality of this provision was upheld in *Winston-Salem/Forsyth County Unit of N.C. Association of Educators v. Phillips*, 381 F.Supp. 644 (M.D.N.C. 1974). Another provision barring government workers from joining any labor organization was ruled unconstitutional. See *Atkins v. City of Charlotte*, 296 F. Supp. 1068 (W.D.N.C. 1969).

[550]See Texas Statutes Annotated, Art. 5154c (Vernon 1971).

[551]See *Commonwealth of Virginia v. County Board of Arlington County*, 217 Va. 558 (1977).

[552]See prohibited subjects of bargaining, 5 U.S.C. 7106(a).

[553]It must be kept in mind that constitutional guarantees run to government action, not private action. Since a governmental entity is the employer of public employee, it must respect their freedom of association under the Constitution. The First and Fourteenth Amendments are not applicable to private employers.

according to public employee representatives. Much depends on the outcome of elections to state and local office. However, from a human rights perspective, the exercise and protection of fundamental rights should not depend on election results. Respect for workers' rights should be constant, not changing with political winds.

The ILO's Committee on Freedom of Association considered a complaint against the United States involving the many restrictions on public employees' rights to organize and to bargain collectively. The Committee rejected U.S. government arguments that "white collar" employees are "engaged in the administration of the State" and urged the United States to bring its laws regarding federal employees into conformance with Conventions 87 and 98. For state, country and municipal workers whose rights are frustrated, the ILO found that "the situation varies widely between jurisdictions . . . where the legal framework for collective bargaining appears to be reasonably appropriate" and " those states that have no public sector collective bargaining legislation . . . or that ban it completely."[554] The Committee called on the United States "to draw the attention of the authorities concerned, and in particular in those jurisdictions where public servants are totally or substantially deprived of collective bargaining rights, to the principle that all public service workers other than those engaged in the administration of the State should enjoy such rights."[555]

* * * * *

A precise count of workers excluded from labor laws protecting one or more of the elements of the right to freedom of association—the right to organize, the right to bargain collectively, and the right to strike—is impossible to provide. But cumulatively, millions of workers in the United States are affected. They include approximately three million farmworkers, one million domestic employees, many of seven million independent contractors, four million supervisors, and ten million managers; 300,000 college professors, 100,000 Indian casino employees, 500,000 employees of religious institutions, millions of public employees—the list goes on.[556]

Within each category, fine distinctions would have to be made to quantify precisely who is excluded under the statute, who is excluded under judicial decisions, and who is excluded because of misclassification. In practice, these

---

[554]See ILO Committee on Freedom of Association, "Complaints Against the Government of the United States of America Presented by the AFL-CIO and Public Services International (PSI)," Case No. 1557, 76 (Series B) ILO Official bulletin, No. 3 at 99, 110-11 (1993).
[555]Ibid.
[556]These estimates are based on an analysis of Bureau of Labor Statistics data for 1997.

issues are resolved in lengthy, complicated proceedings before the NLRB and the federal courts, with attendant delays and frustration of workers' organizing efforts.

Many employees labeled "managers" do not in practice have genuine managerial functions and may desire protection like other workers. Many so-called independent contractors are really dependent contractors with their fate tied to a single employer whose own viability depends on the effort and productivity of these workers. Even after allowing for appropriately excluded categories—true managers and true independent contractors, for example— millions of workers remain exposed under U.S. labor laws to discrimination, dismissal, or other reprisals if they try to organize around basic issues of livelihood and working conditions by exercising the right to freedom of association and related rights to organize, to bargain, and to strike.

Colorado Steelworkers, the Right to Strike and Permanent Replacements in U.S. Labor Law

U.S. labor law lets employers permanently replace workers who exercise the right to strike and allows replacement workers then to vote the union out of existence. No issue arouses as much passion among workers committed to trade unionism. "Just driving around town I look for out-of-state license plates, and I hate that person," a steelworker permanently replaced after nearly thirty years' service in a plant told Human Rights Watch. "I figure he's a replacement worker who took my job."[557] A replaced paperworker said, "I still harbor intense hatred for the scabs that descended like rats to steal our jobs . . . I will take that hatred to my grave."[558]

International human rights and labor rights instruments treat the right to strike in a more nuanced and conditional fashion than the right to organize. Workers must be afforded full freedom to form and join their own organizations. That is really their own affair. But exercising the right to strike implicates other societal interests. Among basic human rights documents, only the International Covenant on Economic, Social and Cultural Rights contains a clause on the right to strike, with the proviso that it be exercised "in conformity with the laws of the particular country."[559]

---

[557]Human Rights Watch interview with CF&I worker Joel Buchanan, Pueblo, Colorado, May 20, 1999.

[558]Cited in Julius Getman, *The Betrayal of Local 14* (Ithaca, New York, Cornell University Press, 1998), p. 215 (hereafter Getman, the *Betrayal of Local 14*). The epithet "scab" for someone who takes the job of a worker on strike is still deeply rooted in workers' language, and has evoked powerful literary portrayals as well.

[559]ICESCR, Article 8 (4).

Among regional human rights and labor rights bodies, the European Social Charter of 1961 was the first express authorization in an international human rights instrument of the right to strike. That clause stated "It is understood that each Contracting Party may, insofar as it is concerned, regulate the exercise of the right to strike by law, provided that any further restriction that this might place on the right can be justified under the terms of Article 31."[560] Article 31 contains a proviso common to many international instruments limiting restrictions on the exercise of specified rights to those "necessary in a democratic society for the protection of the rights and freedoms of others or for the protection of public interest, national security, public health, or morals."[561]

The European Union's Community Charter of the Fundamental Social Rights of Workers states that "[t]he right to resort to collective action in the event of a conflict of interests shall include the right to strike, subject to the obligations arising under national regulations and collective agreements."[562] In Labor Principle 3 of the North American Agreement on Labor Cooperation, the United States and its two NAFTA partners committed themselves to respect the right to strike, defined as "the protection of the right of workers to strike in order to defend their collective interests," without further qualification.[563] These regional statements on the right to strike are not binding instruments that supersede national laws, but they express the political will of the countries and reflect at the international level respect for workers' right to strike.

The right to strike is not expressly mentioned in ILO Conventions 87 and 98 or any other ILO convention. But the right to strike has been carefully considered by the ILO's Committee on Freedom of Association and other supervisory bodies for many decades and is now firmly established by the ILO as an essential element of freedom of association. The general principle is that "the right to strike is an intrinsic corollary of the right of association protected by Convention No. 87."[564]

The ILO recognizes that the right to strike is not an absolute right. It has determined that the right to strike is a legitimate means to defend workers' interests

---

[560]Council of Europe, European Social Charter (1961), Article 6, paragraph 4 and Appendix.
[561]Ibid., Article 31 (1).
[562]See Maastricht Treaty on European Union, Protocol and Agreement on Social Policy, Feb. 7, 1992, 31 LL.M. 247, paragraph 13 under "Freedom of association and collective bargaining."
[563]North American Agreement on Labor Cooperation, Annex 1, Labor Principle 3.
[564]See ILO, *Freedom of association and collective bargaining: General survey of the reports on the Freedom of Association and the Right to Organise Convention (No. 87), 1948, and the Right to Organise and Collective Bargaining Convention (no. 98), 1949*, paragraph 194 (1994).

and that a general prohibition on strikes unduly restricts the right.[565] A general prohibition may be justified in a situation of acute national crisis, but only for a limited period and to the extent necessary to meet the requirements of the situation. This means genuine crisis situations such as those arising from serious conflict or natural disasters in which the normal conditions for the functioning of society are absent.[566]

The committee has articulated the view that the right to strike must be protected and should only be restricted as to military and police forces and in cases which involve essential services or public services implicating public health and safety. Even then, there must be adequate safeguards for workers such as impartial and speedy conciliation and arbitration procedures.[567] The ILO has further established that dismissals of strikers on a large scale involve serious risks of abuse and place freedom of association in grave jeopardy.[568] These principles are now taken to be essential elements of Conventions 87 and 98 binding, like the conventions themselves, on countries that have not ratified them, including the United States.[569]

In a 1991 report on a complaint against the United States filed by the AFL-CIO on the permanent-replacement doctrine in U.S. law, the ILO Committee on Freedom of Association concluded:

> The right to strike is one of the essential means through which workers and their organisations may promote and defend their economic and social interests. The Committee considers that this basic right is not really guaranteed when a worker who exercises it legally runs the risk of seeing his or her job taken up permanently by another worker, just as legally. The Committee considers that, if a strike is otherwise legal, the

---

[565]See ILO, Freedom of Association: Digest of Decisions of the Freedom of Association Committee of the Governing Body of the ILO, Geneva (1996); Report of the Committee of Experts, Vol. 4B, Chapter V (1994).

[566]Ibid., paragraph 152. For a broader discussion of this and other aspects of freedom of association, see Lee Swepston, "Human rights law and freedom of association: Development through ILO supervision," 137 International Labour Review 169 (1998); see also Hodges-Aeberhard and Odero de Diós, "Principles of the Committee of Association concerning Strikes," 126 International Labour Review 544 (1987).

[567]See Ruth Ben-Israel, International Labor Standards: the Case of the Freedom to Strike (Antwerp, Kluwer Publishers, 1988), p.104.

[568]ILO General Survey (1994), paragraphs 176-178; Digest of Decisions (1996), paragraphs 590-600.

[569]Ibid., pp. 66-70.

use of labour drawn from outside the undertaking to replace strikers for an indeterminate period entails a risk of derogation from the right to strike which may affect the free exercise of trade union rights.[570]

The committee's conclusion is formulated in soft diplomatic language. Under its mandate, it does not "level charges at, or condemn, governments."[571] But within this boundary, the ILO's committee on Freedom of Association clearly finds the U.S. permanent-replacement doctrine contrary to the free exercise of trade union rights.

Background: the MacKay Case

The permanent-replacement doctrine was elaborated by the Supreme Court in a 1938 decision not greatly noticed at the time or even for many years afterward.[572] Striker replacement was not the issue presented in the Mackay case. It was not among the issues briefed or argued by the parties. The case involved alleged discrimination in the company's refusal to reinstate strike leaders while reinstating other strikers. Indeed, the workers and their union *won* the Mackay case, with discrimination against the leaders found to be unlawful. In passing, however, the Supreme Court ruled, referring to Section 13 of the NLRA, that "an employer . . . is not bound to discharge those hired to fill the places of strikers, upon the election of the latter to resume their employment, in order to create places for them." It is on the basis of this "dicta"—the legal term for comments in a court decision not related to the formal holding in a case—that the entire structure of the permanent-replacement doctrine depends. It has never been codified in any statute or regulation, but subsequent court decisions have solidified the doctrine into an established element of U.S. labor law.

The permanent striker-replacement doctrine remained a relatively obscure feature of U.S. law until employers began wielding it more aggressively in the late 1970s and early 1980s. Many analysts attribute this development to President Ronald Reagan's firing and permanent replacement of air traffic controllers in 1981

---

[570]See International Labor Organization, Committee on Freedom of Association, *Complaint against the Government of the United States presented by the American Federation of Labor and Congress of Industrial Organizations (AFL-CIO)*, para. 92, Report No. 278, Case No. 1543 (1991).

[571]See ILO, "Procedure for the examination of complaints alleging infringements of trade union rights," at www.ilo.org/public/english/standards/norm/sources/cfa_proc.htm, paragraph 23.

[572]*NLRB v. Mackay Radio & Telegraph Co.*, 304 U.S. 333 (1938).

even though, as federal employees, controllers did not come under coverage of the NLRA and the MacKay rule. They were fired as a disciplinary measure under federal legislation barring strikes by federal employees. In fact, the use of permanent replacements began trending upward before Reagan's action.[573] But the air traffic controllers' case solidified the force of using permanent replacements to block workers' exercise of the right to strike.[574]

Unfair Labor Practice Strikes vs. Economic Strikes

The permanent-replacement doctrine makes a distinction between workers who strike over unfair labor practices committed by the employer and those who strike over economic terms and conditions of employment. So-called "unfair labor practice strikers" must be reinstated to their jobs when they end the strike. "Economic strikers," on the other hand, are unprotected. They can be permanently replaced.[575] And one year after their strike began, replacement workers can vote to decertify the union and extinguish all bargaining rights.

In practice, the distinction between an unfair labor practice strike and an economic strike fails to protect workers' right to strike. As the ILO Committee on Freedom of Association noted, "that distinction obfuscates the real issue . . . [of] whether United States labour law and jurisprudence (the so-called MacKay doctrine) are in conformity with the freedom of association principles."[576]

A practical problem in administering the distinction is that workers and employers only find out years after the strike took place, when an appeals court issues a final ruling, whether it was an unfair labor practice strike or an economic strike. Employers using permanent replacements always declare that workers' strikes are economic in motivation. Workers file unfair labor practice charges with the NLRB arguing that their strike was prompted by the employer's unfair labor practices. As the ILO noted in considering the U.S. permanent-replacement case, "a determination of unfair labour practice . . . may take several years until the last appeal option has been exhausted."[577] Ultimately, courts decide whether the workers were unfair labor practice strikers or economic strikers. But by then, even

---

[573]See Michael H. LeRoy, *Regulating Employer Use of Permanent Striker Replacements: Empirical Analysis of NLRA and RLA Strikes 1935-1991*, 16 Berkeley Journal of Employment and Labor Law 169 (1995).

[574]See Steven Greenhouse, "Strikes Decrease to 50-Year Low . . . as Threat of Replacement Rises," *New York Times*, January 29, 1996, p. A1.

[575]Strikers who are permanently replaced are put on a recall list and must be offered positions vacated by permanent replacements, if the latter quit or are dismissed.

[576]ILO Case No. 1543, para. 89.

[577]Ibid., para. 91.

with a decision in favor or the workers, the strike is often long broken and workers scattered to other jobs.

The Permanent Replacement Threat

The permanent-replacement doctrine is not used only against workers' exercise of the right to strike. Employers aggressively use the threat of permanent replacement in campaigns against workers' efforts to form and join a union and to bargain collectively. In every organizing drive examined by Human Rights Watch for this report, management raised the prospect of permanent replacement in written materials, in captive-audience meetings, and in one-on-one meetings where supervisors spoke with workers under their authority. At Cabana Chips in Detroit, for example, a company letter said that workers

> Can be permanently replaced if the strike is for economic reasons (a strike over wages, benefits, or working conditions) . . . Question: Do you mean that non-strikers could be hired to take my job in an economic strike? . . . Answer: YES. Federal law gives the company the right to hire permanent replacements to continue to serve our customers . . . Question: Isn't the company required to fire the replacements when the strike is over? . . . Answer: NO. The company is NOT required to fire the replacements by law. Strikers are only entitled to get their jobs back when and if openings occur.

Cabana management then reproduced a portion of the NLRB's Guide to Basic Law and Procedures underlining a sentence saying strikers can be replaced by their employer, then wrote below, *"Remember! 'But they can be replaced by their employer'"*[578] (all emphases in original).

In a similar vein, at Precision Thermoform and Packaging company in Baltimore, Maryland, management told employees in a letter that "the law provides that an employer can CONTINUE TO OPERATE AND HIRE NEW EMPLOYEES TO PERMANENTLY REPLACE THE EMPLOYEES WHO ARE OUT ON STRIKE. If this happens, as it frequently does, the replaced strikers have no jobs to go back to when the strike ends" (emphasis in original).[579]

---

[578]See letter to employees of January 7, 1999 from company president Ray Jenkins (on file with Human Rights Watch).
[579]See PTP "Dear Employee" letter, undated (October 1995), on file with Human Rights Watch.

Captive-audience meetings and one-on-one sessions with supervisors lay heavy stress on permanent replacements. "They kept talking about how they can get rid of us for good if we ever went on strike," said Robert Atkinson in an interview with Human Rights Watch describing captive-audience meetings at Smithfield Foods' Wilson, N.C. plant in July 1999.

The permanent replacement threat is not only raised in organizing. An industrial relations researcher found that management threatens permanent replacement during collective bargaining negotiations more often than unions threaten to strike.[580]

The United States is almost alone in the world in allowing permanent replacement of workers who exercise the right to strike. Some of the United States' key trading partners take a polar opposite approach. In Mexico, for example, federal law requires companies to cease operations during a legal strike. Permanent replacements are also prohibited throughout Canada. In Quebec, even temporary striker replacements are banned, and a company may only maintain operations using management and supervisory personnel. In most European countries the law is silent on the subject because permanent replacements are never used and the very idea of permanent replacement of strikers is considered outlandish.

Colorado Steelworkers

When we asked them to hire new people to give us some relief, they told us they couldn't find qualified workers anywhere in Colorado. But when we went out, suddenly they came up with hundreds of replacements.

—A steelworker permanently replaced when he exercised the right to strike

Along Interstate 25 in southeast Colorado, where the central plains meet the Rocky Mountains, the high smokestacks of Oregon Steel Mills' Pueblo plant loom into view as dramatically as Pike's Peak in the distance. Coloradans know the plant as "CF&I," recalling its origins as the Colorado Fuel & Iron company. CF&I began supplying Western coal and hard rock mining firms with steel products for construction, piping, and rail transport in the late nineteenth century.

South of Pueblo is Ludlow, Colorado, the site of an infamous August 1914 massacre of miners and family members, including eleven children, by mine owners' militiamen. The miners and their families had taken shelter in a tent city

---

[580]See Joel Cutcher-Gershenfeld, *The Social Contract at the Bargaining Table: Evidence from a National Survey of Labor and Management Negotiators*, Industrial Relations Research Association, Proceedings of the 51st Annual Meeting, Volume 2 (1999).

after mine operators, under orders from John D. Rockefeller, evicted them from company-owned housing when they went on strike in September 1913.[581]

Today another labor rights crisis besets the area. Oregon Steel permanently replaced more than 1,000 workers who exercised the right to strike in October 1997. Many of the replacements came from outside the Pueblo area, drawn by the company's newspaper advertisements throughout Colorado and neighboring states offering wages of $13-$19 per hour for permanent replacements. A company notice declared, "It is the intent of the Company for every replacement worker hired to mean one less job for the strikers at the conclusion of the strike."[582]

On December 30, 1997, three months after it began, Oregon Steel workers ended their strike and offered unconditionally to return to work. The company refused to take them back except when vacancies occur after a replacement worker leaves. Hundreds of Oregon Steel workers remained jobless two years later, when Human Rights Watch researched the case. The NLRB issued a complaint finding merit in the workers' claim that the strike was caused by management's unfair labor practices.[583]

The board's complaint was upheld by an administrative law judge after an eight-month-long hearing on the complaint that began in August 1998 and concluded in March 1999. More than a year after the hearing ended, the judge issued his decision in the case finding the company guilty of interference, coercion, discrimination and bad-faith bargaining.[584] But management has already vowed to resist the judge's findings and orders, promising years' more delay in the courts.

"How can the government and Congress allow companies to do this?" asks Lloyd Montiel, a twenty-seven-year veteran of the Oregon Steel plant. "They [the company] can plan a strike, cause a strike, and then get rid of people who gave them a lifetime of work and bring in young guys who never saw the inside of a steel mill."[585] "It should not be OK for the company to throw away loyal workers who

---

[581]See Pam Pemberton, "Ludlow Massacre remembered on 85th anniversary," *The Pueblo Chieftain*, April 18, 1999, p. 1.

[582]*See*, e.g., *Denver Post* classified advertising section, October 1, 1997; "Notice to Permanent Replacement Employees," Oregon Steel (notice distributed to replacement workers, 1997).

[583]See Order Consolidating Cases, Consolidated Complaint and Notice of Hearing, *New CF&I, Inc. And Oregon Steel Mills, Inc. and United Steelworkers of America*, Cases nos. 27-CA-15562; 27-CA-15750 (NLRB Region 27, June 30, 1998).

[584]See Decision of ALJ Albert A. Metz, *New CF&I, Inc. and Oregon Steel Mills, Inc. and United Steelworkers of America*, Cases 27-CA-15562 et. al., May 17, 2000.

[585]Human Rights Watch interview, May 20, 1999.

have given their lives and their health to the company," says Linda Friend, a registered nurse who cares for retired steel workers in Pueblo.[586]

Background to the Crisis

Much of the sprawling CF&I mill is silent now. Like many huge, integrated steel companies throughout the United States, the Pueblo plant has shrunk in size since the mid-century heyday of "Big Steel." New steel-making technology, trade competition, open-pit mining that uses trucks instead of rail, a focus on niche products rather than mass production, and other changes have reduced the workforce from over 10,000 in earlier decades to just over 1,000 when Human Rights Watch carried out research into this case.

Despite its smaller size, the Oregon Steel plant is still one of the largest area employers with important "multiplier" effects in the local and regional economy. It has traditionally afforded good wages and benefits to workers under collective bargaining agreements with two local unions of the United Steelworkers of America (USWA). CF&I workers formed their unions decades ago during large-scale organizing drives by the Congress of Industrial Organizations (CIO).

Oregon Steel bought CF&I in 1993 and now calls the facility Rocky Mountain Steel. In a 1993-1997 labor agreement, the USWA agreed to concessions that helped rescue the company from bankruptcy. With profitability restored, workers sought gains in new contract negotiations that began in mid-1997. Two key issues were pension benefits and retirement health insurance, always concerns for workers with long service in a company. With layoffs in previous years taking place by seniority, most of the workers remaining in 1997 were over forty-five years old, and many had well over twenty years of service with the company.

Another vital issue was mandatory overtime. Workers claimed that last-minute compulsory overtime disrupted family life and community involvement like youth league coaching. "I was a widow and a single parent for four and a half years because of forced overtime," said Jan Pacheco, the wife of steel worker Howard Pacheco. "I had to do everything with the house, the kids, their school, teams—everything."[587] Herb St. Clair, an employee with thirty-two years of seniority, said, "They pushed me to work seventy-two hours a week. My wife and I were strangers. When we complained, they told us, 'If you don't like it, go get a job at Wal-Mart.'"[588]

---

[586]Ibid.

[587]Human Rights Watch interview, May 20, 1999.

[588]Ibid.

Oregon Steel management viewed the workers' proposals as a "surprise" and "exorbitant."[589] Worker negotiators saw their pension proposal as one designed "to bring pensions at Oregon Steel up to a level common in the steel industry."[590]

These and other issues were unresolved when the strike began on October 3, 1997. But by that time, massive unfair labor practices had taken place during bargaining. According to the findings of a meticulously documented 111-page decision by the administrative law judge who heard evidence in the case, Oregon Steel management's unfair labor practices before the strike began included:[591]

- spying on a union meeting where bargaining strategies were discussed;

- threatening to close the plant if workers exercised the right to strike;

- threatening to revoke its contract offer if workers exercised the right to strike;

- threatening to close the plant and "reopen non-union in thirty days " if workers struck (as one supervisor said, "Well, I wish you guys would straighten this thing out because Joe's (Joe Corvin, President of Oregon Steel Mills) is going to shut this place down and bring it back nonunion");

- threatening to fire workers if they participated in a strike;

- assigning undesirable, dirty jobs cleaning arc furnaces and cooling towers to union supporters because of their support for the union;

- telling workers if they participated in a strike they would never work for Oregon Steel again (as one supervisor said, "I guaran-f---ing-tee you guys will never be hired back again");[592]

- threatening to "bust" the union if workers struck (as one witness testified, a supervisor said, "within 15 minutes they would have two bus loads of people in the mill to do our jobs and the union would no longer exist");

---

[589]See "Oregon Steel Mills—Chronology of Labor Dispute," company fact sheet (1998).
[590]See "The Rest of the Story," USWA response to company fact sheets (1998), on file with Human Rights Watch.
[591]See Metz decision, May 17, 2000.
[592]Oregon Steel unfair labor practice hearing transcript, pp. 795-796; Metz decision, p. 14.

- promising promotions to workers if they would not support the union during a strike;

- refusing to provide relevant information to the union on 401(k) and other retirement pay and benefit plans.

The judge further determined that after the strike began on October 3, 1997, Oregon Steel management launched a new round of unfair labor practices against workers:

- unlawfully hiring permanent replacements;

- unlawfully refusing to reinstate workers when they ended the strike;

- unlawfully denying workers access to loans from their 401(k) plans by imposing a new requirement that loan repayment must be through payroll deductions (obviously impossible if workers were on strike), when before the strike no such requirement was in place and workers could repay loans from bank accounts or by other payment methods;

- unlawfully revoking its contract proposal to the union after the strike began;

- unlawfully implementing its final offer without having bargained in good faith.

In all, said the judge, Oregon Steel's unfair labor practices "were substantial and antithetical to good faith bargaining."[593]

Even before the judge's ruling, Oregon Steel management had already declared it would not honor it. Company president Joe Corvin called the NLRB "one of the most political of federal agencies" and said "the federal courts will review the facts and law in this case and for that we are not only thankful, but

---

[593]Metz decision, May 17, 2000, p. 92. In a separate case unrelated to the issue of whether the strike is a "ULP" strike or an "economic" strike, the NLRB issued a complaint against the union for picket line misconduct including damage to replacement workers' automobiles. See Complaint, *United Steelworkers of America and its Locals 2102 and 3267 and New CF&I, Inc. and Oregon Steel Mills, Inc.*, 27-CB-3780 et.al. (1998). An administrative judge's decision in that case was pending. when this report went to press.

optimistic . . . [T]he NLRB complaint is just the first step in a lengthy process which will not be concluded for several years."[594]

When the judge's decision was issued, Oregon Steel refused to accept it.[595] "We're looking at years and years of hearings before there's any conclusion to this," declared a company spokesperson.[596] The spokesperson added, "The company will continue to operate as before the decision."[597] A company attorney said , "[T]his decision is no more a victory for the union than was the issuance of a complaint in the first place or the beginning of the trial."[598]

It can indeed take several years for the labor board and the courts to establish that Oregon Steel committed unfair labor practices requiring workers' reinstatement, as the administrative judge ruled, rather than an economic strike allowing management to permanently replace them. In the meantime, union and company attorneys, NLRB staffers, Oregon Steel managers and hundreds of replacement workers are employed and making a living while hundreds of workers who exercised a right guaranteed under international human rights standards and under U.S. law have lost their jobs, lack medical insurance and pension contributions, and cannot provide for their families' welfare as they did before.

Joel Buchanan, a worker with twenty-nine years in the Oregon Steel plant, told Human Rights Watch, "I didn't know the company could do permanent replacements until we ended the strike and offered to go back [on December 30, 1998]. I know the union explained it, but it still didn't seem possible. Before the strike the company was pushing us for forced overtime. When we asked them to hire new people to give us some relief, they told us they couldn't find qualified workers anywhere in Colorado. But when we went out, suddenly they came up with hundreds of replacements."[599]

Conditions for replacement workers have come under scrutiny. Two workers have suffered fatal accidents since management replaced those who exercised the right to strike. Another worker lost both arms in a separate accident. The most

---

[594]See John Norton, "Oregon Steel chief underwhelmed by NLRB ruling," *The Pueblo Chieftain*, March 3, 1998, p. 1.

[595]See Jason Blevins, "Ruling favors steel strikers; Pueblo mill vows to fight decision," The Denver Post, May 20, 2000, p. C-1.

[596]See Erika Gonzales, "Judge's ruling on steel strikers doesn't end dispute: Pueblo operation was told to rehire workers, pay their back wages," Denver Rocky Mountain News, May 23, 2000, p. 3B.

[597]See Tripp Balz, "ALJ finds ULPs by Rocky Mountain Steel, calls for rehires of former strikers, back pay," BNA Daily Labor Report, May 24, 2000, p. A-2.

[598]Ibid.

[599]Human Rights Watch Interview, May 20, 1999.

recent fatality prompted an unprecedented plant-wide safety inspection by the federal Occupational Safety and Health Administration, which normally inspects only areas where a fatal accident occurred.[600]

One of the harshest results of the permanent-replacement doctrine is the breach it causes in the community. Human Rights Watch spoke with a group of Oregon Steel workers who articulated this phenomenon. Ken Louis, a twenty-nine years' service worker, said, "Permanent replacements are turning this city into an 'I hate my neighbor' attitude." Mike Rodriguez told Human Rights Watch, "Just driving around town I look for out-of-state license plates and I hate that person. I figure he's a replacement worker who took my job. I don't trust people the way I used to." Paul Cruz said, "My neighbor's grandson went in and took a job. I couldn't go to my neighbor's funeral when he died, knowing his grandson would be there." "It will take generations to repair the damage," said Jan Pacheco.[601]

Maine Paper Workers

In 1998, Julius Getman, a prominent labor law expert, published an exhaustive study of another major strike that featured permanent replacements. The strike and permanent replacement of workers at International Paper Company's Androscoggin Mill in Jay, Maine, showed the same dynamics of broken faith in the law and community ruptures. "I was naive," said Randy Berry of Local 14 of the United Paperworkers Union, whose members exercised the right to strike at International Paper in June 1987. "I figured as blatant as they were, the Labor Board would have to see our side."[602]

Commenting on the strike, legal analysts brought to life the stakes for workers who are permanently replaced:

> [F]or employees who may have spent twenty years with the company building up a stake of experience and seniority that can rarely be duplicated elsewhere, the stark reality is that if they do go on strike, they can be replaced by the company with people who in less than twenty minutes on the job gain permanent priority over the striking veterans. As the Jay paperworkers learned to their regret, the Supreme Court

---

[600]See Tripp Baltz, "OSHA Investigating Steel Mill Accident That Resulted in Replacement Worker's Death," *Daily Labor Report*, Bureau of National Affairs, March 1, 2000, p. A-11; John Norton, "OSHA Inspects Pueblo, Colo. Steel Mill after Second Fatal Accident," *The Pueblo Chieftain*, March 3, 2000, p.1.
[601]Ibid.
[602]See Getman, *The Betrayal of Local 14*, p. 45.

pictures a strike not as a protected right, but as a gamble with one's job—the most valuable asset that most employees possess.[603]

Within three months International Paper management permanently replaced 1,200 strikers. In October 1988, workers ended their strike, but permanent replacements remained on the job. Maurice Poulin, an International Paper worker whose grandfather, father, brothers and sons had worked at the plant, found it "unbelievable that a company would forget all this service of lifetimes and replace all of us with one swipe . . . It's almost like we had our own holocaust. . . ."[604] In local schools, physical confrontation and mutual taunting took place between the children of strikers and the children of replacement workers.[605]

Summing up the aftermath of the strike years later, a striker who lost his job after thirty-five years as a papermaker said, "I still harbor intense hatred for IP and the scabs that descended like rats to steal our jobs when we left the mill. I will take that hatred to my grave. There have been suicides, early deaths, divorces, alcoholism, broken families, lost homes, and who knows what else. Thank God there were no murders."[606]

Arizona Copper Miners

Another comprehensive, book-length treatment by Jonathan D. Rosenblum, then a journalist and later an attorney and advisor to the International Labor Organization, examined another use of permanent replacements by a major firm. This case is cited here because it was the first major strike broken under the permanent-replacement doctrine in the early 1980s, an action credited with emboldening other employers to permanently replace workers who exercise the right to strike.[607]

---

[603]See Paul Weiler and Guy Mundlak, "Economic Competitiveness and the Law, " 102 *Yale Law Journal* 1907, p. 1917.

[604]See Getman, *The Betrayal of Local 14*, p. 45.

[605]Ibid., p. 120.

[606]Ibid., p. 215.

[607]The earlier air traffic controllers' strike was broken by the Reagan administration's application of federal law forbidding strikes by public employees and did not fall within the scope of the permanent-replacement doctrine under the NLRA flowing from the 1938 Mackay Radio decision. However, the replacement of striking air traffic controllers has been widely noted for sending a "signal" of government approval of the use of permanent replacements. The action of Phelps-Dodge management was one of the first responses to the signal.

In June 1983 at Phelps-Dodge Corporation's copper mines in Morenci, Bisbee, Ajo and Douglas, Arizona, 1,200 miners belonging to the steelworkers union went on strike. In August, the company began hiring permanent replacements, protected by the mobilization of several hundred state troopers and national guardsmen. In an NLRB vote in October 1984, replacement workers decertified the union.

Rosenblum's account provides insights into the effects of the permanent-replacement doctrine both on workers' rights and on family and community ties. For example, one brother speaks about another who crossed the picket line: "When my dad ended up in the hospital, there we were—two sons in the same room—but we didn't talk to each other. At Christmas we would see my mom and stay on separate sides of the room. We were like strangers."[608] The brothers were reunited only when a third brother, a supervisor at the plant, was killed in a workplace accident attributed by workers to strikebreakers' inexperience.

Describing her reaction when a son-in-law took a job during the strike, a striker's mother said, "After our son-in-law went to work we never saw our daughter, never saw our grandkids, never saw our son-in-law. This is a very close-knit place. If we would see them in the J.C. Penney, they would run off. If I was in the meat department and she saw me, she would go to the vegetables so she wouldn't have to face me eye-to-eye."[609]

The dispute ran over to local churches. Most of the strikers were Mexican-American Catholics, and many of the replacements were Mormons. Striking workers charged that Mormon leaders were encouraging strikebreaking. Some Mormon church members confirmed that church leaders counseled going to work at Phelps-Dodge during the strike.[610]

A Catholic church had to establish two lines for communion, one for strikers and one for replacements. One woman left the church, telling the pastor she "couldn't understand how strikebreakers could come to church praying the same prayers and to the same God while taking away her husband's and her friends' jobs."[611] As an example of harsh sentiments, Rosenblum reports: "Entering and leaving the mine gate, the strikebreakers began a ritual of waving paychecks and flicking pennies at the strikers."[612] For their part, the strikers' cause was

---

[608]Ibid., p. 128.
[609]Ibid., p. 129.
[610]See "Church Strikebreaking Charged: LDS members contend they were urged to defy pickets," *Tucson Citizen*, May 24, 1984.
[611]See Rosenblum, *Copper Crucible*, p. 133.
[612]Ibid., p. 154.

undermined by an incident of a shot fired into a strikebreaker's home, wounding his three-year-old daughter.[613]

Jonathan Rosenblum's investigation of the Phelps-Dodge strike uncovered important information about possible unlawful conduct by management during the strike. However, it came too late to help the workers. In a 1986 decision, the NLRB appointed by President Reagan rejected appeals by the workers and ruled that they undertook an economic strike, not an unfair labor practice strike.

In a 1990 interview, company president Richard Moolick told Rosenblum that as of August 1983, "'I had decided to break the union.'" This is significant because Phelps-Dodge was under a continuing legal obligation in August 1983 to bargain in good faith with workers on issues giving rise to the strike. Moolick's admission of a decision to "break" the union when he was obligated to bargain with the union evinces an unlawful refusal to bargain in violation of Section 8(a)(5) of the NLRA.

In an interview shortly before his death, John Boland, who served as Phelps-Dodge's attorney in the strike, told Rosenblum, "'You must keep in mind that dear to the heart of Moolick was to get rid of the unions . . . I'm sure that the decisions by Moolick as the strike progressed were influenced by his long-range decision to obtain a union-free shop. In other words, if a decision is doubtful about 'do this or don't do this'—and the possibility of ultimately getting rid of the union was a factor anywhere in there—why that's the one he'd choose.'"[614]

Rosenblum quotes Moolick as telling him: "'I was born with the thought that you could walk through a picket line. Nobody can keep you out. You walk through.'"[615] Speaking of the union at Phelps-Dodge, he added, "'The first time I sat at a bargaining table there were some card-carrying commies on their side. To me it was an affront to sit across from a goddamned commie.'"[616]

Tangentially, Richard Moolick resurfaced in the Oregon Steel strike in Pueblo in 1999—fifteen years after the strike at Phelps-Dodge. Now retired, Moolick heads a mining museum in Leadville, Colorado. In an April 5, 1999 letter to Joe Corvin, the president of Oregon Steel, Moolick sought a $5,000 contribution to his museum. He supported his request by declaring, "In 1997 I supplied [Pueblo plant manager] Mike Buckentin with the game plan he used so successfully in combating the Steel Workers at CF&I in Pueblo." He added, "In 1983 I took on the Steelworkers coalition at the Phelps-Dodge properties in Arizona and Texas and

---

[613]Ibid., pp. 88-89. The crime was not solved, and no one was charged.
[614]Ibid, p. 194.
[615]Ibid, p. 59.
[616]Ibid.

was successful in breaking some 35 unions." Responding to the appeal, Oregon Steel contributed $5,000 to Moolick's museum.[617]

Workers in Other Major Strikes

The Phelps-Dodge, International Paper and Oregon Steel strikes are only three of many cases of national importance where the permanent-replacement doctrine was used to frustrate workers' exercise of the right to strike in recent years. More than 6,000 Greyhound Corporation bus drivers were permanently replaced in a 1990 strike.[618] In response to a United Auto Workers strike in 1992, Caterpillar Corporation threatened to bring in permanent replacements. Workers ended the strike. But the company's move also ended a thriving program of labor-management cooperation that had taken shape with gains for both parties. Years of unfair labor practice disputes and a poisoned atmosphere of labor-management relations have followed.[619]

In Charlotte, North Carolina, 1,450 workers were permanently replaced at the Continental General Tire factory in a 1998 strike. The company was owned by Continental AG, a German-based multinational corporation. When asked why he treats U.S. workers in ways he would never consider in Germany, CEO Bernd

---

[617]See Dennis DeMaio, "Union-busting plan in Pueblo exposed," *Colorado Labor Advocate*, August 27, 1999, p. 1. In the article, Oregon Steel spokesperson Vicki Tagliafico called Moolick's "game plan" reference "an overstatement" and justified the contribution to the museum as being a "good corporate citizen." Moolick himself blamed "a mole" for leaking the letter. As for the "game plan," Moolick said, "What I told [Buckentin] basically is what you can do and what you can't do. I told him what had worked for me effectively in the past."

[618]See Peter T. Kilborn, "Replacement Workers: Management's Big Gun," *New York Times*, March 13, 1990, p. A24; AP byline, "Strikers at Greyhound Feel Forgotten," *New York Times*, March 4, 1991, p. B7.

[619]See Peter T. Kilborn, "Caterpillar's Trump Card: Threat of Permanently Replacing Strikers Gave Company Big Advantage Against Union," *New York Times*, April 16, 1992, p. A1; Stephen Franklin, "No peace, no contract a year after Caterpillar standoff," *Chicago Tribune*, April 12, 1993, p. 1; Stephen Franklin, "Lessons from a labor-management war: class still not over in dispute at Caterpillar," *Chicago Tribune*, May 15, 1994, p. 1; Barry Bearak, "The Inside Strategy: Less Work and More Play at Cat; Workers stung by strike's bitter end try tactic of t-shirts, balloons and antics; Bosses answer with firings," *Los Angeles Times*, May 16, 1995, p. A1; Barry Bearak, "The Strike at Caterpillar: Staggered by Hits, Unions Need Ways to Regain Punch, Jobs: Balance of power tips to management, leaving workers feeling vulnerable in a cold new business world," *Los Angeles Times*, May 18, 1995, p. A1.

Frangenberg declared, "It's a different culture with different relationships. This country is different. The labor laws are different."[620]

Indeed, the United States is practically alone in the world with its permanent striker replacement policy, despite growing sentiment in favor of changing this aspect of U.S. labor law. In 1991, for example, the House of Representatives passed legislation to prohibit the hiring of permanent replacements in most strike situations. A companion bill in the Senate gathered majority support, but fell under the weight of a filibuster. The Clinton administration in 1995 issued an executive order authorizing denial of federal contracts to firms that permanently replaced economic strikers.[621] A federal appeals court struck down the order for exceeding the executive's authority, concluding that it "is pre-empted by the NLRA which guarantees the right to hire permanent replacements."[622]

Human Rights Implications

The Oregon Steel case and others like it, where workers are permanently replaced when they exercise the right to strike, embody a fundamental breach of the principle of freedom of association and the related right to strike. The *permanence* in what the ILO diplomatically calls "the use of labour drawn from outside the undertaking to replace strikers for an indeterminate period" contravenes international labor rights principles, with its inherently aggressive, intimidating use both against workers who face replacement and as a threat against all workers seeking to exercise rights of association, organizing, and bargaining.

Workers' freedom of association does not abide abstractly in human rights instruments or national laws. Exercising the right only has meaning in a real world of sometimes converging, sometimes clashing interests among workers, employers, governments and other forces in society. Where workers have formed a union, exercise of the right to freedom of association is not static or episodic. It is rooted in a relationship over time between two parties. The relationship includes the possibility of occasional strikes by workers or lockouts by management.

The exercise of economic strength by workers or employers to back up proposals in bargaining is a normal, natural, and accepted right of unions and management. The anticipated sacrifice and pain of economic action propel parties toward compromise. This is why most labor negotiations end in a settlement without a strike.

---

[620]See "Tire chief talks tough on wages," *Charlotte Observer*, January 21, 1999; "Continental General Tire Co. to hire replacement workers," *The Buffalo News*, November 16, 1998, p. 1B.
[621]See Executive Order No. 12,954, 60 Federal Register 13,023 (1995).
[622]See Chamber of Commerce v. Reich, 74 F.3d 1322 (D.C. Cir., 1996).

As noted earlier, employers have many options for continuing operations during a strike. Most obviously, in addition to using managers and supervisors to maintain activity, employers can hire *temporary* replacements. Indeed, most strikes that include the use of replacement workers involve temporary, not permanent replacements, and strikes with temporary replacements are shorter in duration than those with permanent replacements.[623]

A collective bargaining relationship is not indissoluble. Companies close facilities. Workers sometimes choose to substitute a new union for one they are dissatisfied with, or to decertify a union altogether. But as a rule the collective bargaining relationship is a sustained one. Parties in this relationship accept that in the course of collective bargaining they might resort to economic action through a strike or lockout—a realization that creates a powerful force for resolving their differences through mutual agreement.

This basis for coexistence and compromise is recognized as beneficial to the parties and beneficial to society, compared with the alternatives of government control or of unilateral employer power to set employment terms when workers desire representation.[624] But this basis of mutuality is destroyed when employers can seize on workers' exercise of the right to strike as an opportunity to permanently take away their jobs. Workers' exercise of the right to freedom of association and related rights to organize, to bargain collectively and to strike can only be upheld when a balance of rights and interests is forged. Permanent replacement crosses the line by creating an imbalance between the rights of the conflicting parties.

Worker Solidarity and Secondary Boycotts

Workers' right to freedom of association is not limited to the single workplace. They often seek to associate with other workers of the same employer. For example, members of the automobile workers' union have formed a single organization to bargain with large nationwide companies like Ford Motor Co. and General Motors Corp. Members of several different unions—electrical workers, auto workers, steel workers and others—have banded together to bargain with General Electric Co. Beyond that, workers sometimes come together to deal with coalitions of employers, as hospital workers in New York bargain with a single employers' group representing several hospitals.

---

[623]See, e.g., John F. Schnell and Cynthia L. Gramm, "The Empirical Relations Between Employers' Striker Replacement Strategies and Strike Duration," 47 *Industrial and Labor Relations Review* 189 (1994).

[624]The NLRA declares "the policy of the United States" as one "encouraging the practice and procedure of collective bargaining." See 29 U.S.C. § 151.

Such company-wide or industry-wide bargaining relationships are legal under U.S. law. But the situation changes dramatically—in sharp contrast to workers' rights in other countries and contrary to international labor rights norms—when workers seek to associate with employees in other companies with which their employer has a supplier or customer relationship. What workers see as solidarity, U.S. labor law defines as illegal "secondary boycotts."[625]

Freedom of association among workers of different employers, seen as labor solidarity by worker advocates, is severely restricted under U.S. law. Before the ban on secondary boycotts was enacted in 1947, workers could request help from counterparts at other companies. That is, workers involved in a dispute with a "primary" employer could ask workers at "secondary" employers to press their own (secondary) company to curtail business with the primary firm. Now such appeals are prohibited.

A secondary company that continues doing business like selling or purchasing goods and services from a primary firm involved in a labor dispute is helping that primary firm to prevail in the dispute with its workers. However, primary firm workers involved in a labor dispute are not permitted correspondingly to seek help from workers at the secondary company. Moreover, workers at the secondary company may not take action of their own volition to help workers in the primary dispute. Among workers, both appealing for help and offering help are strictly prohibited, while employers can continue doing business with each other as if no dispute existed.

The ban on workers' solidarity is backed up by strict, mandatory injunction requirements and punitive sanctions. These sanctions are harsher than any visited on employers for violating workers' rights, and they are more aggressively enforced.

Under Section 10(l) of the NLRA, the NLRB must seek an immediate injunction to halt an appeal, an offer, or an act of secondary action. Workers' organizations are liable for payment of financial damages for a company's economic losses due to solidarity action.

In contrast to mandatory injunctions against workers' solidarity under Section 10(l), Section 10(j) of the NLRA authorizes only discretionary seeking of injunctions to halt employers' unfair labor practices like firing worker leaders or refusing to bargain in good faith, however egregious and destructive of workers' freedom of association they might be. In further contrast, employers face no punitive measures for violating workers' rights. The only recourse is usually an order to reinstate a fired worker, or an order to bargain with workers' chosen

---

[625]See Section 8(b)(4) of the NLRA, 29 U.S.C. §158(b)(4).

representative, with no further assurance that workers' rights are vindicated or that employer violations are deterred.

In recent years the NLRB has increased its use of 10(j) proceedings for workers from an almost-never to a rare frequency. In 1998, fewer than fifty 10(j) injunctions were sought on workers' behalf—a drop in a sea of some 10,000 meritorious unfair labor practice cases.[626] But even fewer 10(l) injunctions were sought, because the ban on workers' solidarity action is so absolute and the punishment is so swift and resolute that workers rarely test the law's harsh strictures.[627]

International Norms

The U.S. prohibition on solidarity action contrasts sharply with practice of most other countries and runs counter to principles developed by the ILO's Committee on Freedom of Association over many decades of treating cases under Conventions 87 and 98. For example, Japanese labor law contains no prohibition on worker solidarity appeals or action comparable to Section 8(b)(4) of the NLRA. In fact, Japanese labor law proscribes only employer unfair labor practices, tracking the language of Section 8(a) of the NLRA.[628] The only union economic action affirmatively constrained under Japanese labor law involves a narrow issue of safety equipment; namely, that "no act which hampers or causes the stoppage of normal maintenance or operation of safety equipment at factories or other places of employment shall be resorted to even as an act of dispute."[629]

In the European Union (EU), all member states except the United Kingdom recognize the lawfulness of workers' solidarity action. At the same time, they regulate such action to minimize its effects and to channel disputes toward peaceful resolutions.[630]

In many EU countries, especially in northern Europe, employers and unions can agree to no-strike clauses in collective agreements that preclude secondary

---

[626]It should be noted that most unfair labor practice cases involve multiple acts of violations, so the real count against which fifty 10(j) injunctions should be measured is in the tens of thousands.

[627]See 1998 NLRB Annual Report, p. 19.

[628]Much of Japan's labor law was set in place during the post-World War II occupation by the United States, using the Wagner Act as the basic model. See William B. Gould, *Japan's Reshaping of American Labor Law* (Cambridge, MIT Press, 1984).

[629]See Rodo Kankei Chousei Hou (Labor Relations Adjustment Act), Law No. 25 of Sept. 27, 1946, Ch. 5, Art. 36.

[630]See Juri Aaltonen, "International Secondary Industrial Action in the EU Member States," Metalworkers Foundation of Finland (March 1998), on file with Human Rights Watch.

action. In other countries including Spain, Italy and France, the right to strike is constitutionally protected and no-strike clauses are prohibited.[631]

Some countries such as Austria and the Netherlands apply a rule of "reasonableness" or "proportionality" to workers' invoking of solidarity action rights, allowing workers to affect a secondary firm's dealings with the primary company involved in the dispute, but not to influence dealings with other companies not involved in a labor dispute.[632] Some countries, such as Denmark, have a "last resort" requirement for using mediation and conciliation mechanisms before action can be taken.[633]

In some EU countries including France, Spain and Italy, workers engaged in secondary action must share a community of interest with those involved in the primary dispute, giving them some stake in the outcome. As one researcher notes, "Since the right to strike is constitutionally protected in all these countries, it can, however, be presumed that the demand for interest community is not particularly strict. The estimation of interest community probably remains above all to the employees themselves."[634] In contrast, in Sweden and Finland the opposite rule obtains: the permissibility of secondary action is tied to the disinterest of secondary actors. According to the same scholar, "the lawfulness of the secondary action is in these countries the more probable the more remote the interests of the primary and secondary action participants are from each other."[635]

Secondary industrial action is a complex and sensitive matter for any country's labor law system. No country leaves this area of the law totally unregulated. But in nearly every country, secondary action is lawful so long as the primary dispute is lawful and so long as the secondary action is carried out within the bounds of that country's regulations, like those described above. The United States, however, has imposed a blanket prohibition on solidarity action. No effort is made in U.S. law and practice to find a compromise that balances the interests of primary and secondary workers and employers.

ILO Rulings
The United Kingdom under Margaret Thatcher adopted legislation based on the U.S. statutory scheme prohibiting workers' solidarity action. The ILO found

---

[631]Ibid., paragraphs 17.2, 17.3.
[632]Ibid., paragraph 17.4.
[633]Ibid., paragraph 17.3.
[634]Ibid., paragraph 17.2.
[635]Ibid., paragraph 17.3.

these laws to be "excessive limitations upon the exercise of the right to strike."[636]
The ILO went on to say:

> Taken together, these changes appear to make it virtually impossible for
> workers and unions lawfully to engage in any form of boycott activity,
> or "sympathetic" action against parties not directly involved in a given
> dispute . . . [I]t appears to the Committee that where a boycott relates
> directly to the social and economic concerns of the workers involved in
> either or both of the original dispute and the secondary action, and where
> the original dispute and the secondary action are not unlawful in
> themselves, then that boycott should be regarded as a legitimate exercise
> of the right to strike. This is clearly consistent with the approach the
> Committee has adopted in relation to "sympathy strikes.[637]

Upon further consideration of the British legislation, the ILO concluded:

> It was now virtually impossible for workers and unions lawfully to
> engage in any form of boycott activity or sympathetic action against
> parties not directly involved in a given dispute; the protections no longer
> applied to situations where unions and their members had "mixed"
> industrial, social and political motives for what they did; . . .
> Accordingly, the Committee asked the Government to introduce
> amendments . . . which accorded adequate protection to the right to
> engage in other legitimate forms of industrial action such as protests and
> sympathy strikes."[638]

The ILO set forth a general rule on trade union sympathy appeals and action
under Convention 87 as follows:

> Sympathy strikes, which are recognized as lawful in some countries, are
> becoming increasingly frequent because of the move towards the
> concentration of enterprises, the globalization of the economy and the

---

[636] See Report of the Committee of Experts on the Application of Conventions and
Recommendations, International Labor Conference, 76th Sess., Rep. III, Part 4A, 234, 238-
239 (1989).
[637] Ibid.
[638] See Report of Committee of Experts on the Application of Conventions and
Recommendations, International Labor Conference, 78th Sess., Rep. III, Part 4A, 220-221
(1991).

delocalisation of work centres. While pointing out that a number of distinctions need to be drawn here (such as an exact definition of the concept of a sympathy strike; a relationship justifying recourse to this type of strike, etc.), the Committee [of Experts] considers that a general prohibition on sympathy strikes could lead to abuse and that workers should be able to take such action, provided the initial strike they are supporting is itself lawful.

CONCLUSION, 2004

Labor law in the United States is deeply entrenched against even domestic pressure for change, let alone international human rights influence.[639] It is no surprise that the Universal Declaration of Human Rights, UN human rights treaties, ILO conventions, and other international human rights instruments detailed in *Unfair Advantage* have not had a direct impact on American labor law and practice. Nor is it surprising that *Unfair Advantage* has not brought swift reform. On closer examination, however, a climate-changing effect is underway that could help move U.S. labor law toward a human rights foundation. *Unfair Advantage* is an important part of this movement.

Rights Foundation versus Economic Foundation

The rights-oriented thrust of a human rights analysis clashes with the economic thrust of U.S. labor law. The law protecting workers is not grounded in fundamental rights. It rests on the commerce clause of the Constitution, which empowers Congress to regulate interstate business.

International human rights law was undeveloped in the 1930s, and the United States had just joined the ILO when the Wagner Act was adopted in 1935. It would be unfair to blame Congress for not basing the new law on international standards. However, Congress could conceivably have grounded "Labor's Magna Carta," as the Wagner Act has often been called, in fundamental rights provisions of the Constitution such as the First Amendment's protection of speech and assembly, the Thirteenth Amendment's affirmation of free labor, and the Fourteenth Amendment's guarantee of equal protection. Such a fundamental rights foundation to labor law might have made it easier in our own time to apply international human rights standards to labor law reform.

Wagner Act drafters worried that the conservative Supreme Court would declare the new law unconstitutional. They opted for narrow economic grounds to justify passage, citing the commerce clause and Congress's need to address what the act's findings called "forms of industrial strife or unrest . . . burdening or obstructing commerce."[640] The Supreme Court upheld the Wagner Act

---

[639]For compelling accounts of resistance to change in U.S. labor law, see Cynthia L. Estlund, "The Ossification of American Labor Law," 102 *Columbia Law Review* 1527 (2002), and James J. Brudney, "A Famous Victory: Collective Bargaining Protections and the Statutory Aging Process," 74 *North Carolina Law Review* 939 (1996).

[640]For a comprehensive account of this choice and how it was made, see James Gray Pope, "The Thirteenth Amendment Versus the Commerce Clause: Labor and the Shaping of American Constitutional Law, 1921–1957," 102 *Columbia Law Review* 1 (2002).

based on commerce clause arguments that it reduced strikes, not that it advanced workers' rights.[641] The commerce clause similarly underpinned child labor and prison labor laws passed in the 1930s, as well as Title VII of the 1964 Civil Rights Act.

By using a narrow economic base that stressed the free flow of commerce rather than a broader rights-based framework, U.S. labor law set out on a path away from human rights as a guiding principle. Ironically, the only genuinely rights-based feature of our labor law is the "employer free speech" amendment in the 1947 Taft-Hartley Act, which allows employers openly and aggressively to campaign against worker self-organization.

Trade union growth after the Wagner Act masked the dangers that sprang from choosing an economic rather than a fundamental rights underpinning to U.S. labor law. The Supreme Court blithely declared in *dicta* in the Mackay Radio case that employers could permanently replace workers who exercised the right to strike, effectively gutting that right, and no one paid much attention because at the time employers hardly dared do it.[642] The striker replacement issue was not litigated, briefed, or argued by the parties in the Mackay case. Indeed, workers and their union actually won the case, which involved discrimination against union leaders, not striker replacement.

When union membership plummeted in the 1980s (after a more gradual decline that began in the 1960s), and prevailing values shifted away from industrial democracy and social solidarity toward management control and competitiveness, free market economic imperatives trumped workers' fundamental rights. Signaled by President Ronald Reagan's dismissal and replacement of air traffic controllers in 1981, permanent striker replacement became widespread in the 1980s. Without a human rights foundation, employers could argue that workers' organizing and bargaining were in themselves "burdens" on the free flow of commerce. In one landmark case, the Supreme Court ruled that "an employer's need for unencumbered decision-making" and for "speed, flexibility, and secrecy" prevails over and against workers' rights to bargain over workplace closures.[643] In another, the Court ruled that employer property rights take precedence over union organizers' right to distribute leaflets and speak with workers in publicly accessible but privately owned space. The

---

[641]See *NLRB v. Jones & Laughlin Steel Corp.*, 301 U.S. 1 (1937).
[642]See *NLRB v. Mackay Radio & Telegraph Co.*, 304 U.S. 333 (1938). *Dicta* is the term used to describe portions of Supreme Court opinions that do not directly address the issue posed for decision.
[643]See *First National Maintenance Corp. v. NLRB*, 452 U.S. 666 (1981).

Court said that only when workers live at the workplace, as in a remote logging camp, could union representatives communicate with workers on publicly accessible company property.[644]

Labor Rights, Trade, and a New Opportunity

The United States missed the first opportunity in the 1930s to ground labor law in notions of workers' basic rights. But the human rights approach reflected in *Unfair Advantage* presents a new chance to create a rights-based framework for U.S. law.

Human rights concerns first entered U.S. labor law discourse in connection with trade laws and trade agreements, not labor laws. In the mid-1980s Congress adopted a series of labor rights amendments to statutes governing trade with other nations. For example, a 1984 labor rights clause in the Generalized System of Preferences made respect for "internationally recognized worker rights" a condition for trade benefits. The first rights defined in the law were the right of association and the right to organize and bargain collectively.[645]

The GSP labor rights amendment of 1984 was followed by over a half dozen other amendments in which the United States made freedom of association a touchstone of trade relations with other countries. In 1985, Congress added a labor rights provision to legislation governing the Overseas Private Investment Corporation (OPIC), which provides political risk insurance for U.S. companies investing overseas.[646]

In the Omnibus Trade Act of 1988, a labor rights amendment to the trade act's Section 301 made systematic workers' rights violations by *any* trading partner an unfair trade practice against which the United States could retaliate with economic sanctions.[647] The AFL-CIO filed the first-ever Section 301 labor rights petition in March 2004, alleging abuses against workers by the govern-

---

[644]See *Lechmere, Inc. v. NLRB*, 502 U.S. 527 (1992). The space at issue was a shopping center parking lot. The Court said union organizers could instead hold up signs at a nearby grass strip owned by the municipality.

[645]GSP Renewal Act of 1984, Pub. L. No. 98–573, 98 Stat. 3019 (1984).

[646]22 U.S.C.A. § 2191a (a)(1) (West 1990).

[647]19 U.S.C.A. § 2411(d)(3)(B)(iii)(I–V) (West 1999). The AFL-CIO filed the first complaint under the labor rights clause of Section 301 against China in March 2004, citing violations of freedom of association as principal grounds for the complaint. See Steven Greenhouse and Elizabeth Becker, "A.F.L.-C.I.O. to Press Bush for Penalties against China," *New York Times*, March 16, 2004, p. C1.

ment of China involving freedom of association, forced labor, and workplace health and safety.[648]

In 1990, a Caribbean Basin Initiative renewal bill adopted the GSP labor rights formulation[649] The same clause was applied to the Andean Trade Preference Act of 1991.[650]

In 1992, Congress swiftly enacted a bill barring the Agency for International Development from expending funds to help developing countries lure U.S. businesses to countries where workers' right are violated.[651] In 1994, Congress turned labor rights attention to the World Bank, the International Monetary Fund, and other international financial institutions, requiring American directors of those bodies to use their "voice and vote" to screen loan proposals for their effects on workers' rights.[652]

In 2000, Congress passed the African Growth and Opportunity Act, which among other things granted trade preferences to countries that protect internationally recognized worker rights.[653] New trade agreements with Jordan, Chile, Singapore, and Australia all contain labor rights provisions headed by freedom of association and the right to organize and bargain collectively, with mutual commitments by those countries and by the United States.[654]

OECD Guidelines

United States membership in the Organization for Economic Cooperation and Development (OECD) brought multinational employers under OECD "guidelines for multinational enterprises." The OECD is the coordinating body of thirty developed country governments in North America, Western Europe, and the Asia-Pacific region. Under the guidelines, multinational companies are supposed to respect workers' freedom of association, right to organize, and right to bargain collectively.

---

[648]See AFL-CIO, "Section 301 Petition" to the Office of the United States Trade Representative, March 16, 2004; see also Steven Greenhouse and Elizabeth Becker, "AFL-CIO To Press Bush For Penalties Against China," *New York Times*, March 16, 2004, p. C1,

[649]19 U.S.C.A. § 2702(b)(7) (West 1999).

[650]19 U.S.C.A. § 3202(c)(7) (West 1999).

[651]22 U.S.C.A. § 2151 (West Supp. 2002).

[652]22 U.S.C.A. § 262p–264p–4p (West Supp. 2002).

[653]19 U.S.C.A. § 3703(a)(1)(F) (West Supp. 2002).

[654]For information on these agreements and their labor rights provisions, see the Web site of the Office of the United States Trade Representative at www.ustr.gov.

Some U.S. unions have been able to use the OECD guidelines to advance organizing and bargaining goals. The United Mine Workers turned to the OECD following a 1988 labor dispute at a West Virginia mine owned by ENI, the Italian state-run energy company. Following an "exchange of views" among the union, the employers (both the U.S. subsidiary and ENI), and U.S. and Italian government officials the OECD helped resolve the dispute to the UMW's satisfaction.[655]

A U.S. union facing antilabor conduct by the local management of a U.S. subsidiary of the Swedish Electrolux corporation used the OECD guidelines procedure. It led to Swedish unions pressuring their government to persuade parent company managers to convince U.S. executives to halt their objectionable conduct.[656] In 1990, the United Food and Commercial Workers approached the OECD in a dispute with the Belgium-based Carrefour supermarket chain over workers' organizing rights in the company's Pennsylvania stores. International pressure that included solidarity actions by Belgian unions brought about a settlement in April 1991, under which the company recognized the union and entered into bargaining.[657]

NAFTA's Labor Agreement

A further move toward an international labor rights framework came in 1994 with NAFTA and its labor side agreement, the NAALC. Negotiators stressed the obligation to effectively enforce domestic labor laws, not international standards. But they elaborated eleven common "labor principles" covering what later became core labor standards in the ILO's 1998 declaration, headed by freedom of association and the right to organize and bargain collectively.

The NAALC's labor principles created an implicit rights charter for the United States, Canada, and Mexico, the three NAFTA countries. Advocates have used the NAALC to examine and criticize U.S. labor law and practice in freedom of association cases involving Sprint's closure of a California facility after workers formed a union, apple workers' organizing in Washington, H-2A

---

[655]See B. Glade and E. Potter, "Targeting the Labor Practices of Multinational Companies," *Focus on Issues*, U.S. Council for International Business (July 1989).
[656]Ibid.
[657]See David Wallace, "Carrefour, Union Reach Truce in 2-Year Dispute," *Philadelphia Business Journal*, February 19, 1990, p. 1.

workers' organizing in North Carolina, poultry workers' organizing in Maine, and other cases.[658]

The NAALC is not a "hard law" system, so these complaints do not bring enforceable remedies such as reinstatement and back pay or union recognition, which are still left to domestic law enforcement. But the NAALC's "soft law" approach of investigations, public hearings, reports, research, recommendations, and the like put U.S. law under a human rights–labor rights spotlight.[659]

United States

A significant legal case in 2002 brought the relationship between international human rights norms and U.S. labor law into sharp relief in a Norway court. The Norwegian oil workers union (NOPEF) sought judicial permission under Norwegian law to boycott the North Sea operations of Trico Corp., a Louisiana-based company that allegedly violated American workers' rights in an organizing campaign in the Gulf Coast region. Trico's North Sea arm was the company's most profitable venture, and a boycott could have had devastating economic effects.

A key issue in the case was whether U.S. labor law and practice conform to ILO norms concerning freedom of association and the right to organize. NOPEF and Trico's Norwegian counsel each called expert witnesses from the United States to give testimony about whether U.S. law and practice violate ILO core standards on freedom of association. If the Norwegian court found that U.S. law failed to meet international standards, the NOPEF boycott would be allowed to proceed.

Just before the U.S. experts' testimony, NOPEF settled the case when Trico promised to respect workers' organizing rights in Louisiana.[660] The boycott trigger was deactivated. Still, the Trico case had the potential for international labor standards to have a remarkably direct impact within the United

---

[658]Complaints and cases also involve violations of workers' freedom of association in Mexico and Canada. For information, see the Web site of the North American Commission for Labor Cooperation at www.naalc.org.

[659]For a critical analysis of the NAFTA labor agreement, see Joel Solomon, *Trading Away Rights: the Unfulfilled Promise of NAFTA's Labor Side Agreement* (Human Rights Watch 2001).

[660]See Michelle Amber, "Norwegian Court Will Hear Case Involving Labor Dispute in Louisiana," *BNA Daily Labor Report*, November 4, 2002, p. A8; "U.S. Company Agrees in Norwegian Court to Inform Employees of Organizing Rights," *BNA Daily Labor Report*, November 12, 2002, p. A9.

States. Similar cases could arise in the future as trade unions increase their cross-border solidarity work.

Changing the Climate

Arguing that workers' rights are human rights and citing the Universal Declaration and other international human rights instruments are not by themselves going to change U.S. law and practice. Rather, a human rights approach brings a new dimension that can begin a process of change—*can*, not "will," and *begin*, not "finish." The sustained use of *Unfair Advantage* by workers' rights advocates is fostering new ways of talking and thinking about labor law in the United States. Changing the climate is a necessary prelude to changing law, policy, and practice.

Workers and their unions cannot go it alone in today's social and economic context. The cultural drumbeat that unions are "special interests" seeking undue privileges compared with the rest of society is powerful and incessant. Working people and trade unions need allies in other social movements to defend their rights.

The U.S. labor movement has worked hard to join with civil rights, women's, religious, student, and other communities to advance a broad program of economic and social justice. Emphasizing policy issues such as minimum wage and health insurance that protect workers who are mostly *not* union members has helped the labor movement reach out to other sectors of civil society.

Unfair Advantage adds the human rights movement to this coalition. Specific legislative reforms to implement the report's recommendations will have to be fought out in electoral and legislative arenas in years to come. Working people and their unions can get to the point of waging those fights by reframing organizing and bargaining efforts as a human rights mission and attracting new allies to the struggle. In turn, human rights advocates can advance their goal of enhanced respect for fundamental rights and human dignity by defending freedom of association in the American workplace.

HUMAN RIGHTS WATCH

Human Rights Watch conducts regular, systematic investigations of human rights abuses in some seventy countries around the world. Our reputation for timely, reliable disclosures has made us an essential source of information for those concerned with human rights. We address the human rights practices of governments of all political stripes, of all geopolitical alignments, and of all ethnic and religious persuasions. Human Rights Watch defends freedom of thought and expression, due process and equal protection of the law, and a vigorous civil society; we document and denounce murders, disappearances, torture, arbitrary imprisonment, discrimination, and other abuses of internationally recognized human rights. Our goal is to hold governments accountable if they transgress the rights of their people.

Human Rights Watch began in 1978 with the founding of its Europe and Central Asia division (then known as Helsinki Watch). Today, it also includes divisions covering Africa, the Americas, Asia, and the Middle East. In addition, it includes three thematic divisions on arms, children's rights, and women's rights. It maintains offices in Brussels, Geneva, London, Los Angeles, Moscow, New York, San Francisco, Tashkent, and Washington. Human Rights Watch is an independent, nongovernmental organization, supported by contributions from private individuals and foundations worldwide. It accepts no government funds, directly or indirectly.

The staff includes Kenneth Roth, executive director; Allison Adoradio, operations director; Michele Alexander, development director; Carroll Bogert, associate director; Steve Crawshaw, London office director; Barbara Guglielmo, finance director; Lotte Leicht, Brussels office director; Iain Levine, program director; Maria Pignataro Nielsen, human resources director; Dinah PoKempner, general counsel; Wilder Tayler, legal and policy director; and Joanna Weschler, United Nations representative.

The regional division directors of Human Rights Watch are Peter Takirambudde, Africa; José Miguel Vivanco, Americas; Brad Adams, Asia; Rachel Denber (acting), Europe and Central Asia; and Joe Stork (acting), Middle East and North Africa. The thematic division directors are Steve Goose, Arms; Lois Whitman, Children's Rights; and LaShawn R. Jefferson, Women's Rights. The program directors are Arvind Ganesan, Business and Human Rights; Joanne Csete, HIV/AIDS and Human Rights; Richard Dicker, International Justice; and Jamie Fellner, U.S. Program.

The members of the board of directors are Jane Olson (chair), Khaled Abou El Fadl, Lisa Anderson, Lloyd Axworthy, David M. Brown, William D. Carmichael, Jorge Castañeda, Dorothy Cullman, Edith Everett, Jonathan F.

Human Rights Watch

350 Fifth Avenue, 34th floor
New York, NY 10118-3299 USA
Tel: 1-(212) 290-4700, Fax: 1-(212) 736-1300
hrwnyc@hrw.org

1630 Connecticut Avenue, N.W., Suite 500
Washington, DC 20009 USA
Tel:1-(202) 612-4321, Fax:1-(202) 612-4333
hrwdc@hrw.org
2nd Floor, 2-12 Pentonville Road
London N1 9HF, UK
Tel: 44 20 7713 1995, Fax: 44 20 7713 1800
hrwuk@hrw.org

Rue Van Campenhout 15,
1000 Brussels, Belgium
Tel: 32 (2) 732-2009, Fax: 32 (2) 732-0471
hrwatcheu@skynet.be

9 rue de Cornavin
1201 Geneva
Tel: +41 22 738 04 81, Fax: +41 22 738 1791
hrwgva@hrw.org

Web Site Address: http://www.hrw.org

Listserv address: To receive Human Rights Watch news releases by
email, subscribe to the HRW news listserv of your choice by visiting
http://hrw.org/act/subscribe-mlists/subscribe.htm